W9-AUX-612

The Practical Companion

to Your New City,

From Settling In

to Stepping Out

By Jeff Reid

and Amanda Rudolph

MOVING TO LOS ANGELES

alpha
books

A Division of Macmillan Publishing
A Simon & Schuster Macmillan Company
1633 Broadway, New York, NY 10019-6785

International Standard Book Number: 0-02-861280-9
Library of Congress Catalog Card Number: 96-086485
98 97 96   8 7 6 5 4 3 2 1

Interpretation of the printing code: the rightmost double-digit number
is the year of the book's first printing; the rightmost single-digit number
is the number of the book's printing. For example, a printing code of
96-1 shows that this copy of the book was printed during the first printing
of the book in 1996.

Printed in the United States of America

Publisher: Theresa Murtha
Development Editor: Nancy Mikhail
Cover Designer: Michael Freeland
Indexer: Suzanne Simons
Designer: Francine Fishpaw
Creators: James Grace and David Borgenicht

CONTENTS

The Backstreet Philosophy

Don't panic.

Douglas Adams, *The Hitchhiker's Guide to the Galaxy*

Moving is always a traumatic and unsettling experience, but it can be even more insane if you're moving to a new city. Not only do you have to uproot your life from one place, but you need to plant it again in another—all while finding a new place to live, a new job, new friends, new places to hang out, and new places to have fun.

But like the man said, *don't panic.* Because these are not your average guides.

Most guidebooks to the major cities are written for tourists—visitors to the city in question. But Backstreet Guides were created specifically for people who are going to live in the major cities.

These books were created to be your insider perspective on a new city. The information they provide is the kind of information you could get only from a friend who has lived in the city for years. In fact, you can think of these books as your "all-knowing friends," something to refer to, with inside tips about what it's really like in the city, where you might want to live, how to settle in quickly and comfortably, and what to do when you get there and want to start exploring.

These guides don't have everything—they aren't directories or phone books. They're opinionated guides with this point of view:

Cities are a lot of fun once you get to know them.

The problem is that it usually takes several years to really *get to know* a city. And that's where we come in. Our writers grew up in these cities, lived in them, and have loved them for years. The listings in this book come from the "insider's" perspective—from the native's body of knowledge about the city—not from what other guides, magazines, newspapers, and ratings sources say.

Within, you'll find information that no other books have. You'll find sidebars throughout with essential and interesting info.

You'll find easy-to-use maps that will help you navigate the city streets. You'll find great sites to see, restaurants to try, things to do, and places to go—some of which are the essential "tourist" attractions and establishments, but most of which are places where *actual people* (without cameras) go. And the establishments listed in these guides are here because they deserve to be—not because they paid to be. What you'll find here is the best the city has to offer.

But like we said, Backstreet Guides aren't meant to have it all. Instead, they have what you need for your first year in the new city. Backstreet Guides will help you to:

- Select a neighborhood
- Find a place to live
- Move in
- Set up your utilities and your new home
- Decide what to do when you want to explore
- Help you locate good restaurants and bars
- Help you find exciting and fun things to do
- Provide a comprehensive listing of essential numbers and addresses

And much more. We hope you'll find your own favorites in this book, but we know you'll find others on your own. When you do, don't hesitate to drop us a line. Send your comments via e-mail to Book Soup at BookSoop@aol.com.

Have fun in your new city.

THE BACKSTREET GUIDES EDITORS

Chapter
One

GERTRUDE STEIN once complained of Oakland that "there's no 'there' there."

Los Angeles has almost the opposite problem: Every "there" you can imagine is here—but you've got to know where to look. Although you can find whatever you want in this ungainly city, you must beware of smorgasboredom—a curious, and all too common, condition of option overload.

Welcome to sprawling yet oddly self-centered L.A., land of the all-encompassing whatever.

You want to talk geography? Whatever you want, we've got: beaches (wild and mild), deserts (high and low), mountains (preserved and overdeveloped).

Entertainment? Every imaginable diversion is available, and some that we wish had never been invented. But there's no accounting for taste (or the lack thereof).

Outdoor recreation? Where else can you surf and ski on the same day—and then choose among hundreds of stellar eateries (in just about every price range) for the next day's mountain climbing/scuba diving agenda?

Architecture? Whatever you want is here—or can be built. We've got showplaces by Frank Lloyd Wright, Richard Neutra, and Frank Gehry; skyscrapers by all the big names in big buildings; and countless *Leave It to Beaver* housing tracts and Spanish-revival style suburban haciendas—not to mention '50s-futurist Space Age coffee shops (Ships), a hot dog stand shaped like a giant hot dog (Tail o' the Pup) and a record company that looks like an immense stack of records (Capitol).

People? It takes all kinds in this crazy world and we got 'em all (though we might be overstocked on a few varieties of flakes). Los

Angeles is not only the playground of the stars, it's also the nation's top immigrant destination, with an astounding ethnic variety. Folks come here to find themselves or to lose themselves or to reinvent themselves or to whatever themselves.

You want weather? Okay, you've got us there. Los Angeles weather is, generally speaking, too subtle, pleasant, and monotonous for its own good—with only the occasional seasonal monsoon or wind-whipped brushfire to snap us out of our complacency. Nights are cool because it's the desert, but the days are basically room temperature. Summer temps average about 85 (hotter in the Valley, cooler by the beach), and in the brutal chill of winter, daytime highs plunge into the 60s and 70s.

Over the years, Los Angeles has been hit by successive waves of immigration, surfable waves of the Pacific, and seismic waves of destruction. The thing about waves, you just ride 'em. L.A. County, with a population over 8 million, covers almost 5,000 square miles. (The bloated five-county metro area has a population approaching 15 million.) The city's main coastal basin is rimmed by mountains and linked to a chain of valleys that holds more than 100 separate communities. Cars outnumber people, leading to the world's most extensive freeway system and our infamous smog. Nonetheless, thanks to strict auto emission standards, our air is now cleaner and clearer than it's been since the '50s.

And here's another surprising breath of fresh air. According to *Los Angeles* magazine, "California's economy is becoming more diverse, more high tech and more global—and L.A.is at the center of it. The state has recovered all of the jobs lost in the recession, and is now producing jobs 50 percent faster than the rest of the country, once again assuming its traditional role as the beacon for the young, the well-educated, and the ambitious."

That's where you come in—it's called a cue. Don't worry, you'll get the hang of this show-biz thing. This is where you're supposed ask "What's my motivation? Where am I coming from?"

MEET THE CITY

L.A.STORY

In 1542 Spanish explorer **Juan Rodriguez Cabrillo** called the area the "Bay of Smokes," due to the Indian campground haze that hung in the air over what would become the Los Angeles basin. So it was that long before the first Plymouth Duster rocked its smoky way into L.A., 4,000 Native Americans from 30 different tribes were cooking up a benign precursor to smog—but they called it dinner. Cabrillo's expedition was mostly a drive-by situation; the only place he stopped in L.A. county was Catalina Island, where he exchanged gifts with the friendly natives. After that, the peaceful hunter-gatherer tribes who had been here for about 12,000 years had the place mostly to themselves for a couple hundred more years.

Later, in 1769, a missionary settlement in the area was dubbed **Pueblo de Neustra Señora la Reina de los Angeles de Porciuncula** (Town of Our Lady Queen of the Angels of Porciuncula), but the name was wisely shortened (probably by somebody in the publicity department). Not much happened in the sleepy coastal basin (beyond the routine, dehumanizing missionary enslavement of the indigenous people) until Mexican independence in 1821 and the ceding of Alta California to the U.S. in 1848—just in time for the gold rush in '49. Los Angeles cattle ranchers reaped the benefits as hungry miners needed beef on the hoof, pronto. Fortunes were made, and L.A., the cow town, was stampeding toward the future.

After the gold rush, L.A. cashed in on another kind of golden glow—hyping the healthful properties of the orange and the sun-kissed California climate. Promotional train fares dipped as low as $1 for a trip from the Mississippi River to L.A., prompting a deluge of migrating conservative Midwesterners, known generically in Los Angeles as "Iowans." They came for the climate, and their Midwestern life savings fueled many of the area's seemingly endless booms in housing construction and real estate.— (The area's overall conservatism is something of a carryover from those days. The proverbial little old lady from Pasadena was originally from Peoria or Omaha, and she brought her small-town morals to this wide-open frontier town.)

Various water-diversion scams and real-estate hustles later, Los Angeles was well on its way to being a big city, with a unique style of corruption every bit as pernicious the corruption in Chicago, New

York, and Washington, D.C. The discovery of oil fields right in town in the 1890s, and again in the 1920s, prompted more shenanigans. At one time or another, everybody and his dog owned an extra parcel of land and had an oil derrick in the backyard. By the 1920s L.A.'s population was 500,000, surpassing San Francisco's.

Boom went bust again and the Depression hit, but Los Angeles rebounded with the defense industry during and after World War II. Government-subsidized GI bill housing fueled a postwar expansion that sent commuters sprawling every which way around the loose center of Los Angeles. A conspiracy engineered by auto and bus manufacturers squeezed L.A.'s efficient trolley system out of business, and the car was crowned king.

The Making of Hollywood

Hollywood, meanwhile, was building its dream factories, regenerating America's optimistic myths and heroic fantasies on film. If Americans (and others) came west to reinvent themselves, the studios did the same thing on a larger scale. The emphasis on beautiful surfaces is evident in all aspects of L.A. life—from films and television programs to homes and cars and, ultimately, to the residents themselves. Every cheerleader and home-town hunk from across America answered the siren song of Hollywood, which definitely enhanced the local gene pool: generations of wanna-be Valentinos, Garbos, and Brandos came to get famous and stayed here to procreate. The beautiful offspring of these fallen, would-be stars are today's aerobics instructors, manicure mavens, and hair colorists. (Which is not to imply that many of them are not intelligent and sensitive people. Don't be a reverse snob. Remember, in L.A., beauty is *at least* skin deep.)

Personal growth has been a growth industry in Los Angeles since the Mission days, and the spirituality boom never really goes bust. (Tom Wolfe's influential essay about the "me decade" perfectly captured the flavor of this West Coast spiritual reawakening and its supremely self-involved downside—he was writing specifically about the '70s, but . . . what*ever*.) All manner of religions—Eastern,

Western, improvised on the spot—have won adherents among the seekers who flock to the left coast. Over time, part of this self-improvement impulse has been diverted into a cult of the body, the extreme forms of which are marked by exercise mania, dietary fads, and surgical alterations.

Los Angeles sometimes seems like a place where everything is possible but nothing is likely (especially in the film biz, where everybody's pool-boy is one meeting away from a big deal). But even given such dream-like uncertainty, it's nonetheless a pleasant, breathtakingly beautiful place. You can always sit back and marvel at the incredible variety of the vegetation—and the plants are nice too!

The Disasters

Everyone is familiar with L.A.'s chain of disasters: the fires, the floods, the Crips, the Bloods, the ominous rumblings both seismic and social. Yet we're still here—and you're on the way, another migrant to the nation's most populous state. Maybe what draws us all here is akin to the impulse that makes people rubberneck at traffic accidents. Perhaps, as has often been suggested, we're like lemmings rushing pell-mell to the Pacific in some atavistic suicidal urge. Yeah, right.

Still, the lemmings comparison is unintentionally apt. As it turns out, lemmings don't really rush to the sea in a frenzy and jump off a cliff to release mounting population pressures, as we saw in all those nature documentaries. Lemmings, it has been subsequently revealed, only rush to their briny deaths when chased by a nature photographer desperate to enliven a dull bio-pic about some otherwise aimless rodents. So there it is. We all believe it because we saw it in the movies, and that's good enough for us. End of story.

But the beginning of many more. Is this the City of Angels or is it Hell-A? Is it Tinseltown or is it the Capital of the Third World? Is it the Big Orange or just another piece of rotten fruit? The answer, of course, is yes. Which points up the dry humor and sun-baked irony that is central to the mindset of Angelenos: You gotta stay positive, because without optimism, what else is there? Hmmm . . . Whatever are we to make of the city's 464 square miles of contradictions?

What*ever*!

GETTING AROUND IN L.A.

Dog may be man's best friend in the rest of the country, but in Southern Cal your car fills that niche. Forget about Fido's fidelity—what you really need in a ride is dependability, economy, stability, comfort, and durability. And if you have all that, then style never hurts. Because in L.A., a car is both a necessity and an accessory.

The Lay of the Land

But you'll need to know how to get around. And we do mean around—because sometimes it feels like you're going in circles and unfortunately our city planning lacks direction. Things are not marked well here. So let's start off with a few rules.

1.) When getting directions, ask for the number of the freeway. Many people have their own names for freeways, but you want to be able to

INSIDE INFO AND PRONUNCIATION TIPS

How to speak like a native—or at least less like an educated newcomer.

What's in a name? We think Shakespeare covered that one, but this being Los Angeles there's always the chance of a sequel or remake. What's in a name if you mispronounce it? Embarrassment, for one thing. Herewith then, forsooth, verily, and all that, some key pronunciation pointers for the nouveau Angeleno. First off, Mayor Richard Riordan's last name is pronounced "reared-in." [Insert your own joke here.] Also, more than a few of our common street names have counterintuitive pronunciations. Remembering these main ones will help get your tongue started off on the right foot.

La Cienega = Lah-see-EN-ih-gah
Cahuenga = Ko-AIN-guh
Doheny = DOUGH-hee-nee
Sepulveda = Suh-PUHL-vih-duh
Pico = PEE-koh

THE FREEWAY FREE-FOR-ALL

Another local name-game caveat: The freeways all have names and numbers, so get used to the fact that people describe them willy-nilly.

Interstate 10, I-10, the 10 Freeway, and the Santa Monica Freeway are all the same thing (and people also refer to it casually as "the 10" or "the Santa Monica"). That seems simple enough.

More problematic, however, is the fact that different roads merge and diverge with alarming frequency, adding an overlay of confusion onto this proliferation of names. For instance, the Hollywood Freeway and the 101 are the same road near downtown, but further north the 101 splits off to become the Ventura Freeway (which is also the 134) while the Hollywood Freeway continues north, becoming the 170. In other words, some confusion is inevitable for newcomers (and even old-timers here have navigational problems when they drive to areas they don't often visit).

A Few Local Definitions that may Prove Useful

TANDEM PARKING: You've heard of a bicycle built for two? This is a parking spot made for two cars, one immediately behind the other. A favorite of cheap landlords.

SIGALERT: The worst possible traffic tie-up. If you hear that there's a SigAlert on your intended route, change your route.

TEMBLOR: A common synonym for earthquake. Just as the Eskimos have many words for snow, we, sadly, need more than one for quake.

DUDE: Everyone is aware of this quintessential bit of overdone L.A. slanguage, but few outsiders are aware that that dude is now genderless. Chicks can be dudes too, dude, which is a righteous linguistic evolution if there ever was one.

PCH: Stands for Pacific Coast Highway, which is pretty obvious. One peculiarity however: under no circumstances should you refer to it as "the" PCH—it's just not done.

HANG: Is short for a hangout, though if you're just hanging out you have plenty of time to pronounce those extra three letters, but go figure.

look up and easily identify which lane you need to be in. Here are the main arteries:

U.S. 101 (also called the Ventura Freeway in the San Fernando Valley and the Hollywood Freeway in the city of L.A.) runs across L.A. northeast to southeast from the San Fernando Valley to the center of downtown.

California 134 becomes the Ventura Freeway after 101 become the Hollywood Freeway. It runs east through Burbank and Glendale, to I-210, which takes you through Pasadena toward the eastern perimeter of L.A. County.

I-5 (the Golden State Freeway north of I-10 and the Santa Ana Freeway south of I-10) cuts across downtown from San Francisco to San Diego.

I-10 (the Santa Monica Freeway west of I-5 and the San Bernadino Freeway east of I-5) is the main east/west freeway in the city. When taken west, you'll end up at the beach. And going east, you head into downtown L.A.

I-405 (the San Diego Freeway) is the main north/south freeway. It runs from Sacramento up north to San Diego down south. This takes you to the airport.

California 1 (Highway 1, the Pacific Coast Highway, or PCH) runs along the ocean.

As for major boulevards in the city, you should probably memorize the order of these most used routes (starting north and going south): **Sunset, Wilshire, Santa Monica, Olympic,** and **Pico.** These boulevards run east/west and can take you across the entire city. It may not always be the shortest route, but it is important to know these streets so you never feel lost in the city.

In the valley, **Ventura Boulevard** is essential. It runs east/west across the entire valley. Again, there are short cuts, but first learn this main drag because it can take you anywhere you need to get on this side of the hill.

The 101 Freeway also takes you across the valley, but is a major hub for traffic. When it's moving, it's great. When it's not, it sucks. You'll get a feel for it. It will be confusing, but don't let it drive you crazy. You'll get the hang of it.

2.) When in doubt, just look up to the sun as your guide. It sets in the west (at the beach), so if you are headed our for the night in Hollywood, you should be driving away from it.

3.) And the most important rule of all: Everything is about 20 minutes away, so get comfortable in the driver's seat. It's a way of life here.

> *"Between a quarter and a third of Los Angeles's land area is now monopolized by the automobile and its needs—by freeways, highways, garages, gas stations, car lots, parking lots. And all of it is blanketed with anonymity and foul air."*
>
> ALISTAIR COOKE, FROM *AMERICA*

MASS TRANSIT

In an ideal world, we might all prefer clean, efficient mass transit, but in Los Angeles we all prefer to drive. With the nation's most extensive system of freeways and city streets, who can blame us? No one comes to L.A. intending to ride the bus, but, as Elvis Costello pointed out, accidents will happen. Don't despair, mass transit can get you there. It just might take a while.

The Bus: Rattle and Humdrum

Los Angeles has more than 200 bus lines transporting more than one million passengers daily. Service in Hollywood is pretty good, so if you've got to ride the bus do it here (I guess that isn't how it works, though, is it?).

In fact, throughout downtown and across the central city, the bus is workable, particularly if you don't have to transfer from the horizontal to the vertical axis (yeah, right), in which case you may find yourself baking in the sun at Santa Monica and La Brea wondering if maybe the tar pits are opening a branch office. If you must trek from the city basin into the Valley, or vice versa, be prepared for a long ride. Do something different—read a book. Night service is spotty.

Basic transit fare is $1.35 (with transfers $.25 more), but you can get a 10-pack of tokens for $9, so there's a bargain for you. For **transit information and bus schedules countywide,** call (213) 626-4455. **Santa Monica's bus service,** (310) 451-5444, and **Culver City's,** (310) 253-6500, are both rumored to be passable within their areas of operation.

The Subway: Subterranean Carsick Blues

Our expensive, collapse-prone and over-budget subway system has so far delivered more talk-show monologue punch lines than commuters. You've probably seen the sinkholes on the TV news. And the subway project has also been slowed by unanticipated natural poison gas, unexpected underground rivers, and the entirely expected shoddy and corrupt contractors—but we're still hoping for the best and perhaps we'll eventually have a useful subway system.

Taxis: Are You Talkin' to Me?

Also, in a pinch, you can catch a taxi, but the odds are you won't be able to hail one. It's more like call for one and hope. Because L.A. is so large, taxis aren't an economical option for everyday travel—basically an emergency ride of last resort unless money is your middle name. Some reliable taxi options: **Yellow Cab,** (213) 808-1000; **L.A. Taxi,** (213) 627-7000; **Checker Cab,** 1-800-300-5007; **Bell Cab Co-op,** (213) 481-0505.

> " . . . *the freeway experience . . . is the only secular communion Los Angeles has. . . . Actual participation requires a total surrender, a concentration so intense as to seem a kind of narcosis, a rapture-of-the-freeway. The mind goes clean. The rhythm takes over. A distortion of time occurs.*"
>
> JOAN DIDION, FROM *BUREAUCRATS*

A Few Words About Pedestrians

While car is king in Los Angeles, uneasy rests the crown. Pedestrians command respect here, and should one step out in front of your vehicle—even mid-block on a busy street—you are legally required to stop and let them cross. This can lead to unexpected quick stops (and tail-end collisions), so pay attention when peds step off the curb. Once upon a time all of California's alert motorists did so, but the steady influx of new residents has diluted adherence to this law—which makes things even more dangerously erratic for both pedestrians and drivers. Also note that every intersection is considered to have a crosswalk, whether one is painted on the street or not, so pedestrians may abruptly step off the curb when you least expect it.

On the flip side of the pedestrian thing are the hefty fines for jaywalking. When you cross a street against the light or in mid-block, the police can and will cite you. Impatient New Yorkers be advised, crossing against a red light when the road is clear can still cost you plenty. If you hope to avoid driving in Los Angeles, your best bets for living a pedestrial lifesyle are: Larchmont Village, along Fairfax Avenue in Hollywood, near Main Street in Santa Monica, or in Los Feliz Village around Hillhurst.

ANGEL'S FLIGHT

Proudly proclaimed the "shortest railroad in the world" at a mere 298 feet, the fully restored ANGEL'S FLIGHT cable car recently reopened in downtown Los Angeles after lying dormant and disassembled for 27 years. Previous to that, the funky, funicular railway operated steadily for 68 years, groaning up Bunker Hill's steep grade between Hill and Olive streets. Back in those days, thankful loads of weary pedestrians plunked down a nickel each rather than walk the long way around. Times have changed on what is now largely a nostalgia trip; the price has gone sky-high—it costs a quarter!

Roll Reversal

Most neighborhoods are excellent for recreational biking and rollerblading, with unnaturally quiet and beautiful sidestreets everywhere. If you hope to bike or blade as a means of conveyance for basic

CRIME IN L.A.

There's a bit of a debate as to whether or not the crime rate has gone up or down in the last few years. While there have been fewer arrests, many in the city attribute this to a lacking on the part of the Los Angeles Police Department (LAPD). Needless to say, this is a city filled with tension in light of the much publicized events regarding our police department. However, the average person goes about his business in the city without any trouble. In fact the suburb of Thousand Oaks, in the west valley, is one of the safest cities in the U.S. It is a big city, though, and there are always precautions to be taken.

Commonsense Rules:
- *Make it a rule not to stop at ATM machines at night.*
- *Park in populated and well-lit areas.*
- *Always lock your doors, both at your house and in your car.*
- *If you can, carry a cellular phone in your car in case of emergency. And if you get in an accident at night, call a friend before getting out of the car so that someone knows where you are.*
- *Try to find an apartment in a secure building.*
- *Overall, just be smart and always pay attention to what's going on around you.*

transportation, however, you'll run into problems if they don't run into you first—cars by the thousands, that is, driven by morons just like you and me. Also, the everyday distances Angelenos traverse are much greater than those in other cities, so wheeling to work is probably unfeasible—unless you've got a job where being drenched in sweat is not a problem.

Chapter Two

FIRST THINGS FIRST:

Choosing a Neighborhood

L.A. NEIGHBORHOODS

Picking a neighborhood in the gangly megalopolis of Los Angeles can be a little like trying to find a word in the dictionary when you haven't a clue to its spelling—you can't know where to look until you know where to look. With that in mind, we've fingered a few prime locations for nouveau Angelenos, highlighting some key picks for entertainment, shopping, and just plain hanging out. When it comes time to actually make the big move to L.A., you'll want to single out one or two areas from the sprawl, lest you be driven mad by the possibilities. As Devo once aptly observed: "Freedom of choice is what you've got/Freedom from choice is what you want." And we're here to give it to you. But while we've narrowed the options, these are by no means the only sweet spots. As on *Family Feud*, there are no right answers, only the most popular ones. These are them.

L.A. can be pretty darn confusing, but it can be broken down in the following ways:

East Side
    Los Feliz/Silver Lake/Echo Park
    Hollywood/West Hollywood
    Hancock Park/Fairfax (Mid-Wilshire)
West Side
    Beverly Hills
    Westwood/West L.A.
    Culver City/Palms/Mar Vista
    Brentwood
Beaches
    Santa Monica
    Venice
The Valley, from east to west
    Burbank/Glendale
    Sherman Oaks/Studio City
Downtown
Everywhere Else

The map will show you where they all are in relation to one other. Rather than describe each of the neighborhoods in L.A., we've targeted the neighborhoods that are truly considered "L.A. proper." What follows is a key to finding your home there, with full descriptions of the neighborhoods you might want to consider, along with listings of the essential services you'll find there. Get huntin'!

The Neighborhoods in Brief

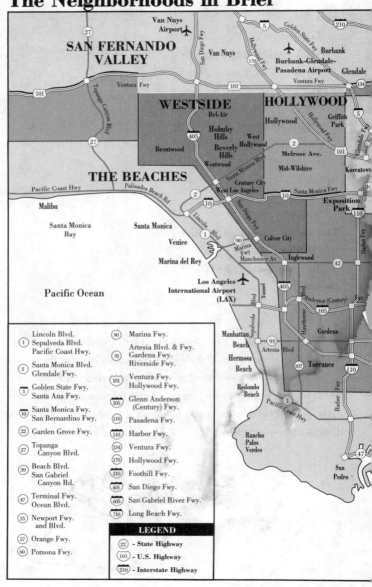

SAN FERNANDO VALLEY

Van Nuys Airport

Van Nuys

Burbank-Glendale-Pasadena Airport

Burbank

Glendale

WESTSIDE

HOLLYWOOD

Bel-Air

Holmby Hills

Brentwood

Westwood

Beverly Hills

West Hollywood

Hollywood

Griffith Park

Melrose Ave.

Mid-Wilshire

Koreatown

THE BEACHES

Century City

West Los Angeles

Exposition Park

Malibu

Santa Monica Bay

Santa Monica

Venice

Marina del Rey

Culver City

Inglewood

Pacific Ocean

Los Angeles International Airport (LAX)

Manhattan Beach

Hermosa Beach

Redondo Beach

Gardena

Torrance

Rancho Palos Verdes

San Pedro

Legend

(1) Lincoln Blvd.
Sepulveda Blvd.
Pacific Coast Hwy.

(2) Santa Monica Blvd.
Glendale Fwy.

(5) Golden State Fwy.
Santa Ana Fwy.

(10) Santa Monica Fwy.
San Bernardino Fwy.

(22) Garden Grove Fwy.

(27) Topanga
Canyon Blvd.

(39) Beach Blvd.
San Gabriel
Canyon Rd.

(47) Terminal Fwy.
Ocean Blvd.

(55) Newport Fwy.
and Blvd.

(57) Orange Fwy.

(60) Pomona Fwy.

(90) Marina Fwy.

(91) Artesia Blvd. & Fwy.
Gardena Fwy.
Riverside Fwy.

(101) Ventura Fwy.
Hollywood Fwy.

(105) Glenn Anderson
(Century) Fwy.

(110) Pasadena Fwy.

(110) Harbor Fwy.

(134) Ventura Fwy.

(170) Hollywood Fwy.

(210) Foothill Fwy.

(405) San Diego Fwy.

(605) San Gabriel River Fwy.

(710) Long Beach Fwy.

LEGEND

(22) - State Highway

(101) - U.S. Highway

(210) - Interstate Highway

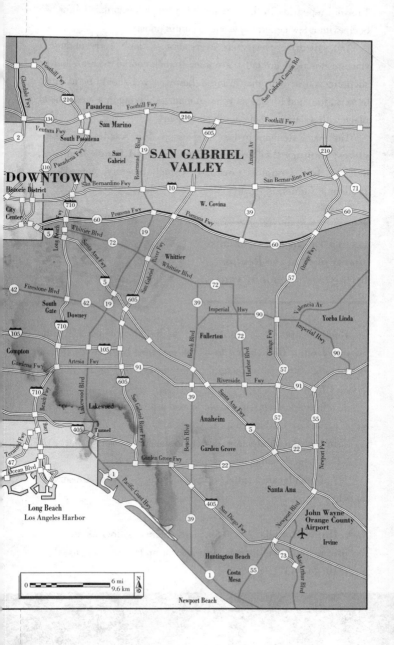

APARTMENT HUNTING TIPS

To avoid repetition in the neighborhood breakdowns that follow, we begin with a few general apartment-hunting notes:

You will drive everywhere every day, so don't worry unduly if you are not right around the corner from potential recreational or shopping zones. With that in mind, however, you should be as close to work, fun, and friends as you can manage. Living in a great cheap place with a painful commute is no bargain.

The major Realtors in Los Angeles are **Jon Aaroe and Associates; Century 21; Coldwell Banker; Fred Sands Realtors;** and the **Jon Douglas Company** (which recently merged with Prudential California Realty).

INSIDER TIP: *In L.A., commission is paid to the Realtors by the owners, not by you.*

Renters who don't go through a Realtor or paid listings company often find their places in the weekly *Recycler* ($2, at convenience stores, newsstands, and drugstores) or in the *L.A. Sunday Times.*

The free *Apartment Magazine* is also a passable source—pick it up at various spots throughout L.A.

Cruising through potential neighborhoods to scope out FOR RENT signs is a good commonsense tactic.

If you can't locate a suitable place on your own, there are services to help you:

L.A. Home Rentals. A $60 fee gives you access to 400–500 private Southland listings per week for up to three months, (310) 441-4371.

HomeHunters. For $50 these friendly folks provide a weekly citywide list of about 300 rentals, which is also good for three months—with a $25 rebate if you find a place through other means, (213) 848-3490

Rentline. A $49 fee gets you three-month listing service or a roommate-matching service, (213) 789-7368

Whatever method you use to locate an apartment or house, always try to get one with a garage, or at least off-street parking—otherwise uninsured maniacs might total your car while you sleep. It happens. Often.

An L.A. peculiarity: Many apartments don't come with stove and refrigerator ("S and R" in classified ad lingo), so ask.

Be persistent. L.A. is full of wonderful places to live, so try to avoid living in a hell-hole (even though, as Spinal Tap noted, "You know where you stand in a hell hole"). If you do initially have to set-tle for something semi-hellish, get a month-to-month lease (very common) and bail ASAP.

When you do find a place you like, feel free to negotiate—it's a renter's market, with vacancies all over town in most price ranges. If the potential landlord likes you and your credit report, he or she may be open to a little negotiation about the rent or the size of deposit required. In other words, it ain't New York.

Palm trees and sunshine can sometimes dazzle apartment hunters new to Los Angeles. It is strongly advised that you pay a nighttime visit to any apartment you plan to rent. Shady behavior increases when there's more shade, and there's nothing glamorous about getting mugged under a palm tree.

It's true what they say "vibes" are big out here, so trust your instincts. If you have none, you may borrow ours.

INSIDER TIP: *If you are looking to buy, the Realtor to contact is FRED SANDS REALTY—Santa Monica, (310) 395-2818; Sherman Oaks, (310) 276-9994; Westwood, (310) 479-1625; Brentwood, (310) 820-6880.*

SCHOOL DAZE

Keeping kids in school isn't the only problem L.A. parents face.
Sometimes the tough part is getting the kiddies into school—
private school that is. Waiting lists can really keep you waiting at
these top notch learning holes.

BRENTWOOD SCHOOL—100 S. Barrington, L.A., (310) 476-9633.
It is mahvelous! So marvelous in fact, that Billy Crystal
sent his kids here, along with the Milken and Schwarzenegger
children. Excellent teachers, excellent facilities and an excel-
lent record with the Ivy League.

CROSSROADS SCHOOL FOR ARTS AND SCIENCES—1714 21st St.,
Santa Monica, (310) 829-7391. Schoolhouse Rock—for those
who are into the artsy scene and not into stringent schedules.
Steven Spielberg likes it well enough for his offspring and so
does O.J. Simpson—Arnelle's an alum.

JOHN THOMAS DYE—11414 Chalon Rd., L.A., (310) 476-2811.
Michael Ovitz has no problem paying the $8,000+ each
year to insure that his children get the finest, if not the
priciest education.

HARVARD-WESTLAKE SCHOOL—MIDDLE SCHOOL: 700 N.
Faring Rd., L.A., (310) 274-7281; UPPER SCHOOL: 3700
Coldwater Canyon, North Hollywood, (818) 980-6692.
They're not using the term Harvard lightly. This school used
to be two (a separate boys and girls school) and recently
merged into one making it the powerhouse for L.A. elite.
Famous grads include: Shirley Temple-Black, Candace
Bergen, Sally Ride, Tori Spelling, and the notorious
Billionaire Boys.

MARLBOROUGH SCHOOL—250 S. Rossmore Ave., L.A.,
(213) 935-1147. Sisterhood prevails at this Hancock Park
all-girls school. It's conservative and structured (with uniforms
to match), and your daughter will get an exceptional educa-
tion. Just keep in mind, prestige is expensive.

OAKWOOD SCHOOL—11600 Magnolia Blvd., North Hollywood,
(818) 752-4400. Proving that not all jocks are dumb, Mitchell

Butler of the Washington Bullets played hoops here while getting his education before going on to UCLA. Highly respected, the curriculum is more liberal than Brentwood or Harvard-Westlake. Elementary and secondary.

POLYTECHNIC SCHOOL—1030 E. California Blvd., Pasadena, (818) 792-2147. It doesn't get as much publicity as all the others, but the education is considered among the best in L.A.

INSIDER TIP: *The ARCHER SCHOOL for girls is making a name for itself despite the fact that it has been open only one year. Started by noted feminist Diana Meehan, whose daughter was a student at Westlake when it went co-ed. Other parents joined in on her crusade for single-sex education. With a new location on prime real estate in Brentwood and a good buzz around town, this is one school to watch out for, and more importantly to consider for your daughter.*

TEMPORARILY YOURS

Because people in L.A. can sometimes be—how shall we say it?—
a little too mellow (okay, flaky), it might take you a bit longer than
you imagine to find a suitable apartment. But where to stay while
you're looking for a place to stay? If you have friends or family
with whom you can crash while you're apartment hunting, that's
the best. If you're on your own, below are a few budget hotels and
motels to consider, but they are by no means luxury accommoda-
tions. Remember, it's always a good idea to stay in a motel for a
day or two to test the waters before you check in for a more
extended stay.

BEVERLY HILLS REEVES—$250/wk., 120 S. Reeves Dr.,
   (310) 271-3006.
DAYS INN—$690/mo., 600 N. Pacific, Glendale,
   (818) 956-0202.
HOTEL DEL FLORES—$260/wk., 409 N. Crescent Dr., Beverly
   Hills, (213) 274-5115.
WILSHIRE ROYALE HOTEL—$475/mo. (and up), 1-800-421-8072.
WILSHIRE ORANGE HOTEL—$210/wk., 6060 W. 8th St.,
   West L.A. (213) 931-0953.$125/wk. (and up),
   (310) 444-8990.
HOTEL HOWARD—$200/wk. 1738 N. Whitley Ave., (213) 466-6943
LA STILLWELL HOTEL—$125/wk, $475/mo., 828 S. Grand St.
   (downtown), (213) 627-1151.
ORCHID HOTEL—$154/wk., 819 S. Flower St., (213) 624-5855.
MILNER HOTEL—$120/wk., 813 S. Flower St., (213) 627-6981.

   Also, the OAKWOOD APARTMENTS offer short-term leases for
decent apartments at several locations:
LOS ANGELES (NEAR UNIVERSAL CITY)—3600 Barham Blvd.,
   (213) 851-3450.
LOS ANGELES—209 S. Westmoreland, (213) 380-4421.
SHERMAN OAKS—4500 Woodman Ave., (818) 981-8060.
WEST L.A.—3636, S. Sepulveda Blvd., (310) 398-2794.

LOS FELIZ, SILVER LAKE, AND ECHO PARK

A wise man once said: Location, location, location. He was probably thinking of this area. Bordered by Griffith Park to the north and the 5, the 101, and the 110 freeways on the east, west, and south, these neighborhoods offer some of the most charming and convenient living situations in Los Angeles (with a few gnarly patches as well). Proximity to downtown businesses, the Burbank studios, and the mixed bag that is Hollywood makes this a good 'hood for work and play.

In these parts, unlike much of over-urbanized L.A., nature can actually be more than a drive-by. The 4,000-plus acres of Griffith Park make it the nation's largest municipal park, with miles of hiking and horseback trails, a modern zoo, a bird sanctuary, and free tennis courts, not to mention the hilltop observatory where James Dean and Sal Mineo rumbled in *Rebel Without a Cause*. A few miles to the south (near Dodger Stadium) is Elysian Park, the city's second-largest park, which features the stunning greenery of the Chavez Ravine Arboretum. In addition to this wealth of civic greenspace, parts of these neighborhoods are almost like parkland—great for walking and gawking—with their world-class architecture, serpentine streets, and superlative landscaping. But beware the air. It can be nasty, downright Valleyish at times, particularly in the low-lying areas around Sunset Boulevard. One other neighborhood caveat: Car thefts are fairly common, so take precautions—use the Club (or a cheap imitation) and rent a garage.

Your neighbors here are a mix of yuppies and guppies, artists and musicians, film-production folks and working-class Latino families. Cafes, restaurants and nightspots are sprinkled liberally throughout the area, but a high concentration of happening joints can be found along Vermont and Hillhurst avenues between Los Feliz and Sunset boulevards. See ya there.

If you are looking to buy:

In this area, be forewarned that housing ranges from plush to plebeian—with prices to match. Multimillion-dollar mansions dot the upper reaches of Los Feliz, on the cusp of Griffith Park, and prices taper off with the elevation, rising again in the Silver Lake hills, and again to a lesser extent in some of the Echo Park hills. An average house in a desirable area would probably hurt you to the tune of $200,000 to $500,000. In most other cities, that's a big ouch, but in L.A. (whose home prices are twice the national average) it's considered just a flesh wound.

<u>If you are looking to rent:</u>
The area is awash with architectural masterpieces from the likes of Richard Neutra, Rudolph Shindler, and Frank Lloyd Wright, but there are plenty of affordable places for rent (one-bedrooms average $500-$600 per month; two-bedrooms $600–$800; houses can be had for $700–$2,000 and up). Generally, you get what you pay for, but bargains are out there for those who persevere.

Essential Neighborhood Resources

<u>Area Code:</u> 213.

<u>Zip Code:</u> 90026.

<u>Police:</u> **Northeast Division,** 3353 San Fernando Dr., 485-2563.

<u>Hospitals:</u>
Hollywood Children's Hospital, 4650 Sunset Blvd., 660-2450;
Hollywood Presbyterian Medical Center, 1300 N. Vermont
    Ave., 413-3000.

<u>Post Offices:</u>
Los Feliz Station, 1825 N. Vermont Ave., 660-3240.
Echo Park, Edendale Station 1525 N. Alvarado, 413-3838.

<u>Libraries:</u>
Los Feliz Branch, 1801 Hillhurst Ave.. 913-4710.
Echo Park Branch, 515 N. Laveta Ter., 250-7808.

<u>Public Schools:</u>
Part of the **L.A. Unified School District** (LAUSD) Cluster Nine;
call 625-6154.

The area's **John Marshall High** is a two-time winner of the U.S. Academic Decathlon.

Banks:

With grocery stores and gas stations offering full-service ATM banking, you may rarely have to queue up at the teller line. But if you do . . .

Bank of America, 2420 Glendale Blvd., 740-9140.

California Federal Bank, 1900 W. Sunset Blvd., 484-8030.

Wells Fargo, 1534 N. Vermont Ave., 1-800-869-3557.

Grocery Stores:

Hughes Market, 2520 Glendale Blvd., 666-5392.

Von's Markets, 1342 N. Alvarado, 483-5573;
4520 W. Sunset Blvd., 662-8107.

Lucky, 2035 Hillhurst Ave., 660-0687.

Mayfair Markets, 2725 Hyperion Ave., 660-0387; 5877 Franklin
Ave., 464-7316. Upscale, high quality and huge selection.

INSIDER TIP: *Leave it to Angelenos to build a cult around a specialty grocer. TRADER JOE'S (at 2738 Hyperion Ave., 665-6774) is part of a quirky citywide chain favored by legions of scruffy well-heeled pilgrims. Whipped into a feeding and shopping frenzy by the store's pun-laden newsletter, the Trader Joe's faithful swear by the great whole-bean coffee, the exotic frozen foods, and the wholesome baked goods. Most cults have their preferred mind-altering substances, and at Trader Joe's it's booze—sold at about the lowest prices in town. Can I get a witness!?*

Drug Stores:

Thrifty Drug Stores, 1433 Glendale (at Alvarado) (213) 483-1128;
2656 Griffith Park Blvd. (at Hyperion), (213) 664-8105;

1533 N. Vermont (at Sunset), 666-5083.

Sav-On Drugs, 5510 Sunset Blvd., 464-2172; 2035 Hillhurst, 662-5105.

Colonial Drug, 1812½ N. Vermont Ave. 666-4044.

Sun Lake Drug, 2860 W. Sunset Blvd. (at Silver Lake). 663-5118.

Dry Cleaners:

Silver Lake Cleaners, 1726 W. Silver Lake Dr., 662-0959.

$1.50 Jasmine Cleaners, 3514 Sunset Blvd., 662-9193.

Griffith Park Cleaners, 2623 Hyperion Ave., 664-5717.

Hillhurst Cleaners, 1804½ Hillhurst Ave., 661-1088.

Laundromats:

Sunset Launderland, 3903 W. Sunset Blvd., 661-5241.

Sparkling Coin Laundry, 2590 Glendale Blvd., 668-2904.

Sunset Coronado Laundromat, 2500 W. Sunset Blvd., 483-8193.

Hardware Stores:

Baller Hardware and Building Materials, 2505 Hyperion Ave., 665-4149.

Cooper Hardware and Paint, 1645 W. Temple, 483-3353.

Orchard Supply Hardware Hollywood; 5525 Sunset Blvd., 871-1707.

Peerless Hardware, 2011 Sunset Blvd. (at Alvarado), 484-8077.

Video Stores:

Video-junkies of the world, unite—you have nothing to lose but your chains. **Video Journeys** (2728 Griffith Park Blvd., 663-5857) has an astounding selection of domestic and foreign releases cheaper than you can find them at Schlockbuster. Nearby **Video Active** (2522 Hyperion Ave., 669-8544) and **Video Hut** (2732 Hyperion Ave., 660-1166) are also good bets.

Main Drags:

Hillhurst and **Vermont avenues** between Hollywood and Los Feliz boulevards; also, the area around the intersection of **Griffith Park Boulevard** and **Hyperion Avenue**.

Landmarks:

The Angelus Temple—Evangelist Aimee Semple McPherson's distinctively curved church is right around the corner from Echo Park, which is a neighborhood landmark in its own right. 1100 Glendale Ave. (at Park Ave.).

The Silver Lake Reservoir—It isn't really a lake, but it's nice to have some open water in these parts in any case. Silverlake Blvd. at about Duane St.

Western Exterminator Sign—From the 101 Freeway, where Silver Lake meets Echo Park, you can see this giant billboard of a cartoon man wagging his finger in warning to a pesky rat— the man conceals a sledge hammer behind his back in case diplomacy fails.

Griffith Park Observatory's gleaming white stone walls can be seen from most of Los Feliz and Silver Lake.

The Great Outdoors:

Griffith Park, 4730 Crystal Springs Dr. (near Los Feliz Blvd. and Riverside Dr.), 665-5188. This 4,000-acre park contains 53 miles of hiking and equestrian trails, a railroad and transportation museum, the Autry Western Heritage Museum, tennis courts (some are free, some require a fee), several sports fields and an Olympic-size swimming pool, not to mention the Los Angeles Zoo, a golf course, picnic grounds, and the famous Observatory. If you can't find something to do in Griffith Park, stay home.

Elysian Park, 1880 N. Academy Rd., 222-9136. Enjoy a daytime hike amid this pleasant, 600-acre glade a stone's throw from downtown, and stop in at the friendly Police Academy Cafe. The city's second largest park has facilities that include ballfields, tennis courts, a gym, and great picnic areas.

Silverlake Rec Center (Silver Lake Blvd. and Van Pelt Place), 660-0556. Always a friendly game of hoops to be had next to a nice playground for the kids and the adjacent dogwalk (if you need to do any showbiz networking).

Echo Park Lake Rec Center, Bellevue Ave. and Glendale Blvd., 250-3578. Quaint (if slightly worn) favorite with tennis courts, ballfields, hoops, lakeside strolling, and pedal/paddle-boat rides.

Cafes and Diners:

Cafe Tropical—Guava cream cheese pie and high-octane Cuban coffee get the unpretentious locals piqued daily. 2900 Sunset Blvd. (at Silver Lake Blvd.), 661-8391.

Backdoor Bakery—Sidewalk scene-making and tasty pastries. 1710 Silver Lake Blvd., 662-7927.

DINNER THE FIRST NIGHT

NETTY'S is the neighborhood's low-budget gourmet spot for succulent chicken, perfect pasta, and a vast array of daily specials. You can relax on the few tables of their dumpy little patio and observe the shaggy trendies at the neighboring Backdoor Bakery, or order your food to go (like most everybody does) and chill at home. 1700 Silver Lake Blvd. (at Effie St.), 662-8655.

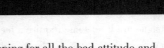

Millie's Diner—One-stop shopping for all the bad attitude and good food you can stomach. 3524 Sunset Blvd., 664-0404.

House of Pies—The blue-hair crowd crosses paths with Gen-X on the road to serious carbo-loading and bottomless cups of Joe. 1869 N. Vermont Ave., 666-9961.

Onyx Sequel—Loiter for hours over a coffee at this funky sidewalk landspill—you'll blend right in. 1804 Vermont Ave., no phone.

Miscellaneous Fun:

Smog Cutter—A hard-drinkin', Karaoke-singin', pool-shootin' dive full of crusty regulars and charming bartendresses. 864 N. Virgil Ave., 660-4626.

Dragonfly—Pogo 'till it's a no-go at the club that proves punk isn't dead, it just smells funny. 6510 Santa Monica Blvd., Hollywood, 466-6111.

Spaceland at Dreams of L.A.—Visit this buzzing alternative club early in the week to avoid a cover charge. Local folk-rap legend Beck drops in occasionally to do a set. 1717 Silver Lake Blvd., 661-4380.

Good Luck Bar—Hollywood hipster flotsam and jetsam washes up at this cozy spot for your amusement. 1514 Hillhurst, 666-3524.

Dresden Room—A throng is always camped out to absorb martinis and capable piano-lounge music. 1760 N. Vermont Ave., 665-4294.

Vida—The next generation of entertainment-biz moguls plans world conquest over high-end eats. 1930 Hillhurst Ave., 660-4446.

INSIDER TIP: *Alcohol anyone? Angelenos never have trouble finding liquor stores—most major supermarkets and many big drug stores have fully stocked liquor departments with decent prices.*

Travel Town—(in Griffith Park, see page 31) An open-air transportation museum with free train rides on Sunday as well as antique cars, planes, trolleys, and trains. Freudians and other children will love the fire trucks. 665-5188.

Gene Autry Western Heritage Museum—This museum of the American West is a great family outing. Educational, interesting, and lots of fun. 4700 Western Heritage Way, Griffith Park, 667-2000.

Dodgers Baseball—It's a great ballpark, and the cheap seats are still cheap enough that you can take the whole family (kids $3, adults $5). Even non-fans will enjoy a pleasant evening in the cool desert air. Dodger Stadium, 1000 Elysian Park Blvd., 224-1500; box office, 224-1448.

Circus of Books—A little bit of porno goes a long way,

but you can get regular mags too at this late-night spot. 4001 Sunset Blvd., 666-1304.

Vista Theater—A classic big, big screen made even better by management wisely removing every other row of seats. You'll be able to see even if Shaquille O'Neal sits in front of you. 4473 Sunset Dr., Hollywood.

You've Got Bad Taste—Exene Cervenka's jaded hipster joint with spoken-word events and groove-some bands doing in-stores. The illegible graffiti sign out front says it all—the store that inarticulately rages against the machine of commerce. Everything's swathed in the campy quotation marks of irony—when that's your trip, stumble in. 3816 W. Sunset Blvd., 669-1718.

Other notable neighborhood stops include **Cobalt Cantina,** 4326 Sunset Blvd., 953-9911; and **Cafe Capriccio,** 2547 Hyperion Ave., 662-5900.

> *"Hollywood is a place where people from Iowa mistake each other for stars."*
>
> ANONYMOUS

HOLLYWOOD, HOLLYWOOD HILLS, AND WEST HOLLYWOOD

There's gold in them thar hills—that's what prospecting '49ers said as they arrived in the Golden State in, well, '49. These days they could be talking about real estate in the Hollywood Hills, with its tony tangle of canyon roads chockablock with flashy yet rustic homes. No place epitomizes the social and economic contradictions of the L.A. experience like Hollywood. Within spitting distance of the rich and famous, the poor and desperate gather in the relentless sun to panhandle and plunder careless tourists along Hollywood Boulevard's star-studded Walk of Fame.

Hollywood, as one wag put it, is where all your dreams become realities and all your realities become dreams. Tinseltown metaphysics aside, in terms of simple geography Hollywood stretches from roughly Vermont Avenue in the east to Doheny Drive in the west, and from the Hollywood Hills down to around Melrose Avenue.

Hollywood is definitely a place where you can get too much of a good thing (and of bad things too—if you like). Young people flock from all over the Southland to sample the neon rainbow of nightlife options—live rock, pop, blues, and jazz joints flourish, as do numerous comedy clubs and discos of unbelievable variety. Bars of every stripe abound, from demimonde dives to cocktail nation campgrounds to glitzy upscale glam-ports. Name your poison.

If you choose to live in the Hollywood Flats, you'll be surrounded by diversity and adversity. When you're living in a melting pot it's easy to get burned, but poverty and cultural variety have their upside: affordable ethnic eateries abound, including Japanese, Thai, Chinese, Armenian, and Indian joints. Plus the streets run brown with cappuccino as chains like Starbucks and independent espresso bars proliferate. Depending upon the exact area, Hollywood can be a good daytime pedestrian neighborhood, with energetic urban density and some relaxing side streets. The commercial strip along Franklin Avenue (around Bronson) has a nice village feel to it, and the streets around Fairfax have urban presence without undue grit. Although parts of central Hollywood are plagued by crime, sleaze and drugs, the biggest danger as you approach the trendoid Melrose strip is likely to be your escalating Visa balance. In Hollywood, cheap thrills are often the best, and cafe-hopping on Melrose remains a people-watching smorgasbord of the first order.

When Horace Greeley said, "Go West, young man," you can be sure he wasn't thinking of the discos in West Hollywood, but many other folks have that covered—so not to worry. Predominantly gay West Hollywood, an independent city since 1984, manages to be gay-oriented without being hetero-hostile. It's a much safer, more upscale neighborhood than the scabrous central stretch of Hollywood proper. High-end shops, first-rate restaurants and packed nightclubs flourish, especially near the convergence of Melrose Avenue and Santa Monica Boulevard.

If you are looking to buy:

A shack in the hills runs about 200 Gs, and prices ascend swiftly from there into the millions. Hyper-developed WeHo is also steeply priced, with houses starting at $300,000; condos are also fully raging.

If you are looking to rent:
In Hollywood, a one-bedroom will run $300–$600 per month, two-bedrooms, $600–$800, and houses $600–$1,000. In the Hills, add $200–$300 for apartments and at least as much for houses. In West Hollywood, a one-bedroom will cost $500–$700 per month; a two-bedrooms $700–$900 per month, and houses $1,000–$1,300 per month.

Essential Neighborhood Resources
Area Code: 213.

Zip Codes: 90004, 90026, 90038, 90046, 90069, 90048.

Police:
Hollywood Division, 1358 N. Wilcox Ave., 485-4302.
West Hollywood, Los Angeles County Sheriff's Department,
   720 N. San Vicente Blvd., 855-8850.

Hospitals:
Kaiser Perminente Hospital, 4867 Sunset Blvd.,
   667-4011.
Hollywood Presbyterian Medical Center,
   1300 N. Vermont Ave., 413-3000.
Hollywood Community Hospital, 6245 DeLongpre Ave.,
   462-2271.

Post Offices:
Hollywood, 1615 Wilcox Ave., 464-2194.
Sunset, 1425 N. Cherokee, 460-4819.
West Branch, 820 N. San Vicente Blvd., (310) 652-2345.

Libraries:
Goldwyn Hollywood, 1623 N. Ivar Ave., 467-1821.
West Hollywood, 715 N. San Vicente Blvd., 652-5340.

Public Schools:

Part of LAUSD Cluster 11. For info,
call 742-7572.

INSIDER TIP: *The LOS ANGELES UNIFIED SCHOOL DISTRICT
(LAUSD) is extremely large and is broken up into different
clusters. Overall, there are 420 elementary schools, 72
middle schools, 49 senior high schools, 44 continuation
schools, 14 opportunity schools and centers, 18 schools
for the handicapped and 211 magnet schools and centers.*

Banks:

Wells Fargo, 6320 Sunset Blvd., 1-800-869-3557.
Bank of America, 1811 N. Western Ave., 730-9140.
Coast Federal, 1600 N. Vermont Ave., 662-3151.

In addition, most supermarkets and chain gas stations have ATMs
at the checkout.

Grocery Stores:

Jon's, 4520 W. Sunset Blvd., 662-8107; 5311 Santa Monica Blvd.,
461-9382.
Mayfair Markets, 5877 Franklin Ave., 464-7316;
1234 N. La Brea Ave., 464-2171.
Pavilion's, 727 Vine St., 461-4167.
Ralph's, 5420 W. Sunset Blvd., 871-8011.

INSIDER TIP: *GIBSON AND COOKE is a gourmet market great
for special occasions when you really want to impress
someone with classy appetizers or fancy cooking. It's also
a perfect place to stop when you need to bring something
over to a friend's house as a gift. 508 N. Doheny Dr.,
West Hollywood, (213) 272-7400.*

Drug Stores:

Thrifty Drug Stores, 1132 N. La Brea Ave. (at Santa Monica),
461-4295; 6130 Sunset Blvd. (at Gower), 467-8608;
5422 W. Sunset Blvd. (at Western), 464-0586; 1841 N. Western,
461-6170; 7900 W. Sunset Blvd. (at Fairfax), 876-0070.

Sav-On Drugs, 5510 W. Sunset Blvd., 464-2172;
7302 Santa Monica Blvd., West Hollywood, 850-6839.

Dry Cleaners:

Lido Cleaners and Laundry, 1905 Wilcox (at Franklin),
874-9600.

Paragon Dry Cleaners and Laundry, 1310 Vine St., 465-4663.

Hollywood Hills Cleaners, 1900 N. Highland Ave., 874-9491.

Laundromats:

Sanfair Cleaners and Laundry, 7877 Santa Monica Blvd.,
654-3852.

Hollyway Cleaners, 8359 Santa Monica Blvd., 654-1271.

Melrose Automatic Laundry, 619 N. La Brea Ave., 939-1497.

Vine Street Laundromat, 722 Vine St., 462-8038.

Hardware Stores:

Orchard Supply Hardware Hollywood, 5525 Sunset Blvd.,
871-1707.

Fred's Curb Hardware, 4583 Melrose (at Normandie),
663-7232.

Rompage Hardware, 5916 Hollywood Blvd., 467-2129.

Laurel Hardware, 7984 Santa Monica Blvd. (between Crescent
Hts. and Fairfax in West Hollywood), 656-9605.

Koontz, 8914 Santa Monica Blvd. West Hollywood,
(310) 652-0123.

Video Stores:

Rocket Video, 726. N. La Brea Ave. (at Melrose), 965-1100.
Selection, location and delivery—what else do you want?

Holly Hills Video, 1931 N. Bronson Ave., 463-1750.

Blockbuster Video, 7833 W. Sunset Blvd., 851-2688.

Main Drags:

Melrose (especially) as well as **Santa Monica** and **Sunset Boulevards** west of La Brea.

Landmarks:

The Hollywood sign—The clearest landmark in town, which originally read "Hollywoodland" when the 50-foot sign in the Hollywood Hills was erected in 1923 to promote a real estate development.

Capital Records—This circular office building wasn't really designed to look like a stack of records, but it sure turned out that way. 1750 Vine St. (near Hollywood Blvd.).

The Great Outdoors:

Runyon Canyon Park, A 15 minute walk up Curson Ave. from Hollywood Blvd. and you've escaped the doldrums of the Hollywood Flats. If you keep hiking for an hour you'll hit the top of the ridge—and get a panoramic view of the city and the Pacific.

Griffith Park, 4730 Crystal Springs Dr. (near Los Feliz Blvd. and Riverside Dr.; see page 31), 665-5188.

Frank Lloyd Wright's Hollyhock House, 4800 Hollywood Blvd. (near Vermont Ave.), 485-2116.all hidden right out in the open on a bluff rising right out of a rundown section of shabby old Hollywood.

Poinsettia Recreation Center, A gym, an auditorium, eight lighted tennis courts, handball courts at Willoughby and Poinsettia, 876-5014.

Cafes and Diners:

Authentic Cafe—The real thing gets real strange. Great Chinese and southwestern chow in a pleasantly crowded spot. 7605 Beverly Blvd., 939-4626.

Joseph's Cafe—Neighborhood staple for Greek and Mediterranean food—and star spotting. Actress Ione Skye and bassist Flea of the Chili Peppers, among others, have been known to stop in. 1775 N. Ivar St. (at Yucca St.), 462-8697

Bourgeois Pig—Work your van dyke (if you've got one) in this dark coffee bar with pool tables in the back. 5931 Franklin, 962-6360.

Ben Frank's Coffee Shop—Rock around the clock at this 24-hour breakfast favorite of the high-mileage hipster crowd. 8585 Sunset Blvd., (310) 652-8808.

Who's on Third—There's always a crowd for Sunday brunch and with one bite, you'll know why. 8369 Third St, 651-2928.

DINNER THE FIRST NIGHT

HIGHLAND GROUNDS—It's a coffee bar. It's an acoustic music venue. And it's also an excellent healthy restaurant with a good selection of beer and wine. Check the board for the specials, which are invariably good, but when in doubt opt for the blue-corn tacos. Relax and enjoy the cool night air on the patio, or come inside for some first-rate strumming. Hollywood casual. 742 N. Highland Ave., 466-1507.

Miscellaneous Fun:

Coconut Teaser—Young and rockin'. 8117 Sunset Blvd., 654-4773.

Thailand Plaza—E. Hollywood minimall crammed with Thai eateries and entertainment—"Thai Elvis" is a local favorite. 5321 Hollywood Blvd., 993-9000.

Viper Room—Johnny Depp's joint manages to be hip and relaxed—no mean feat. 8852 Sunset Blvd., West Hollywood, (310) 358-1880.

Rage—Everything a throbbing gay disco should be. 8911 Santa Monica Blvd., (310) 652-7055.

Musso and Frank Grill—This is either the oldest restaurant in Hollywood that serves the best martini or the best restaurant in Hollywood that serves the oldest martini. After a while, it's hard to tell. 6667 Hollywood Blvd., 467-7788.

House of Blues—Tasty Cajun eats paired with blues-roots music—from big names who often deserve to be much bigger. 8430 Sunset Blvd., 650-0247.

Checca—Gregarious and mostly gay with friendly drinking, dining, and dancing. 7231 Santa Monica Blvd., 850-7471.

Jones—Celebrities used to come here to drink, but now it's only people looking for celebrities—but they're fun to watch, too. 7205 Santa Monica Blvd., 850-1727.

Formosa Cafe—People who were famous decades ago used to hang out here, but they're all dead—in contrast to the lively crowd here. The Chinese food served here is mostly decorative. 7156 Santa Monica Blvd., 850-9050.

Family Fun:

Walk of Fame—The family will enjoy strolling Hollywood Boulevard and stepping on the stars (between La Brea and Vine).

INSIDER TIP: *Hearing the L.A. PHILHARMONIC at the Hollywood Bowl can be an expensive proposition, but you can often eavesdrop on rehearsals for free around midday. Pack a lunch. 2301 N. Highland Ave., 850-2000.*

HANCOCK PARK AND THE FAIRFAX DISTRICT (Mid-Wilshire)

These residential neighborhoods are full of character and relaxed charm. The area—which is part of what is called **Mid-Wilshire**—is roughly bounded by La Cienega to the west, Western Avenue to the east, Melrose to the north and Wilshire to the south.

Larchmont Village, near Beverly and Larchmont, is the perfect neighborhood for newcomers with auto anxiety—everybody in the neighborhood strolls to the plaza, which has a small-town, back-east feel to it. It's a pleasant area favored by families and low-key singles. And if you're overcome by a burning need to check out the latest advances in hairstyle technology or goatee grooming, hipster-haven Melrose is just a short hop, and restaurants and cafes aplenty can be found between La Brea and La Cienega. It's a stone's throw to Paramount and CBS, and downtown's an easy trip even in rush hour.

The Fairfax district offers an interesting ethnic mix, with a large community of Hasidic Jews and a variety of ethnic restaurants. Kosher everything can be found on Fairfax Avenue. The **Farmer's Market** at 3rd and Wilshire is a jumbled amalgam of open-air restaurants, fresh produce stands, tchotchke merchants, and big-time eavesdropping. This is one of the few spots in town that has a cosmopolitan big-city buzz—though maybe that's just the cappuccino.

Nightlife is pretty sparse in Hancock Park, but jumpin' Fairfax, Hollywood, and the Westside aren't so far away. The good news: When you get home, it's quiet.

If you are looking to buy:

Forget about the old-money mansions on the east side of Hancock Park until you make a big bucket of new money in the movie business. But in the more distressed areas farther west, some big old places can be had for $250,000 to $350,000. In the quaint Larchmont Village area, nice little houses with tidy yards can be found for under $200,000.

If you are looking to rent:

Houses can be pricey ($900–$2,000 per month) but the occasional Kato-guesthouse thing happens, so keep your eyes peeled. Often, officially renting these spots out can be a violation of zoning ordinances, so doing some service in lieu of rent is a situation that works out for all involved. One-bedrooms run from $500–$600; two-bedrooms $600–$1,000.

Essential Neighborhood Resources

Area Code: 213.

Zip Codes: 90004, 90019, 90036, 90048.

Police:
Hollywood Division, 1358 N. Wilcox Ave., 485-4202.
Wilshire Division, 4861 Venice Blvd., 485-4022.

Hospitals:
Cedars Sinai Hospital, 8700 Beverly Blvd., (310) 855-5000.

Westside Hospital, 910 S. Fairfax Ave. 938-3431.
Hollywood Presbyterian Medical Center,
  1300 N. Vermont Ave., 413-3000.

Post Offices:
Bicentennial Station, 7610 Beverly Blvd., 933-8448.
Miracle Mile, 5350 Wilshire Blvd., 933-5746.
Oakwood Station, 265 S. Western Ave., 383-3605.

Libraries:
Fairfax Branch, 161 S. Gardner St., 936-6191.
Memorial Branch, 4801 Wilshire Blvd., 934-0855.

Public Schools:
Part of LAUSD cluster 11. For info, call 742-7572.

Grocery Stores:
Farmer's Market, W. 3rd St. and Fairfax Ave., 933-9211.
Erewhon, 7660 Beverly Blvd., 937-0777. Pricey but good
  health-food grocery with a large selection.
Jon's, 3667 W. 3rd St., 382-5701, and also at 5311 Santa Monica
  Blvd., 461-9382.
Ralph's, 1010 S. Western Ave., 731-8525; 3410 W. 3rd St.,
  480-1421
Von's, 1831 W. 3rd, St., 483-1053, and also at 1430 S. Fairfax
  Ave., 939-9335, and 3461 W. 3rd St., 384-6342.

Drug Stores:
Thrifty Drug Stores, 334 S. Vermont (at 3rd), 381-7054;
  3420 Wilshire (at Mariposa) 380-9797.
Sav-On Drugs, 6360 W. 3rd St., 937-3030; 6155 W. Pico Blvd.,
  651-0440; 5570 Wilshire Blvd., 936-6123.

Dry Cleaners:
Larchmont Cleaners, 415 N. Larchmont Blvd., 461-9519.
Fairfax Laundry and Dry Cleaning, 1058 S. Fairfax, 939-6980.
Chapman Cleaners, 3450 W. 6th (at Kenmore), 386-6816.

Laundromats:

Launderland, 5960 W. Pico.

Maytag Coin Laundry, 1606 Beverly Blvd., 975-1277.

Hardware Stores:

Larchmont Hardware, 152 N. Larchmont (btwn. 3rd and
 Beverly), 463-5783.

Callahan Hardware, 139 S. Western Ave.(between 1st and 2nd),
 387-3336.

Video Stores:

Rocket Video—Tons of titles, and they even deliver. 726. N. La
 Brea Ave. (at Melrose), 965-1100.

Blockbuster Video—You know the drill. 5353 Wilshire, 934-8367.

Main Drags:

Melrose Avenue, west of La Brea.

Larchmont Boulevard (at Beverly).

Fairfax Avenue.

DINNER THE FIRST NIGHT

In L.A., Thai food is the hamburger and French fries of the '90s—everyday food that can often be mediocre. Get your taste buds off on the right foot at CHAN DARA with some Pad Thai, Satay, and sweet Crispy Noodles. Caution: Flammable—this location of Chan Dara (there are two others) tends to go pretty hot on the spices. Ask for yours mild, unless you prefer the authentic tongue-flambé type of Thai food. If you're too tired to venture out, they deliver. 310 N. Larchmont Blvd., 467-1052.

Landmarks:

The CBS Television City at Beverly Boulevard and Fairfax is an air-
plane hangar you can't miss when you're driving by. 800 Beverly Blvd.

The Beverly Center's hulking form can be seen for miles down Beverly Boulevard, so you can use this upscale mall as a navigational aid if need be.

The Great Outdoors:

If L.A. starts to drag you down, remember that things could always be worse. Visit those fossil fools down at the **La Brea** tar pits and imagine yourself neck-deep in black slime like some extinct Mastodon. Wilshire Boulevard and Curson avenue.

Queen Anne Rec Center—All your urban recreation needs can be met here: tennis, volleyball, hoops, picnic areas, and ballfields. At West and Pico, 237-1726.

Cafes and Diners:

The Living Room—Fashionably funky types take their cappuccino breaks here when they tire of antique shopping along La Brea. 112 S. La Brea Ave., 933-2933.

red—Slightly smug but definitely happenin' wine bar. 7450 Beverly Blvd., 937-0331.

King's Road—A cafe where people go to be seen and overheard—with a great newsstand outside. 8363 Beverly Blvd., 655-9044.

Gingham Garden—Go elbow-to-elbow with your neighbors at this chatty cafe in Larchmont Village. 123 N. Larchmont, 461-1677.

Insomnia Cafe—Sleep is for wimps at this energetic java joint. 7286 Beverly Blvd., 931-4943.

Miscellaneous Fun:

Canter's Deli—Bright and sprawling favorite on Fairfax Avenue's kosher corridor. 419 N. Fairfax Ave., 651-2030.

India's Oven—Excellent, economical fare with polite yet painfully relentless service. 7231 Beverly Blvd., 936-1000.

Du-pars—Legendary heavy-duty pancakes. 6333 W. 3rd St. (in the Farmer's Market), 933-8446.

Pink's Famous Chili Dogs—Doyens of the dog dig this one to death. 709 N. La Brea Ave., 931-4223.

Gengis Cohen Cantina—Folk 'till ya choke at this ultra-hip haunt for up-and-comers. 740 N. Fairfax Ave., 653-0640.

Lucy's Drive-In—Tasty 24-hour drive-thru Mexican place.
1373 S. La Brea (at Pico), 938-4337.

INSIDER TIP: *THE BARGAIN CIRCUS (also known as La Brea Circus) is a bizarre bazaar that includes several different stores within its labyrinthine confines. There's an economical Armenian deli, an intermittently good produce stand, and a vast array of off-brand and way-off-brand merchandise. Consider picking up a bar of 1st-Date Deodorant Soap or a can of Rusty Dog Food just for laughs. Or stroll amid long aisles of canned goods, household items, and small appliances until you locate the serious brand-name bargains. 852 La Brea Ave. (near Melrose), 466-7231.*

<u>Family Fun:</u>

George C. Page Museum of La Brea Discoveries— Actually part of the Natural History Museum, the La Brea tar pits outside the museum proper are an L.A. landmark. Kids will want to check out the holographic displays, fossils, and bones, and learn all about L.A. in the dinosaur age. 5801 Wilshire Blvd., L.A., 857-6306.

LACMA Art Classes for Kids can help draw the whole family together. 5905 Wilshire Blvd., 857-6110.

THE WESTSIDE: PRELUDE

Unlike most other major cities, downtown in L.A. isn't the only mecca for business and nightlife. The Westside exerts a strong pull and exhibits its own peculiar quasi-autonomy. One Realtor explained, "People coming from Manhattan are the only ones who can really relate to the Westside. Century City, not downtown, is our midtown Manhattan. Downtown is like Wall Street. So if you live in Brentwood, you have to think of it as 20 minutes from midtown." This analogy captures the mindset of many egotistical Westsiders who consider their turf the real center of Los Angeles.

How Do You 'Do?

If you don't look good, they don't look good, which is probably why so many people always look so damn good in this town. Here's a list of the top-notch hair stylists in town:

CHRIS MCMILLAN—*Estillo Salon, 7402 Beverly Blvd., L.A., 936-6775. This list would not be complete without the man who turned Jennifer Aniston's haircut into the only haircut to have. Trendsetter McMillan also does Cameron Diaz, Patricia Arquette, and Christian Slater.*

ART LUNA—*Art Luna, 8930 Keith Ave., West Hollywood, 247-1383. Los Angeles Magazine called this "the ultimate insider salon" probably because it is located in a bungalow on a side street in West Hollywood—you either know about it or you don't. Anjelica Huston, Lauren Hutton, and Kelly Lynch certainly do.*

COREY POWELL—*Jonathan Salon, 910 Westbourne Dr., West Hollywood, (310) 855-0225. After you leave your car with the valet, head upstairs to the private loft where it is rumored Michelle Pfeiffer can be seen from time to time.*

STUART GAVAERT—*Umberto, 416 N. Canon Dr., Beverly Hills, (310) 274-6395. This colorist famous for his work with blondes has been written up in so many women's magazines, it's hard to keep track. His latest clients include Courtney Thorne-Smith and Christina Applegate.*

LORRI GODDARD—*Cristophe Salon, 348 N. Beverly Dr., Beverly Hills, (310) 315-0455. She'll actually send you away if she doesn't think she can give you the exact color you want. But considering she works wonders with all her clients, including Kate Capshaw and Pamela Anderson, it isn't likely you'll leave disappointed.*

If you don't need to look that good, you can shorten your hair without shorting your bank account at SUPERCUTS or FANTASTIC SAM'S, two chains that offer reliable snipping at several outlets citywide.

WHO'S THAT GIRL?

One of the first L.A. rites of passage is driving down La Cienega or Sunset Boulevard and getting a glimpse of that famous pink poster girl. Who's the girl of indeterminate age on the billboard with the balloon-like breasts looking seductive and sexy with a phone number running across her body? May we introduce you to Angelyne, a local Los Angeles celebrity who doesn't really do anything but pose for her billboards and make herself seem very busy. For years, these billboards have bombarded the streets of the city, and yet Angelyne still hasn't made it in Hollywood. In fact, she rarely ventures out, making some suspect that she relies heavily on air-brushing.

Still, she is something of an icon in this star-studded city. You may have seen some close-ups of her billboards in Get Shorty. Gene Hackman's fictitious office was directly under an Angelyne photo. It was something of an inside joke, and well, now you are on the inside.

The **Westside** is somewhat amorphous, however. In addition to the zip codes that are actually considered to be West L.A., several other smaller neighborhoods also make up the Westside. Brentwood, Beverly Hills, Century City, Westwood and Mar Vista can all be considered West L.A.

Much of the city's business is done on the Westside. In fact, Century City is home to over 220 law firms, in addition to countless entertainment production companies, ad agencies, and public relations firms. UCLA is located in Westwood, which is in the heart of West L.A. As a result, bars, coffeehouses, and pool halls proliferate. Westwood Village boasts 17 movie theaters. But the Westside is much more than a hopping student ghetto.

Many of L.A.'s best restaurants are located on the Westside, and there is certainly no lack of shops there either, with the **Century City shopping center and market place** (10250 Santa Monica Blvd.), **the Westside Pavilion** (10850 and 10800 W. Pico Blvd.), and **Santa**

Monica Place (395 Santa Monica Place, 394-5477), not to mention several hundred specialty stores and boutiques. Here's a look at some of the most popular Westside neighborhoods.

BEVERLY HILLS

Believe it or not, you can (well, maybe) afford to live in Beverly Hills — 90212, that is, not 90210. The mansions of the rich and famous are located north of Wilshire Boulevard, up in the hills. However, south of Wilshire, there are actually much older buildings with reasonable rents.

The advantage of being a Beverly Hills resident is that you are entitled to Beverly's municipal services, which are generally considered to be far superior to those of Los Angeles. Beverly Hills schools are independent of LAUSD, so they have more money and better facilities. Greenery is also abundant in Beverly Hills—Roxbury Park is a great place to exercise, shoot some hoops, or just go for a walk. Green also lines Wilshire to the north, where there is almost always some kind of show or festival taking place. On the outskirts of Beverly Hills, east of Doheny, is an L.A. address with a great young neighborhood that boasts trendy cafes, popular shops, and the everything mall—otherwise known as the Beverly Center. If you live in Beverly Hills right on the boundary, you get the best of both worlds: BH zip codes with all of their financially stable municipalities to the west, and a hip, younger neighborhood to the east.

When they are available, the side streets near Beverly Hills High School are full of duplex-type apartments that have the charm most places in L.A. are missing. These are few and far between, and snagging a place is usually about timing. Easier to find are apartments on the side streets around Beverly Dr., and the side streets near Doheny, which is really the farthest area to the east considered Beverly Hills.

If you are looking to buy or rent:

In addition to the previously mentioned sources, *The Beverly Hills Post* and *The Beverly Hills Courier* are also good if you are looking to buy or lease. These papers can be picked up at various markets, restaurants and stores located throughout Beverly Hills. Singles can go for as little as $700, but there are also nicer places with rents of $1,000. Most doubles go for $1,100-plus, but you should be able to find a comfortable place and stay at $1,100. As mentioned, the buildings are older and may not come with a dishwasher, garbage disposal, air-conditioner, parking spot or laundry facilities. Make sure to ask about all of this. (Liebes Properties, 1821 Wilshire Blvd., 264-7712, may be a good source to check with).

INSIDER TIPS:
- *Beware that even if you find a reasonably priced place here, car insurance rates are sky high if you have a Beverly Hills zip code. Make sure to check with your insurance company before you sign your lease.*
- *Check out the parking situation carefully, because most parking in Beverly Hills is by permit only. You will have to buy a permit for yourself, but it may be best to buy an extra one so your visitors can park without piling up painful parking tickets.*

Essential Neighborhood Resources
<u>Area Code:</u> 310.

<u>Zip Codes:</u> 90210, 90211, 90212.

<u>Police:</u> **Beverly Hills Police Department,** 464 N. Rexford Dr., 550-4800.

<u>Hospitals:</u> **Cedars-Sinai Medical Center,** 8700 Beverly Boulevard, 855-5000.

<u>Post Offices:</u>
Beverly Branch, 312 S. Beverly Dr., 247-3458.
Crescent Branch, 469 N. Crescent Dr., 247-3451.
Eastgate Station, 8383 Wilshire Blvd., 247-3461.

<u>Library:</u>
Beverly Hills Library is an excellent library with wonderful resources

and a very helpful staff. Their computer system is logical and user-friendly, in contrast to L.A.'s clunker. 444 N. Rexford Dr., 288-2220.

Public Schools:
Beverly Hills School District—Four elementary schools, one high school. For information, call 277-5900.

Banks:
Fidelity Federal, 403 N. Beverly Dr., 278-7200.
California Federal Bank, 9720 Wilshire Blvd., 550-8667.
American Savings, 9090 Wilshire Blvd., 859-6572.

Grocery Stores:
Pavilion's, 9467 W. Olympic Blvd., 553-5734.
Gelson's—10250 Santa Monica Blvd., 277-4288. Most 90210-ers do their shopping here—the produce is superb, the prepared food is delicious, and the prices unfortunately reflect this.

Drug Stores:
Rox-San Pharmacy, 465 N. Roxbury Dr., 273-1644.
Pay Less Drug Stores, 463 Bedford Dr., 247-0840.

Dry Cleaners:
The Cleaning Spot, 308½ Beverly Dr., 556-1121.
Beverly Wilshire Cleaners, 8302 Wilshire Blvd., (213) 653-0525.

Laundromat:
Sparkling Coin Laundry, 8959 Santa Monica Blvd., 274-1395.

Hardware Stores:
Carter Hardware Inc., 153 N. Robertson Blvd., 657-1940.
Pioneer Lucerne Hardware, 315 N. Crescent Dr., 276-1167.

Video Stores:
Blockbuster Video, 270 S. Robertson Blvd., 854-0991.
Videocentre—large selection with a small neighborhood feel—145 S. Beverly Dr., 550-1092.

Main Drags:

Rodeo Dr.—It's not the Champs-Elysées but it is a sight to see.

Beverly Dr.—It's the boom in Beverly Hills at the moment. With clothing chains such as The Gap, Victoria's Secret, and the Limited, it's also the most user-friendly street in this area.

DINNER THE FIRST NIGHT

NEWSROOM CAFE—120 N. Robertson Blvd., 652-4444. The food is absolute L.A.—veggie burgers and natural juices. The staff too is oh, so L.A.—out-of-work actors and frustrated screenwriters. And in case you get bored, there is a fully stocked newsstand to choose from, not to mention a radio running at all times and the constant news from CNN broadcast on two different TVs.

For a quick bite or to take out, try BAJA FRESH. It's healthy-ish Mexican with tasty guacamole and sensational salsas. The Baja burrito is fantastic. Just remember that they'll make it anyway you like it, so it can be healthy—minus the cheese, sour cream, and guacamole. 475 N. Beverly Dr., 858-6690.

Landmarks:

The Beverly Hills Hotel—Often called the big pink, it's a part of Los Angeles history, and like most all Hollywood legends, it's recently had a face-lift. 9641 W. Sunset Blvd.

Beverly Hills Municipal buildings —A beautiful display of architecture, these buildings look a little (well, a lot) different than the city buildings downtown. 270 N. Canon Dr.

The Great Outdoors:

Roxbury Recreational Center, 471 S. Roxbury Dr., 550-4761. There's always some type of game going on—whether it's soccer, B-ball, or softball. A great place to escape on a Sunday afternoon. And of course, this BH park is not without its celebs: Rod Stewart and Rachel Hunter have been spotted playing with their offspring.

Cafes and Diners:

Larry Parker's Beverly Hills—The quintessential diner gone Beverly Hills (open 24 hours). 206 S. Beverly Dr., 274-9007.

Brighton Coffee Shop—A charming old place that's been serving Beverly Hills brats for who knows how many years. 9600 Brighton Way, 276-7732.

Armani Cafe—Located upstairs at Emporio Armani, it's dark, stark, and quiet with over-priced dishes and under-valued "dish" from the tables nearby. 9533 Brighton Way, 271-9940.

Il Fornaio—Great for a leisurely breakfast outside especially if you order the pancakes. 301 N. Beverly Dr., 550-8330.

The Hollywood Hot Dog—It's the best, well only-hot dog stand in Beverly Hills. The turkey dogs are a neighborhood favorite. 9527 Santa Monica Blvd., 278-4674.

Miscellaneous Fun:

Balducci's—Family-style dining with huge portions and wine on the honor system. 300 N. Beverly Dr., 858-0445.

Barney Greengrass—Extremely pricey, and snooty too, but if you can suck it up, the breakfast is amazing—the best whitefish in town. In Barney's New York at 9570 Wilshire Blvd., 777-5877.

Kate Mantilini—One of the only places around that's open late every night and until 3 a.m. on weekends. 9101 Wilshire Blvd., 278-3699.

WESTWOOD AND WEST LOS ANGELES

UCLA students dominate **Westwood,** which is great if you are looking for reasonable prices, friendly neighbors, loud music, and frequent pizza deliveries. If you're not, don't even consider living north of Wilshire near Westwood Village. However, south of Wilshire between Westwood all the way to Bundy is a whole other story. While some still think this neighborhood is reserved for the blue and gold, graduate students and young professionals make up a large percentage of the population.

Living here puts you right smack in the middle of everything. You are close to the beach and to great nightlife, and shouldn't be more than a 20-minute commute to work or school unless it's USC or downtown.

A decade ago, Westwood Village was the happening place to be. Unfortunately, gangs moved in and turned this boomtown into a bust town. Slowly Westwood has recovered from the fall and is rising to the top again. With lively bars, a new microbrewery, a latte on every corner, and movie theaters galore, Westwood is once again attracting crowds. In fact, if you are planning on seeing a new movie in the Village, it's wise to buy your tickets ahead of time. (Between the students and the show-biz folks, getting into a new flick takes strategy.)

Hidden in a small area of West L.A. is a mini "Little Tokyo." Along Sawtelle Boulevard between Wilshire and Olympic is a mix of wonderful Asian cuisine, specialty markets, and some of the best sushi the city has to offer. With so many good places, just let your nose lead the way. And for the best Ramen in town? Ramenya, 11555 W. Olympic Blvd., 575-9337.

If you are looking to buy or rent:

In Westwood, try the **Roberts Companies** at 312-9090. They own a lot of nice buildings throughout West L.A., Also, call **R. Scott Tucker and Associates,** 11941 Santa Monica Blvd., 479-2565. The *Daily Bruin* is a great source for apartment listings in this area, too. Also check out the community paper, **Westwood News.** Both of these free papers can be picked up in several locations throughout Westwood Village. The *Daily Bruin* sits alongside the *Los Angeles Times* on most ever corner where they have news boxes. Generally, one-bedrooms go for $800 to $1,100, depending on size. Doubles go for around $1,100. Most places south of Wilshire come with parking as well as a dishwasher and garbage disposal. But beware, parking in Westwood is horrible, and when you do find a meter, it'll cost you. A quarter only buys you eight minutes in some parts of Westwood Village.

Essential Neighborhood Resources
Area Code: 310.

Zip Codes: 90024, 90025.

Police: **West Los Angeles Division,** 1663 Butler Ave., 575-8401.

Hospital:
UCLA Medical Center, 10883 Le Conte Ave., 825-9111.

Post Offices:
West Los Angeles Branch, 11420 Santa Monica Blvd., 477-1539.
Village Station, 11000 Wilshire Blvd., 575-7771.

Library: **West Los Angeles Regional Branch,** 11360 Santa
Monica Blvd., 575-8323.

Public Schools:
Part of LAUSD Cluster 10 which includes **Hamilton, Palisades**
and **University High School.** Call 473-5743.

Banks:
Great Western Bank, 10901 Wilshire Blvd., Westwood
208-0195.
Coast Federal Bank, 11766 Wilshire Blvd., 820-5692.
First Interstate Bank of California, 11836 San Vicente Blvd.,
826-6611.

Grocery Stores:
Ralph's, 11727 W. Olympic Blvd., 473-5238. Huge supermarket with
reasonable prices and a delicious make-your-own-pizza station.
Gelson's, 10250 Santa Monica Blvd., 277-4288.
Trader Joe's, 10850 National Blvd., 470-1917.

Drug Stores:
Westside Village Pharmacy, 1391 Westwood Blvd., Westwood,
474-4222.
Thrifty, 11321 National Blvd., 473-6517.

Dry Cleaners:
Sterling Cleaners, 1600 Westwood Blvd., 474-8525. You'll pay for
the convenience so make sure and tell THEM when you
want your clothes returned.
Carriage Trade Cleaners, 11803 Wilshire Blvd., 477-8088.

Laundromat:

Westwood Coin Laundry, 1874 Westwood Blvd., 474-5233. Because you're in a college town, it's safe and can front for a pick up spot on Sunday afternoons.

Hardware Stores:

Boulevard Hardware, 1456 Westwood Blvd., 475-0795.
Ayres Hardware, 10577 W. Pico Blvd., 475-1720.

Video Stores:

Blockbuster Video, 12112 Santa Monica Blvd., 447-2481.
The Wherehouse, 1860 Westwood Blvd., 470-7959.
Laser Video West, 11701 Wilshire Blvd., 479-4069.

Main Drags:

Westwood Blvd.—It's a main boulevard that leads directly into Westwood Village and on into UCLA.

Wilshire Blvd.—Another major boulevard, Wilshire can get pretty busy in this area because it is a mini-Century City in that many businesses are located in the highrises here.

Landmarks:

UCLA—405 Hilgard Ave. Tanned coeds blade to class and then take time off to study—well, soak up the sun.

Mann Bruin theater—9560 Broxton Ave. If you're a frequent *Entertainment Tonight* viewer, you'll recognize this spot immediately. Major movie premieres take place here while celebs take turns walking up and down the red carpet.

INSIDER TIP: *BORDERS BOOKSTORE has become something like the Babysitter's Club on Saturday nights around 9:00. It's a family hangout where there is something for everyone, including music and snacks. 1360 Westwood Blvd., 475-3444.*

The Great Oudoors:

UCLA has beautiful grounds that make for a perfect morning or afternoon walk. Also, the park located next to the Federal Building at Wilshire Blvd. and Veteran is always crowded with families picnicking, seniors strolling, and sweaty Gen-Xers plus or minus a few years giving it their all at a sport of choice—usually basketball.

Cafes and Diners:

Lulu's Alibi—1640 Sawtelle Blvd., 479-6007.

Cacao—11609 Santa Monica Blvd., 473-7283.

Sandbags—Brown-bag it in style at this small sandwich spot with big college-town charm. 1134 Westwood Blvd., 208-1133.

Jerry's Deli—It's coming to Westwood (Weyburn Ave.) soon, maybe even by the time you get here. It's sure to do well with the college crowd—it's open round the clock.

Coffee Bean and Tea Leaf—There's actually two in Westwood to meet the high demand for caffeine. 1001 Gayley Ave., 208-1991 and 10887 Weyburn Ave., 208-8018.

INSIDER TIP: *For good Chinese take out, call 1-800-WOK-FAST.*

Miscellaneous Fun:

Q's Billiard Club—The crowd is young, the routine is old, but shooting pool never goes out of style. 11835 Wilshire Blvd., 477-7550.

The Sushi House—Small and crowded but definitely worth the wait. 12013 W. Pico Blvd., 479-1507.

DINNER THE FIRST NIGHT

ISLANDS—Great burgers, salads, and soft tacos if you can stand eating under posters of perfect bikini-clad women. The most popular item on the menu is probably the Pelican chicken sandwich, but most important, you must order their legend__ry fri__ seasoned

Maloney's On Campus—A college bar with all the amenities: beer, loud music, smoke, sports, and shots of tequila. What could be better? 1000 Gayley Ave. (Westwood), 208-1942.

Main Line Brewing Co.—Westwood's very own microbrewery, with continuous sports coverage on multiple screens. 1056 Westwood Blvd., 443-5401.

Ramayani—Nuff said. 1777 Westwood Blvd., 477-3315.

JR Seafood—Great Chinese food at great prices with very little atmosphere so bring along a crowd you really like and make your own fun. 11901 Santa Monica Blvd., 268-2463.

CULVER CITY, PALMS, AND MAR VISTA

People who realize that being in the heart of the action also means paying through the nose might prefer the low-key convenience of these economical and comfortable neighborhoods. Culver City, Palms, and Mar Vista—south of the 10 Freeway down to around Slauson, east from Centinela over to about Jefferson—are centrally located yet out of the way. Venice Beach, Santa Monica, LAX, DreamWorks' new studio, and Westside nightspots are all just a short drive—and you'll soon come to appreciate being where the action isn't.

Excellent eateries along Venice Boulevard, Washington Boulevard, and Motor Avenue cater especially to the Sony Studios lunch crowd, but residents whose only contribution to the industry is squandering $7.50 on the *Last Action Hero* also get to share the culinary benefits with the big shots.

Young families favor independent Culver City for its excellent schools, and young professionals and working stiffs in the nearby neighborhoods of L.A. proper appreciate the shot of stability that family life supplies. Housing is relatively cheap here, and the bustling Fox Hills Mall on Jefferson simplifies shopping into that oddly calming quasi-suburban mall-rush we all know too well. The *Leave It to Beaver* atmosphere is shattered somewhat by a bit too much burglary and vandalism spilling over from Venice (especially in Palms), but these eternally transitional neighborhoods never seem to make the really bad transition into free-fire zone.

The mostly flat terrain makes for great casual bike escapes to the beach in Venice. Depending on the winds, you're either cooled by gentle ocean breezes or fouled by nasty freeway dust. If you have a long rush-hour commute, you will come to know the 405 Freeway as Satan's parking lot. And the 10 isn't much better. (When Angelenos say an area is convenient to freeways, they often only mean it's convenient right up to the entrance ramp—and not an inch farther. Be warned: L.A. humor is sometimes as dry as the air.) If your car should go down, bus service from over here to the rest of the city is awful. **Culver City Bus info:** (310) 253-6500.

If you are looking to buy:
Small homes in Culver City will set you back $200,000–$300,000 and condos $90,000–$150,000. In Palms and some parts of Mar Vista, you can get a lot more home for the same money—or something small for less.

If you are looking to rent:
These areas are a mid-price bonanza with plenty of places always available, especially in Palms. one-bedroom, $450-$650; two-bedroom, $600–$800. Houses, $600–$1,400 and, of course, up.

Essential Neighborhood Resources
<u>Area Code:</u> 310.

<u>Zip Codes:</u> 90230, 90232, 90034.

<u>Police:</u>
Culver City Police Headquarters, 4040 Duquesne Ave., 837-1221.
Palms and Mar Vista, L.A. Pacific Division, 12312 Culver Blvd., 202-4502.

<u>Hospitals:</u>
Brontman Medical Center, 3828 Delmas Ter., 836-7000.
Washington Medical Center, 12101 W. Washington Blvd., 391-0601.

<u>Post Offices:</u>
Culver City Main, 11111 Jefferson Blvd., 391-6374.
Fox Hills Station, 6083 Bristol Parkway, 645-0173.

Gateway Station, 9942 Culver Blvd., 204-1051.
Palms Station, 3751 Motor Ave., 839-1181.
Mar Vista Station, 3865 Grandview Blvd., 390-3491.

Libraries:
Culver City Library, 4975 Overland Ave., 559-1676.
Palms-Ranchero Park Branch, 2920 Overland Ave., 838-2157.
Mar Vista Branch, 12006 Venice Blvd., 390-3454.

Public Schools:
Culver City Unified School District, five elementary schools, one middle school, one senior high school, one continuation school, one adult school and one children's center. Call 842-4200.

Grocery Stores:
Lucky Food Centers, 3456 S. Sepulveda Blvd., 839-3577; 5750 Messmer Ave., 390-2373.
Pavilion's, 11030 Jefferson Blvd., 398-1945.
Von's, 9860 National Blvd., 836-4161; 4030 Centinela Ave., 391-1503.
Gelson's, 13455 Maxella Ave., 306-2953.

Drug Stores:
Thrifty Drug Stores, 8708 W. Pico Blvd., 652-5141.
Sav-On, 5748 Messmer Ave., 915-9652; 6299 S. Bristol Pkwy., 641-3901.

Dry Cleaners:
Baronet Cleaners and Laundry, 12831 Washington Blvd., 306-7976.
Cheviot Palms Cleaners, 3371 Motor Ave., 839-1554.
Raintree Cleaners, 10774 Jefferson Blvd., 559-6580.

Laundromats:
18 Minute Wash, 9838 National Blvd., 202-1685.
The Neighborhood Coin Laundry, 11127 Venice Blvd., 842-7536.

Hardware Stores:

Culver City Hardware, 5429 Sepulveda Blvd., 398-1251.
Dick's True Value Hardware, 12210 Venice Blvd., 397-3220.
Mar Vista Lumber Co., 3860 Grandview Blvd., 870-7431.

Main Drags:

Venice Boulevard
Washington Boulevard

Landmarks:

Columbia/Sony Studios on the old MGM lot just off Venice
Boulevard, where a heap of classics and many recent bombs
have been made.

The Fox Hills Mall at Sepulveda at Slauson is impossible to miss,
and you really shouldn't.

DINNER THE FIRST NIGHT

Culver City's bustling VERSAILLES—*10319 Venice Blvd., 90034,
558-3168—is no palace, but there is often an unruly mob outside.
Don't worry, they're just waiting to eat. This road house's nothing
decor and raucous atmosphere doesn't detract from the hearty, reasonably priced food however. Roasted garlic chicken served with
black beans, fried plantains and rice is the hands-down favorite, but
the pork chop dinner is an excellent choice for those of us with a
thing for swine (you know who you are). After a filling meal and a
couple of Bohemia's or Corona's you may need to re-stoke with a
double espresso. Don't you have some unpacking to do?*

The Great Outdoors:

Kenneth Hahn State Recreational Area—315 acres of
reclaimed parkland set on the site of a former oil reserve,
which offers hiking trails, two small fishing lakes, picnic areas,
a basketball court, and a welcome expanse of green. 4100 S.
La Cienega Blvd. (between Rodeo Road and Stocker Street.)

Culver Slauson Park—Fields and hoops and picnic areas. 5070 Slauson Ave., 398-5291.

Mar Vista Recreation Center—Small strip of park just where it's needed. 11430 Woodbine St., 398-5982.

Culver City Park—It's not that easy being green in industrial/ residential Culver City, but this is a good bet. Jefferson Blvd. and Duquesne Ave..

Cheviot Hills Recreation Center—With 14 lighted tennis courts, Cheviot Hills is the biggest and busiest of the city's public racquet centers. They also have basketball courts, a gymnasium, and well-maintained ball fields. Call 836-5186 for specific info.

INSIDER TIP: *MRS. GOOCH'S NATURAL FOODS offers slightly pricey but wholesome foods such as free-range chicken, earth-enslaved vegetables, and organic what-have-you. It's a friendly, quintessentially L.A. place, which, even if you don't go in for competitive healthsmanship, is definitely worth the trip. 3476 Centinela Ave., 391-5209 (and other locations citywide).*

And if you tire of the typical suburban subdivision fare, take a culinary excursion to the subcontinent at INDIA SWEETS AND SPICES, specializing in import Indian and British foods. 9409 Venice Blvd., 837-5286

<u>Cafes and Diners:</u>

Ships—Space Age futuristic '50s diner with toasters at every table. 10705 Washington Blvd., 839-2347.

Peterson's Frisch Rost—Comfy spot for jazz, folk, and word. 10019 Venice Blvd., 839-3359.

Coffee Bean and Tea Leaf—When you need that double-decaf mocha mint latte done just so. 13440 Maxella, Marina del Rey, 823-0858.

Bob's Big Boy—A California classic. 5350 Sepulveda, 397-9044.

The Burger Factory—This is the kind of factory work that's easy to stomach. Fox Hills Mall, 398-5559.

George's Coffee Shop—Maybe not the grill of your dreams, but she'll do in a pinch. 5439 Sepulveda, 391-9303.

Miscellaneous Fun:

D.B. Cooper's Restaurant and Saloon—Throngs slosh and nosh in a kinda yuppie kinda sports bar kinda place. 3387 Motor Ave., 839-2500.

Jabberjaw—It's a bit out of the Culver area—into Crenshaw no-man's land—but the youngish crowd that thrashes to alternative bands swears by it. 3711 W. Pico Blvd., (213) 732-3463.

Culver Saloon—Yee-haw crowd stomps to live local country music. 11513 Washington Blvd., 391-1519.

Jazz Bakery—Great place to savor the ever-tasty blue note and some pastries from the adjacent cafe. 3233 Helms Ave., 271-9039.

Sarna's Lounge—Darts, drinks, and pool in an unpretentious corner bar. 10899 Venice Blvd., 839-6197.

Family Fun:

Centinela Adobe—Take the kids back to the 19th century—and leave them there. A joke, just a joke. This 1834 adobe house, which preserves some of the original planting, is packed with antiques and offers free tours. 7634 Midfield Ave. (near La Cienega), 677-1154, 649-6272.

Allied Model Trains—Tiny fun for big kids and little ones. 4411 Sepulveda Blvd., (310) 313-9353.

Life's a Beach—so get your ship together. One of the best family things to do in Culver City is leave town-cross the city limits and head to the nearby beach in Venice or take a Sunday stroll through Marina del Rey.

BRENTWOOD

After the trial of the century, you probably think you know all there is to know about Brentwood. Believe it or not, there was a time when Brentwood was well known for something other than O.J. This community of wealthy families, fresh-faced yuppies and UCLA types is actually known for its multitude of restaurants and trendy shops. In fact, Brentwood is a kind of laboratory for capitalism, a grand experiment of chain eateries gone ballistic. The results are generally positive—especially if you happen to own one of these places.

Brentwood is a safe community. It is residential, clean, and in close proximity to all of West Los Angeles. The public schools are good, and improving. While Brentwood is part of the bureaucratically mired Los Angeles Unified School District (LAUSD), Brentwood schools have teamed up with nearby Pacific Palisades schools to form their own charter school system. This allows them to devise independent educational programs while still remaining part of LAUSD. The private school, Brentwood is considered one of the finest in the city.

Being close to the beach helps to keep the weather beautiful and the air cleansed by sea breezes. Best of all, you can actually walk to bars, restaurants, and shops from many different locations. This is quite a rarity in L.A. where cars are our second homes.

With a population of around 10,000, Brentwood is small enough to retain a community feeling. The action in this otherwise quiet neighborhood happens along San Vicente Boulevard, between Bundy Dr., and Wilshire Boulevard. Lined with about 300 upscale shops, restaurants, coffee bars, and bookstores, San Vicente is definitely Brentwood's town square.

There are many different ways to search for a place here. UCLA's free *Daily Bruin* can be picked up at nearby newsstands. The *Brentwood News*, a free, monthly publication, can also be helpful. Because good rentals go so quickly, it is actually best to drive or walk around the area and take note of the FOR RENT signs. Although it would seem that Sunday would be a good day to go apartment shopping, most Realtors do not answer their phones until Monday, so make a big push on Saturday instead. Also, check the building's tenant list for the manager—it's best if you can see the apartment immediately. Apartments are expensive in this very desirable location. According to Sally Sussman, associate manager of the Brentwood Fred Sands Realty, "Most people rent between San Vicente and Wilshire and Barrington and Bundy. These are people past the age of UCLA students." North of San Vicente prices are a little higher than south—but no one gets off easy in Brentwood.

San Vicente Boulevard runs throughout the whole city with more curves than Anna Nicole Smith. Call it L.A.'s version of Lombard Street, except San Vicente isn't for tourists. It is an essential route for Angelenos. Luckily, the part that runs from Brentwood down to the ocean is not only straight, but beautiful. With a wide grassy island in the middle that runs for three residential miles, it has become one of the city's most popular exercise spots. Families in the area call a walk on the boulevard together time. But early morning weekends, you'll see the best and not-so-best bods of L.A. on display. And of course, besides being a great place for exercise, it is also an excellent pickup alternative to the bar scene. Please note, if you have a dog, bring him/her along. Rumor has it old rover is an excellent tool to help you meet someone.

If you are looking to buy:
Contact is **Fred Sands Realty** at **Fred Sands Brentwood**, (310) 820-6880.

> *"It's like paradise, with a lobotomy."*
>
> NEIL SIMON, FROM *CALIFORNIA SUITE*

If you are looking to rent:
For a 1 bedroom, the price is steep: $900-$1200 lands you a spacious, well maintained place. Two bedrooms go up from there. Even at these stratospheric prices, parking isn't always included, so be sure to ask. It is best to look around on your own. But if you really need help, try contacting these management companies:

The Roberts Companies, 10990 Wilshire Blvd., 312-9090; **PBM Quality Apartment Homes,** 476-1205; **Miller and Desatnik Management Company,** 3623 Motor Ave., 838-1828.

Essential Neighborhood Resources
<u>Area Code:</u> 310.

Zip Code: 90049.

Police: **West Los Angeles Division,** 1663 Butler Ave.,
575-8401.

Hospital: **UCLA Medical Center,** 10833 Le Conte Ave. 825-9111.

Post Office: **Barrington Branch,** 200 S. Barrington Ave.
476-3065.

Library: **Brentwood Branch,** 11820 San Vicente Blvd., 575-8016.

Public Schools: **Part of LAUSD cluster 10.** For info, call
(310) 473-5743.

INSIDER TIP: *BRENTWOOD AND PACIFIC PALISADES have
teamed up to form their own charter school district. This
means that while they are still part of LAUSD, the teachers and administration are not forced to stick with
districtwide curriculum or spending habits. The charter
system has been hailed as a huge success, and many parents in this area are taking their children out of private
school and putting them in the public school system.*

Banks:
Bank of America, 11911 San Vicente Blvd., 247-2080,
24-hour customer service, with other branches all over Los
Angeles and an accessible ATM machine.
Glendale Federal Bank, 11666 San Vicente Blvd.,
820-0406,—two other locations on the Westside.
Cenfed Bank, 11726 San Vicente Blvd., 826-5537.

Grocery Stores:
Vicente Foods, 12027 San Vicente Blvd., 472-5215.
Westward Ho, 11737 San Vicente Blvd., 826-4666.

Drug Stores:

Brentwood Plaza Pharmacy, 11980 San Vicente Blvd.
820-1496.

Vicente Pharmacy, 12027 San Vicente Blvd., 476-1237.

Dry Cleaners:

Fazio Cleaners, 11702 San Vicente Blvd.

Brentwood Village Cleaners and Laundry,
11722 Barrington Ct., 472-6919.

DINNER THE FIRST NIGHT

Once you are moved in, go out and take a stroll down to San Vicente. For dinner, definitely stop in at the BRENTWOOD GARDENS located at 11677 San Vicente Blvd., an upscale shopping center that boasts some of L.A.'s trendiest eateries. The fact that it's in a mall is the bad news. The good news is that the prices are decent and the food is really good. And, you aren't sick of any of these places . . . yet.

In the Brentwood Gardens, you'll have your choice of the DAILY GRILL (442-0044), OLE LA (826-5352), TAIKO (207-7782) and CALIFORNIA PIZZA KITCHEN (CPK to seasoned Angelenos). CPK makes a great first night dinner: filling dishes, quick service and typical L.A. alfresco-style dining. (11677 San Vicente Blvd., 826-3573). After dinner, head up to the top level for HUMPHRY'S FROZEN YOGURT, an L.A. must. And don't be surprised if you catch a celeb or two dining out. Many stars call Brentwood home, including Roseanne, Mark Harmon, and Steven Bochco. But don't bug them. In L.A. to appear as jaded and blase as possible.

Laundromat:

Sparkling Coin Laundry, 11927 W. Pico Blvd., 312-8831.

Hardware Store:

Barrington Hardware, 253 26th St., 576-0590.

Video Store:
Blockbuster Video, 11770 San Vicente Blvd., 207-3837.

Main Drags:
San Vicente Blvd.—It's the lifeblood of this city.

Barrington—It's a major street that runs perpendicular to San Vicente and up into Brentwood Village.

Landmarks:
The Brentwood Gardens—A fancy shopping center that boasts such luxury stores as Boulmiche and Ron Herman. 11677 San Vicente Blvd.

The Brentwood School— Passing this L.A. institution lets you know you've just entered into the wealthy zone. 100 S. Barrington Pl.

The Great Outdoors:
Santa Monica Pier—Games, food, sun, fun, and lots of people from all walks of life doing the boardwalk thing. Recently, the pier has had a facelift to the tune of 12 million, and there are plans for an all new "fun zone."

Cafes and Diners:
Arrosto—One of the more notable coffee chains in the city; the desserts are terrific and some are even fat-free (if you believe the signs). 11652 San Vicente Blvd., 207-4802.

Hamburger Hamlet—It's a typical eatery—mediocre— with something for everyone. 11648 San Vicente Blvd., 826-3558.

Kelly's Cafe and Bakery—A great morning stop before work. 11740 San Vicente Blvd., 826-5282.

Krystine's Bakery—Heaven for those who don't let anything but fat-free touch their lips. 13050 San Vicente Blvd., 451-2191.

Authentic Kitchen—A less casual version of the Authentic cafe, this is a popular eating hole. Make sure to try the tamales. 11690 San Vicente Blvd., 571-0868.

Miscellaneous Fun:

Noah's Bagels—The line on Saturday mornings makes it seem like they are giving bagels away. They're not! 11911 San Vicente Blvd., 472-5651.

The Juice Club—Located right next door to Noah's, the Juice Club mixes anything and everything into a blender and what comes out is oh, so California. Try the most popular blend: Strawberries Wild! 11900 W. San Vicente Blvd., 476-5823.

JAVA GOOD TIME?

The COFFEE BEAN and TEA LEAF'S iced mochas. Vanity Fair *paid homage to these caffeine dreams, and* Los Angeles *magazine named it the* Best Hip Addiction of 1995. *What's all the fuss? Iced Mochas are L.A.'s answer to milkshakes, but without the calories. The tricky part is ordering the perfect blend. If you don't know all your options as you step up to the counter, it can be difficult when the pressure's on and impatient patrons behind you get surly. It's tough to say "a decaf, iced vanilla, with whipped cream to go" all in one breath. So rehearse, people! Here are a few pointers to help you overcome Mondo Mocha Ordering Anxiety.*

- *Decide if you want it decaf or regular;*
- *Clearly state if you want an iced mocha, a vanilla iced mocha, a pure blend chocolate or a pure blend vanilla;*
- *Decide if you want or need it sugarless;*
- *Specify if you want whipped cream on top;*
- *Make sure you say if it is for here or to go;*
- *Always have them punch your coffee-bean card so you can eventually get a free iced blend;*
- *If you are ordering for a child, they will blend it without.*

Chin Chin—This is not the place to go if you are in the mood for real Chinese food. This is healthy-ish, California-style Chinese food, which doesn't mean it's bad. This has also become a chain restaurant, but Brentwood can boast that it has the original.

11740 San Vicente Blvd., 826-2525.

Mezzaluna—Famous for great pasta—among other things . . .
11726 San Vicente Blvd., 447-8667.

Father's Office—An intimate microbrewery pub where everybody really will know your name. 1018 Montana Ave., 451-9330.

Eiger Ice Cream—This is one place in the area where low-fat does not rule. It's the real thing at this ice cream parlor that's a favorite with kids. Still, mom and dad won't have to be persuaded too much to stop in. 124 E. Barrington Place, 471-6955.

SANTA MONICA

You can't be uptight and live in Santa Monica, the liberal beach community that local satirist Harry Shearer once called "the home of the homeless." Santa Monica has long been home to grungers, senior citizens, beach bums, and even yuppies—all sharing the same neighborhood, which consists of just 8.3 square miles. But the profile of this ocean city is about to change.

In 1995, the California State Legislature eliminated Santa Monica's long-standing rent control ordinance. As of January 1, 1996, rents in vacated apartments can now rise 15 percent in the next couple of years, and by 1999 to whatever the market bears. This former lefty enclAve., once tagged "the People's Republic of Santa Monica," is quickly becoming The DINK (double income, no kids) Republic. *Los Angeles* magazine described Santa Monica as ". . . a hotbed, not of revolution but of developers of every stripe. Big houses north of Montana now go for a million plus; commercial rents rival those in Beverly Hills; there are more Starbucks than hardware stores; and the Third Street Promenade has replaced Westwood as L.A.'s largest singles scene. Sniffing a no-hassle opportunity, the movie and record industries have also crowded in."

Despite this upscale stampede, there are still some great deals to be had in Santa Monica but they're getting scarcer—and you have to realize you're paying to live by the beach. Midwesterners might think this is a deal worth a million bucks. Luckily, prices aren't quite that high . . . yet.

In recent years, Santa Monica's pedestrian Third Street Promenade has gone through a major facelift and become one of the most popular nightlife spots in town. Filled with movie theaters,

MOVIN' TO MONTANA SOON?

Here are some of the Highlights. CAFE MONTANA, very popular for breakfast, 1534 Montana Ave., 829-3990; PLANET EARTH, a fat-free heaven because the food actually has taste, 1512 Montana Ave. 458-3096; WOLFGANG PUCK CAFE; and of course this street wouldn't be complete without a STARBUCKS, NOAH'S AND COFFEE BEAN.

OTHER THAN FOOD:

ROOM WITH A VIEW, expensive but worth its linens, 1600 Montana Ave. 998-5858; NUMBER ONE BEAUTY SUPPLY, where they have any product you could ever want—plus miracle products to help straighten those curly locks, 1426 Montana Ave. 656-2455; OPTICAL DESIGNS, Eyeglasses for the very chic—and their kids with an adjoining junior shop next door, 1235 Montana Ave., 393-4322.

restaurants, bars, pool halls, coffee house, bookstores, and shops, Third Street is always hopping on the weekend. On a warm night, street musicians line the promenade and there is the occasional clown and acrobat show. The crowds can get to be too much at times, but locals keep coming back to the Promenade for its many sports bars and dance clubs.

Montana may be the new state of choice for Hollywood celebs, but when they are not on their million-dollar ranches, they can also be seen walking and shopping on Montana Avenue in Santa Monica. Montana Avenue has become the new Melrose—it's hip, happening, and a great place to people watch.

If you are looking to rent:

North of Montana, the real estate is big-sky high, but south of Montana, prices are much more reasonable. Typically, one-bedrooms run at $1,000-plus and doubles at $1,200-plus. This price should include a parking spot underground and a view of the water.

If you are looking for the soothing vibe of a beach community, you'll need to be further west on Montana. But trying to find a place can be anything but relaxing. Usually referred to as Ocean Park, this area is bordered by Lincoln to the east, Rose to the south and Pico to the north. If you can afford it, there are small houses that look like cottages and rent for $1400-$1700, which are charming with hardwood floors, bay windows, and fireplaces. Harder to find are rooms for rent or even duplex type apartments in older, large homes. The apartments are '50s vintage and therefore don't include modern luxuries such as a dishwashers, garbage disposals, or parking. In fact, parking is problematic and permits are almost always a necessity. One bedrooms go for $800 to $900 and doubles range from $1100 to $1500. The rent control units are a lot less but unless a black market develops, don't count on cheaper prices in Santa Monica.

INSIDER TIP: *Check listings in* THE OUTLOOK, *Santa Monica's daily paper. Also, pick up* THE ARGONAUT, *a local beach paper which can be found in various locations around the* THIRD STREET PROMENADE *and* DOWNTOWN SANTA MONICA. *You can also try:* MOLLOY REALTORS INC., *458-0013 and* LAMBERT INVESTMENTS INC., *453-9656.*

Essential Neighborhood Resources

Area Code: 310.

Zip Codes: 90401, 90402, 90403, 90404, 90405, 90406.

Police:
1685 Main St., 395-9931.

Hospitals:
Santa Monica Hospital Medical Center, 1250 16th St., 319-4000.
St. John's Hospital and Health Center, 1328 22nd St., 829-5511

<u>Post Offices:</u>
1248 5th St., 576-2626.

2720 Neilson Way, 576-2620.

1217 Wilshire Blvd., 576-2616

<u>Libraries:</u>
Main Library, 1343 6th St., 458-8600.

Fairview Branch, 2101 Ocean Park Blvd., 450-0443.

Ocean Park Branch 2601 Main St. 392-3804.

Montana Avenue Branch, 1704 Montana Ave., 829-7081.

<u>Public Schools:</u>
Santa Monica-Malibu Unified School District—Nine elementary

SANTA MONICA CANYON STAIRS

With rents mostly sky-high over here at sea level, here's a way to reduce your health club costs. Call it Santa Monica's StairMaster. Take San Vicente to 4th St. going west and 4th St. to Adelaide and you're there. At first glance, it may look like a Baywatch casting call, but it is actually one of the hottest workouts in the city. Just be careful you don't get hit with someone's script, because almost everyone is carrying one. Rarely, however, is anyone reading.

Word has it that there are four different ways to do the stairs.

1.) For a great cardio work-out, jog up the stairs one step at a time.

2.) For toning, take two stairs at a time, keeping a rapid rate with your hands held by your side.

3.) Specifically for the tush, keep your hands behind your back and move very slowly, while putting pressure on your extending leg and taking two stairs at a time.

4.) To work the back of the thigh, walk backward, but please only one step at a time.

Most important, everyone has their own rate, so be polite and observe proper stair etiquette. Let people pass if they are moving schools, two middle schools, two senior high schools, one continuation high. Call 450-8338.

Banks:
American Savings, 2701 Wilshire Blvd., 828-3158.
Coast Federal Bank, 720 Wilshire Blvd., 393-0746.
First Federal Savings Bank of California, 2827 Main St.,
   399-9261.

Grocery Stores:
Pavilion's, 820 Montana Ave., 395-1682.
Von's, 710 Broadway, 260-0260; 1311 Wilshire Blvd.
Wild Oats, 1425 Montana Ave., 576-4707.

Drug Stores:
Horton and Converse Pharmacy, 2001 Santa Monica Blvd.,
   829-3401.
Sav-On Drugs, 2505 Santa Monica Blvd., 828-6456
   (open 24 hours).

Dry Cleaners:
A-1 Chinese Hand Laundry, 1006 Montana Ave. 394-7413.
Noble-Gateway Cleaners, 2723 Ocean Park Blvd., Santa Monica
   and other locations, 450-7878.

Laundromat:
Westgate Cleaners and Laundry, 11853 Santa Monica Blvd.,
   478-2039.

Hardware Stores:
Busy Bee Hardware, 1521 Santa Monica Blvd., 395-1158.
Best Hardware, 1440 4th St., 451-5542.

Video Stores:
Vidiots—Great selection of foreign flicks, cult pix and dour docs.
   302 Pico Blvd., 392-8508.
Blockbuster Video, 625 Montana Ave., 393-5131.

Main Drags:

Montana Ave.—What Melrose used to be, only more yuppies and a lot more strollers.

Main St.—Living up to its name, it's a charming, yet beachy, street running parallel to the Pacific.

Landmarks:

Santa Monica Pier (322 Santa Monica Pier) and **Bergamot Station** (2525 Michigan Ave.)—The best way to combine a day of culture with a day at the beach.

The Great Outdoors:

Rustic Canyon Park, 601 Latimer Rd., Pacific Palisades, 454-5734.

Temescal Canyon Park, Temescal Canyon right before Pacific Coast Highway.

Cafes and Diners:

Wednesday's House—When the young and the restless need coffee, sweet snacks, and bargain entertainment, they linger here. 2409 Main St., 452-4486.

Novel Cafe—Laptop-friendly, 24-hour used book store, coffeehouse, and healthy dining haven. Always a scene. 212 Pier Ave. 396-8566.

Thomas Restaurant—Popular diner that's packed on weekends. 2645 Lincoln, 452-2265.

DINNER THE FIRST NIGHT

WOLFGANG PUCK CAFE—Original California Cuisine from the man who invented it. It's over-priced and over-decorated but a perfect example of L.A. chi-chi cuisine which can be really tasty—make sure you order the famous spring rolls. 1323 Montana Ave. 393-0290. If you just can't deal with Wolfgang and aren't interested in a scene, check out Johnnie's New York Pizza, with delicious indi-

Rose Cafe—A popular hang-out for brunch on Sunday; check out their fabulous baked goods. 220 Rose Ave.. 399-0711.

World Cafe—Sit outside and enjoy the beach air. 2820 Main St., 392-1661.

Miscellaneous Fun:

Schatzi on Main—Arnold Schwarzenegger's restaurant, where cigars are all the rage. 3110 Main St., 399-4800.

Circle Bar—A charmingly dank oval bar with jukebox spinning fab tunes while patrons spin fab yarns. 2926 Main St., 392-4898.

Gilliland's—A mix of Irish specialties and Cal-Asian delicacies— great for business lunches. 2424 Main St., 392-3901.

Rockenwagener—Atmosphere is everything at this upscale sandwich place. 2435 Main St., 399-6504.

Santa Monica Beach—If you live in Los Angeles, Santa Monica beach is probably the closest paradise in proximity. The only problem with this Southern California (So-Cal) landmark is that the water is polluted and for years there have been off-and-on-again warnings to steer clear of the water. For a walk on the beach or a heavy-duty tan, Santa Monica is great, but for water sports, it's probably best to head further south to Manhattan Beach or up north towards Malibu.

Color Me Mine—Part of a major trend, this is a do-it-yourself store where art projects become home furnishings with a little help from the professionals. Make yourself a plate, coffee mug, or vase, and bring the kids too. It keeps them interested and very busy. 1109 Montana Ave., 393-0069.

VENICE

Founded in the early 1900s by Abbot Kinney, Venice was originally supposed to be a sister city to its namesake in Italy. Unfortunately, it falls far short of the charm of that most romantic city in the world.

California's Venice does have canals running through the city, but they are filled with dark ooze and you're not likely to see a gondolier passing through. Venice does, however, have its own charm . . . especially if you are an artist. The Beyond Baroque Literary Arts Center (681 Venice Blvd., 822-3006) is one place where the community comes together—for concerts and lectures and poetry readings. The former jail next door has become an art gallery and community outreach center.

But it's the famous boardwalk that gives Venice its funky carnival atmosphere. Life here is centered around the beach, and while the freaks come out at night, they also fill the streets on Saturdays and Sundays to soak up the sun, panhandle, and entertain. In fact, more than 150,000 people visit Venice Beach on a typical weekend summer day. Dead Heads and flower children will love to call this home. For everyone else, Venice is a great place to visit, but, well, you know the rest.

If you are into rollerblading, you'll definitely want to give the Venice boardwalk a try. There is a path by the beach that runs from Redondo Beach down south to Malibu up north. The portion in Venice, however, is the most famous because it is filled with street musicians, side shows, muscle men, and itsy-bitsy-teeny-weeny bikini-wearing women—not to mention overly tattooed men carrying a variety of reptiles and stuck-in-the-'60s activists urging you to help in the fight to legalize hemp. The vendors too will want your help and your money. You'll have your choice of trinkets, "silver" jewelry, Mexican leather bags, bikinis, used Levis, and neon-colored T-shirts emblazoned with a message for the geographically impaired: VENICE BEACH.

INSIDER TIP: *There is one good thing to shop for on the boardwalk—posters. Already framed posters are really cheap and will help complete your new living space so it feels like home. Movie posters, sports heroes, prints of famous artworks, and more adorn the walls of the Venice poster shops. So grab a friend to help you carry the goods and you will save yourself a lot of hassle and money.*

On a sunny day, Venice is packed and parking is going to cost you. But if you are new to L.A., this is a rite of passage. No excuses. There is a great bike path, too; many people just choose to walk, jog, or run.

Whatever you do, do it here—at least once.

Unfortunately, Venice has recently suffered from gang violence, especially in the Oakwood area. As a result, the crime rate is one of the highest in Los Angeles. Also suffering: the Venice public schools, which are not rated among the highest in the city. Hopefully, things will turn around. Discussions are underway for a $7 million make-over of the oceanfront walkway. But for now, Venice remains far from the city Kinney once imagined it would be.

If you are looking to rent or buy:

Housing is an eclectic mix of quaint beach cottages and low rent apartments—with a few beautifully restored blocks here and there to remind you of the glory that was Venice. If some of the rents seem too good to be true, they may be. Make sure to look in and around the building thoroughly. *The Argonaut* is a local beach paper with cur-rent listings—a great inside-the-neighborhood source for rentals. Even if you don't find a place through the paper, it should give you a clear picture of average rental rates. If your rent is lower than $650 for a one-bedroom, be cautious-something might not be kosher. One-bedrooms go from $650 to $900, and doubles tend to run anywhere from $850 to $1,100—depending on your need for luxury. On the average, two-bedroom houses rent for $1200 and up, but there are some bargains out there. If you are looking to buy a house, the going rate is anywhere from $125,000 to $200,000 for a two- to three-bed-room, according to Bob Peisen, sales associate with **Fred Sands Realty.**

Essential Neighborhood Resources

Area code: 310.

Zip code: 90291.

Police:
Pacific Division, 12312 Culver Blvd., 202-4502.

Hospital: **Daniel Freeman Marina Hospital,** 4650 Lincoln Blvd., 823-8911.

<u>Post Office:</u>
Venice Post Office, 1601 Main St., 396-3191.

<u>Library:</u>
Venice Abbot Kinney Library, 501 S. Venice Blvd., 821-1769.

<u>Public Schools:</u> **Part of LAUSD cluster 14.** For info, call
(310) 473-5743 (Despite what they say when they answer the
phone, you've got the right number).

<u>Banks:</u>
Great Western Bank, 1415 Lincoln Blvd., 823-9261.
Olympic National Bank, 2221 Lincoln Blvd., Santa Monica,
450-6700.

<u>Grocery Stores:</u>
Ralph's, 910 Lincoln Blvd., Santa Monica, 392-4854.
Gelson's, 13455 Maxella Ave., Marina del Rey, (310) 306-3192.

<u>Drug Stores:</u> **Thrifty Drug,** 888 Lincoln Blvd., 392-9683.

DINNER THE FIRST NIGHT

*THE SIDEWALK CAFE. It's a smorgasbord! Not the restaurant, the
endless carnival of humanity streaming past your table on the
asphalt boardwalk. The drinks are not exactly cheap and the food
is not exactly gourmet, but you're exactly where you want to be:
50 yards from the Pacific and a million miles from the workaday
world. What with the sun and the sea breeze and the half-naked
people—it's not half bad. After you down your meal and the proper
number of beverages, do something tres L.A. like having your for-
tune told by a sidewalk charlatan. Why not, you only live once.
Or do you? You're starting to get the hang of this California thing.
If you haven't done so already, go get yourself some cheap sunglasses, put them on, and address somebody as "dude." Now
you're arrived. 1401 Oc__ n Front Walk, (310) 392-4627.*

Sav-On Drug, 219 Lincoln Blvd., 392-3983.

Dry Cleaners:
Bestway Cleaners, 2805 Abbot Kinney Blvd.
   821-7710,
Park Cleaners, 115 Rose Ave. 392-0740.

Laundromat: **Thrifty Wash,** 1865 Lincoln Blvd., 399-5880.

Hardware Stores:
Builder's Emporium, 1400 Lincoln Blvd., 392-5771.
Lincoln Hardware, 1609 Lincoln Blvd., 821-1027.

Video Store:
Vidiots—It's almost unanimous that this is the best video store in
   L.A. 302 Pico Blvd., 392-8508.

Main Drags:
Venice Blvd.—Taken west, it leads you right to the beach.
Abbot Kinney—An emerging trendy street great for a morning
   mocha and some funky shopping.

Landmarks:
The Venice Boardwalk and **Venice High School.** It's been a
favorite with tourists ever since it fronted for Rydell High School in
the movie "Grease." 13000 Venice Blvd.

The Great Outdoors:
Venice Boardwalk—The best freak show on earth, and it's free for
the whole family.

Cafes and Diners:
The Cow's End—34 Washington Blvd., 574-1080.
Abbot's Habit—1401 Abbot Kinney Blvd., 399-1171.
Van Go's Ear—24-hour hipsters hang for super breakfast, hyper
   java, and major whatever. 796 Main St., 314-0022.
Cafe 50's—Playfully faux '50s malt shop with seriously good

(and delightfully fattening) food. The kids will be happy with everything—except, maybe the music. 838 Lincoln, 399-1955.

<u>Miscellaneous Fun:</u>

72 Market Street—Co-owned by Dudley Moore and Tony Bill. 72 Market St., 392-8720.

Hama (sushi)—A laid-back joint with sensational sushi. 213 Windward Ave., 396-8783.

Casablanca Restaurant—Noted for their homemade tortillas— you can't eat just one. 220 Lincoln Blvd., Venice, 392-5751.

Chaya Venice—The fabulous food should be enough, but the patrons seem much more intent on each other. Their seared tuna is the catch of any day, and the specials really are. 110 Navy St., 396-1179.

Singapore Express—Don't miss this easy-to-miss, excellent, cheap Thai restaurant hidden in a Marina del Rey mini-mall (a couple doors down from Starbucks, but then again, what isn't). 4236 Lincoln, 578-6668.

BURBANK AND GLENDALE

These East Valley sisters are as different as two sibs can be—even through they share the same bad air and bake in the same oppressive heat (Valley summer temps average 10 degrees hotter than the rest of the city). If you're one of those primitives who feel that air should be transparent, maybe you just don't have the right stuff to hack it (literally) out here.

Burbank is the glamorous sister; Glendale's the sensible one. Both, however, are convenient and economical gal pals—especially if you toil for The Mouse (read: work for Disney) or one of the other Valley-based studios. The Glendale commute into downtown isn't too bad once you get used to it, and Burbank-Glendale-Pasadena airport is an excellent alternative to LAX. The schools are good, as you might expect in family-friendly suburbs, but these two little cities have their fair share of pubs and clubs.

The malls of choice highlight the contrast between the two burghs. Glitzed-out Universal Citywalk, over on the Burbank side, combines tourist trappings with postmodern pastiche architecture—it's chaos theory transposed to commerce. The Glendale Galleria, meanwhile, is as comfortably understated as a complex of more than 150 busy shops can be. There are no tourists at the Galleria, just the gorgeous mosaic (or was that prosaic?) of L.A.'s multi-ethnic middle class shopping to the max.

For nightlife options, Burbankians will likely spend a lot of time cruising Ventura Boulevard to restaurants, cafes, and nightspots in North Hollywood (NoHo to some) and Sherman Oaks (S.O. only to Realtors)—and then over the mountains into Hollywood. Glendalites will probably be doing the same, but will also feel a pull to the scene percolating in Pasadena's Old Town.

If you plan to hold your breath until you get rich in the entertainment industry, Glendale or Burbank could be the perfect place to hunker down. And when you need to come up for a breather, as you invariably will, Griffith Park is nearby, and the refreshing green hills of Glendale's Forest Lawn Cemetery also offer some respite from what can be an ugly part of town. Also, on the northern fringe of Glenbank, several large parks in the Verdugo Mountains give a better sense of nature. In terms of housing, the prevailing L.A. hierarchy holds: If it's in the hills it kills, if it's down low . . . well, y'know.

If you are looking to buy:
More home for the money can be had up here, according to the Glendale Board of Realtors, with median prices of $200,000-$300,000 (depending on the area). The houses in Glendale are a little bit older, on the average, and many of them evidence a conservative Midwestern mood that dates to the first big wave of migration to this suburb in the '20s. Burbank, which boomed a bit later with the aviation industry, has a slightly different character.

If you are looking to rent:
You can find one-bedrooms for $400-$500 and two-bedrooms for just a little more. Depending on the neighborhood, a cozy house might be a mere $800—or of course a lot more if you want a big place with all the bells and whistles in a prime spot.

Essential Neighborhood Resources
Area Code: 818.

INSIDER TIP: *Fishmonger of the Valley. It's easy to forget that you're living in a coastal area when you're over here in the Valley, but let* FISH KING *remind you—with an astounding piscean cornucopia. (That's a lot of fresh fish to you!) 722 N. Glendale Ave., 244-2161.*

Zip Codes: 91202, 91205, 91206, 91208, 91501, 91502, 91504, 91505, 91506, 91523.

Police: 140 N. Isabelle, Glendale, (818) 548-4840.

Hospitals:
Glendale Memorial Hospital and Health Center,
1420 S. Central Ave. (at Los Feliz Blvd.), 502-1900.
Verdugo Hills Hospital, 1812 Verdugo Blvd., 790-7100.
Verdugo Medical Center, 1510 W. Verdugo Ave., 954-0593.

Post Offices:
Glendale, 339 N. Central, 265-9202.
Burbank, 2140 Hollywood Way, 846-3155.

Libraries:
BURBANK
Central, 110 N. Glenoaks, 238-5600.
Buena Vista, 401 N. Buena Vista, 238-5620.
Northwest, 3323 W. Victory Blvd., 238-5640.

GLENDALE
Central, 222 E. Harvard St., 548-202.
Brand Art and Music, 1601 W. Mountain St. (At Grandview),
548-2051.
Grandview, 1535 5th St., 548-2049.

Public Schools:
Burbank Unified School District, Eleven elementary schools,

three middle schools, three high schools, one adult school, one special school.

Glendale , Nineteen elementary schools, four middle schools, three senior highs, one continuation high, one school for the handicapped. Call (818) 558-4600.

Grocery Stores:

BURBANK

Hughes Market, 1100 N. San Fernando Blvd., 845-6424.

Von's, 101 N. Pass Ave., 848-9542; 1011 N. San Fernando Blvd., 845-1447.

GLENDALE

Mrs. Gooch's Whole Foods Market, 826 N. Glendale, 240-9350.

Trader Joe's, 130 N. Glendale, 637-2990.

Ralph's, 1416 E. Colorado, 548-0945.

Von's, 311 W. Los Feliz Rd., 246-7161; 561 N. Glendale Ave., 242-5926.

Drug Stores:

BURBANK

Sav-On Drugs, 511 North Hollywood Way, 841-0700; 1015 N. San Fernando Blvd., 841-0800; 1011 W. Alameda Ave., 845-5002.

Thrifty Drug Stores, 3618 W. Magnolia Blvd., 841-2835, and also at 1606 W. Magnolia Ave., 841-0623.

Burbank Tower Pharmacy, 500 E. Olive Ave., 843-2241.

Jay Scott Drugs, 2200 N. Glenoaks, 845-8313.

Medisco Drugs, 1100 N. San Fernando Blvd., 842-2115.

GLENDALE

Western Drugs, 501 Western Ave., 242-56887; 416 E. Colorado, 243-2231; 445 W. Broadway, 241-5996; 433 W. Colorado, 241-0415.

Thrifty Drug Stores, 130 S. Central Ave., 243-2507; 531 N. Glendale Ave., 241-9773.

Arden Medical Pharmacy, 435 Arden St., 247-1842.

Sav-On Drugs, 1000 S. Central Ave., 246-5679; 1855 W. Glenoaks Blvd., 246-4934.

Dry Cleaners:

BURBANK

Holly Cleaners, 531 Hollywood Way, 848-6433.

Milt and Michael Master Dry Cleaners, 4021 W. Alameda
(at Pass Ave.), 846-4734.

Felix the Cat Cleaners, 1113 North Hollywood Way, 846-7540.

GLENDALE

Border Bros. 1901 Riverside Dr., 846-3667.

The Cleaning Store, 1225 N. Pacific Ave., 507-8834.

Ninty-Nine Cleaners, 916 E. Colorado, 246-5416.

Laundromats:

BURBANK

Maytag Coin Laundry Fluff and Fold, 521 Hollywood Way,
843-6845.

Gene's Coin-Op Laundry, 508 S. Glenoaks Blvd., 563-4112.

GLENDALE

Stop 'n' Wash, 1141 E. Chevy Chase Dr., 243-7345.

EZ Wash, 1649 W. Glenoaks Blvd., 244-9728.

Thrifty Wash Coin Operated Laundry, 1268 S. Glendale Ave.,
507-6945.

Hardware Stores:

BURBANK

Orchard Supply Hardware, 641 N. Victory Blvd., Burbank,
(818) 557-2755.

Burbank Paint Company, 548 S. San Fernando Blvd., 845-2684.

GLENDALE

Virgil's Glendale Hardware Center, 520 Glendale Ave., 242-1104.

AA Baker's Super Hardware Center, 3925 San Fernando Rd.
(at Los Feliz Blvd.), Glendale, 242-7467.

Video Stores:

Sure, you'll be able to find a Blockbuster on every corner, but it might be worth a drive over to **Eddie Brandt's Saturday Matinee** at 6310 Colfax in North Hollywood (506-4242). This is video heaven, where you can get rarities, out-of-print films, and old TV shows unavailable elsewhere. The Beatles *Let It Be* and Peter Cook and Dudley Moore's comic gem *Bedazzled* are two tough-to-find favorites among the thousands on hand.

Main Drags:

Forget about Burbank and go over to nearby **Universal Citywalk.** In Glendale, **Brand Boulevard** near the Glendale Galleria is a pedestrian paradise and a nightlife magnet.

Landmarks:

NBC Studios at 3000 Alameda is way culturally significant, especially if you work there, but the ultimate Burbank landmark is the Bob's Big Boy restaurant nearby. 4211 Riverside Dr. (at Alameda Ave.).

Forest Lawn Cemetery is a literal bit of greener pastures, whatever your views may be on the afterlife. Glendale near San Fernando Road.

The Great Outdoors:

Brand Park (548-2000) is 851 acres of escape north of Glendale and Burbank on the slopes of the Verdugo Mountains. If Brand's 20 miles of hiking and biking trails can't make you forget it all, maybe the tranquil Japanese teahouse can. If that doesn't do it, you're probably remembering it all, whatever it is, for a very good reason. **Stough Park** (238-5300) and several other large preserves in the Verdugo's ensure outdoorsy variety. **The Descanso Gardens** are 165 astonishing acres of flowers—azaleas, roses, and especially camellias. 1418 Descanso Dr., (at Verdugo Blvd.), Glendale, 952-4400.

Cafes and Diners:

Stage Left Coffeehouse—Spacious coffee bar and restaurant. Low-key fun with no cover. 208 N. Brand Blvd., Glendale, 551-9791.

Piacere Espresso Bar—1101 Air Way (at Grandview Ave.), 240-7335.

Priscilla's—Comfortable coffeeshop. 4150 Riverside Dr., (at Evergreen Rd.), 843-5707.

Miscellaneous Fun:

Scarantino—Moderately priced Italian with generous portions. 1524 E. Colorado St., Glendale, 247-9777.

Milano's Italian Kitchen—Fast-food Italian that's wholesome and gives the Louise's chain a run for its money. Nobody's running much of anywhere, however, after such heavy eating. 525 N. Brand Blvd., Glendale, 244-1150.

Mo's—Great burgers, convenient to the studios. 4301 Riverside Dr., Burbank. 845-3009 (and several other locations).

DINNER THE FIRST NIGHT

How about a slice of Americana cheese? BOB'S BIG BOY in Burbank is the only surviving original store of this famous chain, circa 1949. (The meat in the famous burgers is guaranteed of more recent vintage, however, so come on in and take a bite out of history.) The grinning big boy holding up the sign out front is, in a word, large. 4211 Riverside Dr., (at Alameda Ave.), 843-9334.

Clancy's Crab Broiler—Everyday fish at reasonable prices. Red Lobster with a clue. 219 N. Central Ave., Glendale, 242-2722.

Mr. Burrito—Try the great big Cubano burrito with black beans or many other foodstuffs way too good to be coming out of what looks like a converted Burger King. 6424 San Fernando Road, Glendale, 243-8587.

Pickwick Five Horseman Inn Restaurant—Schlocky decor does not hurt the solid American fare—in fact, the schlock is almost a condiment. 921 Riverside Dr., (at Main St.), Burbank, 846-2668.

Choosing a Neighborhood p.87

<u>Family Fun:</u>

Pickwick Ice Center—1001 Riverside Dr., Burbank, 846-0032. It's where the L.A. Kings practice and so can you and your kids. Great family fun, and perfect for birthday parties. No high-sticking, unless you bring a pinata.

Brand Library—The exotic Brand Library (circa 1904) and the surrounding park are an ideal family place for a picnic. Or to check out a library book from this, Glendale's music and art library, or just enjoy the occasional free concerts and art events. 1601 W. Mountain St. (at Grandview), Glendale, 548-2051.

SHERMAN OAKS AND STUDIO CITY

The only stars to see in Hollywood these days are those that line the cement on the walk of fame. Believe it or not, much of the biz is based out of "beautiful downtown Burbank," as Johnny Carson dubbed the place. With Warner Brothers, NBC, Rysher, Columbia, Disney, and several other production companies headquartered in the valley, many of the people who work there choose to live close by and dodge the commute.

Studio City is popular with studio execs and celebs. It sort of feels like the Westside without having to go over the hill—the same energy and trendy eateries. Sherman Oaks is just a little bit farther west and has easy access to all the canyons and Sepulveda Boulevard.—alternates to the freeway for getting over the hill into the city. Once a charming community, Sherman Oaks has lost some of its sparkle to strip malls and shabby commercial facades. Still, the area between Kester Avenue and Van Nuys Blvd. on Ventura Blvd. is a happening street that frequently fronts as Melrose Place on the hit series. It's typical L.A., with Noah's Bagels, Starbucks, The Gap, Banana Republic, and a huge Tower Records that often features famous names signing their new albums.

Typical of suburbia, the schools are better and you can still hear the faint sound of an ice cream truck every so often. Also, because it is the Valley and not the Westside, you get a lot more for your money. Despite the bad rep, this part of the valley offers excellent shopping and delicious eating. The **Sherman Oaks Fashion Square** (14006 Riverside Dr., 783-0550) is the Beverly Center with fewer people and less hassle. **Chic Ron Ross boutique** (12930 Ventura Blvd., 788-8700) caters to the rich and famous, while **The Bistro Garden** (12950 Ventura Blvd., 501-0202) and **Cafe Bizou** (14016 Ventura Blvd., 788-3536) are rated among L.A.'s top dining spots. And *Los Angeles* magazine voted the **Bigg Chill yogurt shop** (12050 Ventura Blvd., 508-7811) as the best place to spot TV stars.

If you want a nice place, but can't quite afford the high prices of the Westside, this neighborhood is an excellent alternative. On a good day, your commute will average 30 minutes to the Century City area. When it rains or there is an accident, tack on another 15. The people of Los Angeles are used to sunshine and tend to freak out at the sight of moisture in the air.

If you are looking to rent:
Much of this area was hit hard during the quake of January 1994, but most of the buildings have been rebuilt and are stronger than ever. Almost every place comes with new appliances and guaranteed secure parking. A nice one-bedroom may go for as little as $600. Doubles go for $900 to $1,000 and are often located in buildings with a gym, pool, and hot tub.

Essential Neighborhood Resources
Area Code: 818.

Zip Codes: 91403, 91404, 91405, 91406, 91407, 91408, 91409, 91410, 91411, 91412, 91413, 91414, 91415, 91416, 91417, 91418, 91419, 91420, 91421, 91422, 91423, 91604.

Police: **Van Nuys Division,** 6240 Sylmar Ave., 756-8343.

Hospital:
Sherman Oaks Hospital and Health Center,
4929 Van Nuys Blvd., 981-7111.

Post Offices:
Sherman Oaks, 14900 Magnolia Blvd., 778-1800.
Studio City, 3950 Laurel Canyon Blvd., 506-0087.

NOTORIOUS L.A.

BUGSY SIEGEL'S HOUSE—*810 Linden Ave., Beverly Hills. Rumored to be the house where Bugsy met his fate when gangsters shot him through those famous long windows.*

HEIDIWEAR—*1247 Third Street Promenade, Santa Monica, (310) 394-7488. When she's not in court or jail, infamous Hollywood madam Heidi Fleiss really does work here selling her line of clothing. If she's not in, her sales staff is quite helpful and, well, noticeably beautiful.*

THE MENENDEZ MANSION—*722 N. Elm Dr., Beverly Hills. Don't be embarrassed to stop and stare. Tons of tour buses slow down daily to catch a glimpse of this famous house where two Beverly Hills brats shot their parents and somehow deadlocked their first juries even after confessing. Huh? The sequel had a better ending, but didn't do as well at the box office.*

FLORENCE AND NORMANDIE—*It's a deadly intersection, as the world now knows. If you must, take a drive-by to see where Reginald Denny was beaten during the Los Angeles riot of 1992.*

O.J.—*His house, her house, and that now famous restaurant. 360 N. Rockingham Avenue, L.A.*—*It's really not that interesting since you can't see much from the street. Still, if your curiosity gets the best of you, come see for yourself what the limo driver was describing in his testimony.*

875 S. BUNDY DR., L.A.—*If you're driving, you'll have to glance quickly, because the locals have had enough and will give you the horn if you seem to be slowing. If you are going north, it's on the left as you come around the bend. If you are headed south, it's on your right.*

MEZZALUNA—*11726 San Vicente Blvd., Brentwood, (310) 447-8667. Join the hundreds of others who've given this business a boost simply because they want to be part, in any way, of the trial of the century.*

Libraries:

Sherman Oaks Library, 14245 Moorpark St., 981-7850.

Studio City Library, 4400 Babcock Ave., 769-5212.

Public Schools:

Part of LAUSD cluster 7 and 8. For info, call 997-2552 and 997-2490 respectively.

Banks:

Fidelity Federal, 14475 Ventura Blvd., Sherman Oaks, 1-800-434-3354.

Glendale Federal Bank, 12191 Ventura Blvd., Studio City, 766-6141.

American Savings Bank, 12185 Ventura Blvd., 752-2300.

Grocery Stores:

Mrs. Gooch's, 12905 Riverside Dr., 762-5548/4520; N. Sepulveda Blvd. 382-3700.

Ralph's, 14049 Ventura Blvd., Sherman Oaks, 784-2674.

Drug Stores:

Marks Valley Drugs, 4556 Van Nuys Blvd., Sherman Oaks, 788-5531.

Thrifty Drug Stores, 12100 Ventura Blvd., Studio City, 766-8628.

Dry Cleaners:

Oaks, 14445¾ Ventura Blvd., Sherman Oaks, 783-4797.

Ultimate Cleaners, 12754 Ventura Blvd., Studio City, 509-8700.

Laundromats:

Sherman Oaks Laundry, 14840 Burbank Blvd., 901-6924.

Larry's Coin Laundry, 10504 Victory Blvd., North Hollywood, 766-8244.

Hardware Stores:

GD Builders Hardware and Plumbing, 13241 Ventura Blvd., 784-6274.

North Hollywood True Value Hardware, 4397 Tujunga Ave.,
980-2453.

Video Stores:
Blockbuster, 13303 Riverside Dr., 501-8335.
Dave's Video The Laser Place, 12144 Ventura Blvd.,
760-3472.
The Wherehouse, 12123 Ventura Blvd., 769-1444.

Main Drags:
Ventura Blvd.—Cruising this street is a rite of passage for valley kids.
Laurel Canyon—It's a shortcut to the city.

Landmarks:
Sherman Oaks Galleria—15301 Ventura Blvd. A monument to
the Valley Girl craze.
The Gap—14622 Ventura Blvd. It sounds strange (and a little sad),
but this Gap housed in the former La Reina movie theater is
actually a landmark.

The Great Outdoors:
Beeman Park/Studio City Recreational Center—12621 Rye St.,
769-4415—A popular playground for kids and a good resting place
for moms and dads.

Cafes and Diners:
Insomnia—Lounge on the couches while sipping cappuccinos with
a mostly young crowd of wannabe Ethan Hawkes and imitation
Alanis Morissettes. 13718 Ventura Blvd., 990-9945.
The Coffee Roaster—Delicious coffee in a relaxed venue.
13567 Ventura Blvd., 905-9719.
Dupars—The best and most fattening pancakes in L.A. Just ask
the waitresses, they've been there forever.12036 Ventura Blvd.,
766-4437, 1-800-434-3354.
Tiramisu—It's amazingly close to a small Italian cafe anywhere
in Florence. 13705 Ventura Blvd., 986-2640.
Marmalade Cafe—A cozy inside with furnishings actually for sale

right off the wall. The food is pretty good too. 14910 Ventura Blvd., 905-8872.

DINNER THE FIRST NIGHT

JERRY'S FAMOUS DELI—This is the original Jerry's without all the fanfare of the newer establishments. Beware the menu; it is so large you might need the cliff notes. 12655 Ventura Blvd., Studio City, 980-4245.

Miscellaneous Fun:

Ventura Blvd.—Between Coldwater Canyon and Laurel Canyon. A great place to walk, stop for coffee, have a bite to eat, and do some major damage shopping, especially for furniture. Every other place is full of antiques and home furnishings. It's a perfect Sunday afternoon.

La Loggia—Outstanding Italian meals but it is a little loud— the good news is soap celebs frequent the place making for good conversation to overhear.11814 Ventura Blvd., Studio City, (818) 985-9222.

Tokyo Delve's—It's always a party at this sushi house perfect when you get a group of friends together. And if the lucky lantern lands on you, your food up to that point is free. It gets pretty wild waiting to see whose lantern will light up.5239 Lankershim Blvd., North Hollywood, 766-3868.

Pickwick Ice Center—It's a great place to cool down and have some fun, especially when outside temperatures reach over 100 degrees in the summer. The L.A. Kings practice here and so can you. 1001 Riverside Dr., Burbank, 846-0032.

Sports Center Bowl— Arcade games and bowling have never been this fun probably because the crowd is always eclectic and energized. 12655 Ventura Blvd., Studio City, 769-7600.

DOWNTOWN

Last and probably least on most potential neighborhood lists is Downtown. However, many people believe this is about to change.

One up-and-coming Downtown area is usually referred to as THE ARTISTS' LOFT AREA between Little Tokyo and the Los Angeles River. Old warehouses there are being rehabbed one-by-one into lofty living spaces. Prices vary according to size, but because this area is being developed for the art community, the rental has to be under $1 a foot. For instance, 1,000 square feet might go for as little as $500.

The other area attracting attention is the HISTORIC CORE on the northern end of Downtown—a area that's great for grad students from USC (a couple of miles away) and students at the Fashion Institute (which is basically right next door).

The best part of moving to the center of this centerless metropolis is that because Downtown is in its early stages of residential renovation, rents are cheap. Units in the Historic Core run from roughly $400 a month for a studio to about $800-900 for a two bedroom.

Downtown doesn't quite have the feel of a trendy neighborhood just yet. It is still a gritty part of town where you are right on top of the Metro and within feet of industrial L.A. But if you've got a touch of that urban pioneer spirit, this might be the neighborhood for you.

WHERE ELSE TO LOOK?

Obviously, there are more swell places to live in Los Angeles than the ones we've briefly sketched in this chapter.

Many of your other best bets would be communities adjacent to the areas we've mentioned. Just to the east of CULVER CITY, for instance, BALDWIN HILLS, VIEW PARK, LADERA HEIGHTS, and parts of INGLEWOOD all have much to recommend them.

Similarly, ATWATER VILLAGE, across the L.A. River from LOS FELIZ and SILVER LAKE, is a decent discount alternative to these somewhat trendy locales. And farther to the east, MOUNT WASHINGTON and S. PASADENA are two other unpretentious, economical, and comfortable residential centers.

Farther south and east, on the periphery of downtown (and in other semi-industrial no-man's-lands), artists and their poser pals are always angling to live the low-budget lofty life.

But upscale options are also plentiful, especially in the far west. If you can afford it, by all means consider living in MALIBU or the PACIFIC PALISADES (up the coast and up the hill, respectively, from Santa Monica). These spots will be especially appealing if you are independently wealthy or if your high-paying job is on the WESTSIDE (otherwise, the commute can be hairy, especially in mudslide season).

And let's not forget that more than a million people live in the SAN FERNANDO VALLEY, though every summer when the smog gets bad there are millions more of us who are happy that we are not among them. While much of the Valley is an eyesore—pancake flat and laid out in an endless grid of residential tracts and commercial strips—it is also a place of unexpected ethnic variety and good old-fashioned cheapness. If you feel like braving the heat and smog, the areas nearest the city's central basin are the most convenient: ENCINO, VAN NUYS, NORTH HOLLYWOOD. Farther to the east, on the far side of Burbank and Glendale, PASADENA is a pleasant, mostly affordable place with its own nightlife nucleus and ample family-oriented housing.

The southern coastal communities of MANHATTAN BEACH, REDONDO BEACH, and HERMOSA BEACH (and maybe even far-off LONG BEACH) also have their advantages, especially if you've fantasized about living near the beach.

Once again, proximity to work, play and pals are central to the "where" equation. You've got to enjoy driving in order to like Los Angeles, but you shouldn't do any more driving than you must. Many people, we're given to understand, actually live in such quasi-mythical places as ORANGE COUNTY, SAN BERNARDINO, and SIMI VALLEY, but we're not sure why. If you know people who live in such distant zones, in what is laughingly considered part of the metropolitan area, you can figure on seeing them about as often as you see friends on the East Coast.

Chapter Three
THE CAR CHAPTER

YOU'LL WANT TO HAVE A CAR IN L.A. It's possible—though not pleasurable—do without, but you won't really be enjoying L.A. until you're a vehicular free agent. Public transportation is, shall we say, not so good. The buses are okay when they're running, but they are rarely ridden by professionals with schedules to meet, and they tend to be plagued by graffiti and prone to breakdown. And that's about it for public trans. Our new subway operates for 3.2 miles within the city, so while it is clean, it's not very useful—L.A. county is roughly 70 miles across by 70 miles top to bottom. And the biggest problem of all for Angeleno commuters, even those with cars: traffic. Obviously, it is important to like your car, like being in your car, and to be able to start your car on a consistent basis. So, let's go car shopping.

BUYING OR LEASING A NEW CAR

We'll start with some Common Sense Rules, okay?

1.) Shop around.

2.) Get *Consumer Reports* new-car buying guide, and determine the best value.

3.) Locate your financial neighborhood and try to stay in it.

4.) Take your time and be methodical (it's cheaper to rent a car for a while than to get duped into buying the wrong car).

5.) Don't get so frustrated that you let a salesperson hard-sell you into something you don't really want.

6.) Credit is easily extended to the employed, but don't get in over your head.

7.) Shop around for your loan, too. (Work-related credit unions often have the best loan rates—take advantage of this if you can.)

8.) Read the small print. Leases sometimes offer enticingly low payments, but can require a significant chunk down or a big balloon payment at the end. If you don't end up buying the car at the end of a lease, all the money you paid is simply gone when the car is.

9.) A "hidden" cost for new vehicles is insurance: When you buy on

CAR TALK

Check it out: If you're going to hang with the performance-art hipster crowd in Silver Lake, you'll probably want to get a slightly weathered old Cougar, Rambler, Falcon, or Dart (or some such American beast). If your new life in L.A. takes you onto studio lots for potentially important meetings you'll soon feel pressure to get a Jeep, a Range Rover, or a Bronco (or a similar urban survivalist assault vehicle). And, of course, if you find yourself in an upscale milieu where you simply must drip money (becoming a literal wheeler-dealer endlessly yakking on the car phone), you'll find yourself magnetically drawn to the three Bs: Beemer, Benz, and Bentley (not to mention Infiniti, Continental, Rolls, and maybe even Ferarri).

Like it or not, many people are going to judge you by your car (just as folks elsewhere interpret social status through shoe styles), but you needn't succumb to peer pressure and spend more than you can afford. If you want something dependable and unpretentious, we'll see you out there in your Volvo, Honda, Toyota, Ford, or Chevy. It's all good, as we like to say.

credit, the owner of the car (the bank) often mandates that you get full insurance coverage to cover their investment. Depending on your driving record, this can exceed the cost of your monthly car payments.

Buying a Used Car (from a Dealer)

When it comes to bars and cars in L.A., the same rule applies: Don't be fooled by a beautiful body. Any idiot can go to the gym; and any old car in California can look like new—even after 15 or 20 years. The mechanical aspect of a used car is the tricky part. Unless you really know cars, your safest bet is to avoid corner car lots and go to large, established used-car dealers where you have a better chance of getting some sort of effective warranty.

In any case, you should always have an independent mechanic check out any vehicle you are seriously considering. There are many services that will drive to meet you and thoroughly examine your potential new chariot—for a small fee. **(310) BUY-RITE** is one such service that will check out a car in about an hour for $40-$50, and unlike the mechanic from your neighborhood garage, the car checker has nothing to gain from diagnosing potential repairs. Make sure to have them do a compression check, which might cost a bit more, but will tell you a lot about the engine's prognosis. Whatever you do, never buy a car from someone who won't let your mechanic give it the once over. (If a dealer or individual should balk, you should walk.)

INSIDER TIP: *California was one of the first states to crack down on lemons—cars, that is. If you have to take your car in four times in the same 30-day period within the first year or 12,000 miles, you're car is legally considered sour. By law, the manufacturer must buy the car back from you. And as of January 1, 1996, such vehicles' titles must be marked as a "lemon law buyback" when a vehicle is repurchased by the manufacturer. So make sure to ask for the vehicle title when leasing or purchasing a car.*

Prices and financing charges at car lots are often inflated, so you might have better luck buying from a private party. But California car prices are generally higher than other parts of the country, so there's no guarantee. Plus, after a certain mysterious number of years some old cars become "vintage" and begin to appreciate.

CLASSIFIED ADSPEAK: YOU AUTO KNOW

Brevity is the soul of wit, but automobile want ad abbreviations can make you lose your wits. Most of it is common sense, but there are a few local wrinkles you might not be familiar with. A typical ad:

'81 Honda Accord. 4dr, auto, ps/pb, snrf, vy cln, xnt. in and out. 150 k, gd, rnng cond, grt trans. car, nds mnr bdy rpr. Tags til '99, smog. $1,800 obo.

Translation: This 1981 Honda Accord four-door comes with automatic transmission, power steering, power brakes, sunroof, very clean, excellent interior and body, odometer reads 150,000 miles, good running condition, great transportation car (as opposed to a prestige-mobile), needs minor body repair, registration is paid until 1999, the owner has had it smog-checked at a state approved inspection station as required by law for all sellers. A few others:

4cyl = 4 cylinder engine.   *16vlv = 16 valve engine.*

lthr int. = leather interior.   *chrm = chrome.*

cpe = coupe.   *Gd lk 2 U.*

Buying a Used Car
(through the Classifieds)

Your best deal, or your biggest headache, awaits you in the world of buying a used car through the classified ads of the *L.A. Times* or the weekly *Recycler*. Be prepared for people without answering machines, people who only have beepers, shady car dealers pretending to be individual sellers, people who don't speak English, people who only want you to see their cars at night, people selling the car for a friend (c'mon, who does this?), people who say they're in a rush because they're moving overseas next week, people who go on vacation after placing their ads and call you back weeks later. But be persistent. There are plenty of swell regular folks out there selling their cars, too. The good news is that the sellers are probably just as frustrated by flaky potential buyers as you are by flaky would-be sellers.

As with a purchase from a dealer, have a mechanic or car-check service examine a car if you drive it and like it (if the car is determined to have some looming repairs, you can usually talk the seller down). In any event, haggling is expected.

To avoid costly and annoying headaches at the **Department of Motor Vehicles** (see below), make sure that the car is currently registered, has a valid smog certificate (meets stringent state air-quality standards), and that the owner listed on the title is the person you're buying it from.

INSIDER TIP: *Sometimes it's best to leave it up to the professionals, and buying a car may be one of those times. To get the best price and a fair deal, you may want to go through an auto broker. LCS in Van Nuys is an excellent service that does the dirty work for you and you don't pay a thing—the dealers do. (818) 997-3060.*

Renting

If you need to rent your wheels until you find the car of your dreams, here are a few resources:

Rent-a-Wreck—Let Dave and his sardonically charming crew put you in the driver's seat of a somewhat distressed but mechanically sound older used car. Monthly rates can be as low as $500 (including insurance). 1233 W. Pico Blvd., West L.A., 1-800-535-1391.

DNR Rentals—(Formerly Ugly Duckling Rent-a-Car) Provides alternative low-rent wheels for as little as $109 per week. 10620 Venice Blvd., Culver City, (310) 837-7752 or (310) 451-4724.

Alamo—1-800-327-9633.

Avis—1-800-331-1212.
Budget—1-800-527-0700.
Dollar—1-800-421-6878.
Enterprise—1-800-325-8007.
Hertz—1-800-654-3131.
National—1-800-328-4567.

INSIDER TIP: *Here's how to get the best rate out of rental car giants. Once you determine when your move will take place and when you'll need a car, call to make a reservation. Call them every week or two to check the rates—if they quote you a lower rate, tell them your confirmation number and lock it in. This will annoy them, but you'll end up with the lowest rate possible. Monthly rates are sometimes as low as $500, and if you return the car early, it's generally pro-rated so you only pay for the days you use. If you rent with a "gold" credit card, your insurance is usually covered by the card.*

INSURANCE

State law requires motorists to maintain at least $15,000 in liability coverage for others they may injure in an auto accident and up to $30,000 per collision if more than one victim is injured. The state also requires at least $5,000 in additional insurance to cover property damage. California's Department of Insurance found that about 28 percent of California motorists—at least 5 million drivers—hit the road without auto insurance. While this is illegal, it can also be a big problem for you—to avoid serious nastiness you should consider getting "uninsured motorist" coverage, which covers you if you're hit by one of these maniacs.

Insurance can be expensive, especially if you've had accidents or moving violations within the last three years. You should definitely shop around to get the best insurance rates; most companies will give you price quotes on the phone. A good time to comparison shop is

DISCOUNTS WITH AAA

Having an AUTO CLUB OF SOUTHERN CALIFORNIA card is a must for safety reasons. The annual fee is $58, and that includes three free roadside assistance stops (and towing, city maps, and trip-plan services. But many don't know that having "the card" enables you to much more. Check the "Auto Club Values" page in every issue of members' Avenues magazine for special discounts and deals available to cardholders.

You must have a California driving license in order to become a member of AAA. In order to do this, make an appointment at the DMV and bring your current "out of state" license and a birth certificate or passport and your social security number. Next step, pay your $12, and then, yes, you have to take the driver's test—written that is. They have study guides at the DMV, but also, Los Angeles Magazine published the answers to the actual tests (there are several) in their February 1994 issue. So your best bet is to look it up at the library. Here's a peek at what to take advantage of:

DISCOUNT PHOTOS—Present your automobile club card when you bring in photos to be developed at Fox photo stores located throughout Los Angeles. There are no signs, so be in the know yourself and get a 50% discount on your first set of prints and $1 off the developing cost.

AIRPORT PARKING—Long-term parking at the airport can be as costly as flying to your destination. But by using your AAA card, you can save some cash when you park at Wally Park (977 Bellance Ave., L.A., (310) 337-1944) and take their shuttle to the airport. It's not very time consuming and well worth it anyway. Best for a weekend trip. (Self-park daily rate is $9.75 but if you stay between three and six days, you'll get one day free. And after six days, it's $1.50 off per day).

TRAVELER'S CHEQUES—There's no service charge for American Express Travelers Cheques when you purchase them at an Auto Club office

DISCOUNT CAR RENTAL—Hertz rental offers exclusive deals with AAA members. For more information, call 1-800-654-3080.

CELLULAR DISCOUNTS—AirTouch Cellular offers a 10% discount on all Cellular accessories.

HOTEL DISCOUNTS—You can save up to 25% at Hyatt and Hilton hotels. Make sure to ask about discounts for AAA members when making your reservations.

SPECIAL DISCOUNTS—Each month, the Auto Club offers a Member $aver guide that features special values on everything from travel accommodations to sporting events. All you have to do is contact any office and ask for a free copy.

CAR BUYING SERVICES—AAA has a vehicle pricing service that lets you buy or lease new vehicles at just about lowest price with the least hassle. The Club's membership of 4 million gives them the clout to work a volume discount deal with some of the area's most reputable dealers.

REGISTRATION—Perhaps the best thing about AAA is that they function as your surrogate DMV (state-authorized to perform most DMV transactions such as car registrations and transfers—and they do it in a friendlier, more helpful atmosphere).

MOTORISTS TAKE NOTE

- You just can't escape the camera in this town. A new law allows cameras to film drivers at specific intersections. If you run such a red light, a citation will be sent to you by mail. Drivers will have the opportunity to contest the ticket. Just remember, they've got you on tape.

- Attention all speedracers—things are moving pretty quickly in L.A. these days. The speed limit on many major freeways has been increased from 55 mph to 65 mph. In fact, the new law allows California to raise speeds to 70 mph on certain highways—but don't hit the pedal to the metal yet. Most of those highways are up north.

- Don't leave home without it. No, we're not talking about your American Express Card, or your driver's license, or even another I.D. If you are stopped for a vehicle code violation and you don't have proper I.D., California law now says that it's okay to let your fingers do the talking: they'll accept thumbprint on the citation.

while you're car shopping (you may decide that the hidden costs of the sporty model make it less desirable). In addition, some neighborhoods' rates rise due to higher levels of theft, vandalism, and accidents involving parked cars. (Having a garage and a car alarm will often lower your rate.)

Start shopping with these reputable, competitively priced insurers (and let your fingers do the walking to discover others):

AAA—(213) 525-0018.
AIS—(310) 478-2500.
Farmer's—1-800-400-9990.
Mercury—(213) 653-5293.
Prudential—(213) 954-3740.
State Farm—(213) 876-6653.
20th Century—(818) 704-3700.

INSIDER TIP: *The most comprehensive maps of the city and surrounding areas are found in THOMAS GUIDES, detailed spiral-bound maps of the city that include all the sneaky little streets you'll never find on those fold-out gas-station specials. It is worth the $25 or so to pick one up at your local bookstore and keep it in your car. Even if you are one of those stubborn types who refuse to ask for directions, at least you can quietly surrender to the Thomas Guide and get where you need to be going. There are some areas you just don't want to be lost in.*

LICENSE AND REGISTRATION, PLEASE

Tread carefully when entering the Kafka-esque bureaucratic labyrinth of the **DMV.** They have many rules and regulations and required paths of paperwork to follow. As is the case with many states' motor vehicle departments, the answers you get from the employees sometimes vary with whom you ask, but in general the folks at California's DMV are courteous if typically weary civil servants.

Happily, you can limit your exposure to lengthy queues by calling tto make an appointment—which, mysteriously, many people don't do. Let's see, you have the option of going to the DMV on the spur of the moment and standing in line for an hour or more, or planning ahead a couple of days and getting your transaction over in 10 minutes. It seems like a no-brainer.)

To make an appointment with the DMV, call (213) 744-2000. Bring your out of state license, another form of I.D. and proof of local residence (such as a utility bill). You will be asked to take a written test of California's rules of the road. Stop in beforehand to pick up a booklet to study them; they may differ slightly from your old state's laws.

A couple of key laws:

1.) Cars purchased in California must be registered within five days of purchase. Cars from out of state must be registered within 20 days (and there is an import fee for out of state vehicles of about $300). Some people take things too far—trying to circumvent the DMV by keeping their cars registered and insured out-of-state. They, in effect, pretend to be visiting in order to enjoy the benefits of cheaper out-of-state insurance rates. This of course is illegal, and can cause problems if you have an accident, but some people prefer to pinch pennies any way possible.

2.) New residents are supposed to surrender their out-of-state licenses for California's own within a month of establishing residency.

L.A.'S NASTY DRIVING HABITS

"Red Light? I Didn't See Any Red Light . . ."—While Angelenos are, in general, excellent and experienced drivers, too many fly through red lights a second or two after they change. Always wait a beat after the light goes to green, and never sneak into an intersection as it's changing.

"I Own the Road . . ."—Tailgating and relentless lane shifting are common dangerous modes of driving, which should be avoided. Keep a close eye peeled for motorcyclists when you change lanes (for some mysterious reason, it's legal for them to ride the white line between lanes out here).

COMMON SENSE RULES FOR CAR OWNERSHIP

If the worst should happen, report the theft immediately—the police often do find cars stolen for joyrides after they've been cruised and abandoned. And, at the very least, you can avoid liability for tickets that the thieves incur if you've reported it stolen. The possibility of theft is another reason to make sure your car is properly registered with the DMV; if your car is located and towed into custody, the police impound lot is a bureaucratic quagmire in its own right if your paperwork is not in order. File this info in The Adding Insult to Injury Department: The impounders can ticket you for illegal parking where they find your car, they will charge you for towing, they will charge you for storage, they will charge you for whatever they can think of—get your vehicle out of there ASAP.

"Turn Signal? Oh, That's What That Is . . ."—Another mystery of the California roads is why so few people use their turn signals (though we have no shortage of people who leave their turn signals on for miles when they're not turning). If, as a newcomer, you'd like to do something to improve California's culture, we suggest that you lead by example and use your turn signal.

KEEPING THE CAR CLEAN

Keeping your car looking shiny and new is very important in this town. People are quite particular about who gets the job of washing their "baby." Still, there are some car washes that have earned the trust of Los Angeles big-wigs. If it's good enough for a 600 SL, well . . .

HANDY J—Whether it's just a wash or detailing you want, Handy J leaves your car looking better than it did the day you first got it. A few years back, Los Angeles Magazine named this car wash as one of the 101 reasons not to leave L.A. 14311 Ventura Blvd., Sherman Oaks, (818) 788-3011.

SEPULVEDA WEST CAR WASH—The wash you get here is excellent, but it's the gift shop that Angelenos rave about. 2001 S. Sepulveda Blvd., L.A., (310) 478-9274.

MAJESTIC CAR WASH—When you're running late, this is a reliable quickie that leaves your car sparkling clean. If you shop at Ralph's, you're in luck—coupons can be found on the back of their receipts. 8017 W. Third St., L.A. (213) 933-7393.

SANTA PALM CAR WASH—A 160-foot-long hallway displays more than 200 autographed photos garnered over the years from the celebrity clientele at this upscale bathing spot for fancy wheels. In fact, they boast of washing more Rolls-Royces here than at any other car wash in the world—500 per month. Still, feel free to drive up in your "practical" car. Everybody gets the star treatment. 8787 Santa Monica Blvd., L.A., (310) 659-7888.

Chapter Four
MOVING IN AND SETTING UP THE ESSENTIALS

UNFORTUNATELY, HOMES ARE LIKE TOYS—most often, not all the necessary parts are included, and they come bearing that ominous warning—some assembly required. Lucky for you, your new house or apartment comes with these easy-to-read instructions. Follow them closely and in no time at all you'll have yourself a beautiful dream house fit for a . . . well, Barbie or Ken. Kidding aside, however, Los Angeles is the perfect place to reconfigure your life—and your home can reflect the new you, whatever that might be. Or, if you prefer, you can just rebuild the old you with a few minor improvements, or sans a couple of pieces of that battered personal baggage you've always secretly hoped to jettison somewhere.

But for the stuff you want to keep, it pays to take proper care of it in your new city. In case you have any last minute moving that needs to be done from this end, here's a list of well-known companies who'll move and store you with the least amount of hassle possible:

Moving Companies
Allied—1-800-624-5938.
Bekins—1-800-994-MOVING.
Mayflower—1-800-984-6683.

Starving Students—1-800-441-6683, (310) 477-8261,
(818) 989-5886.

Wetzel and Sons—(310) 859-1028.

If you're the type who likes to do it all on your own, try some moving equipment rental companies known for being user-friendly:

Ryder Truck Rental—1-800-467-9337; 2489 Lincoln Blvd.,
Venice, (310) 301-6628; 4095 Glencoe Ave., Marina Del Rey,
(310) 301-1507; 15111 Ventura Blvd., Sherman Oaks, (818)
789-6881; 121 S. Victory Blvd., Burbank, (818) 841-0489.
Call for other locations.

U-Haul Co.—1747 Lincoln Blvd., Santa Monica, (310) 450-6947;
10321 National Blvd., L.A., (310) 202-1645; 3250 Olympic
Blvd., Santa Monica, (310) 829-4109; 11666 Victory Blvd.,
North Hollywood, (818) 763-4381; 7610 Van Nuys Blvd., Van
Nuys, (818) 786-6400.

INSIDER TIP: *If you are considering using a moving company unfamiliar to you, make sure they are properly licensed. Many companies are not, which can result in unnecessary headaches. To find out, call the CALIFORNIA PUBLIC UTILITIES COMMISSION at 1-800-366-4782.*

SETTING UP THE UTILITIES

Moving is a hassle. There is no question about that. To make the big transition a little easier, plan ahead so that the day you are ready to take up residence in your new pad, your gas, heat, electricity, and phone are also ready.

BANKS

Before you do anything, you'll need to set up a bank account. Money might not grow on trees, but it does come out of machines on almost every corner, so don't worry about choosing a bank with a local ATM. ATM's are more abundant in L.A. than sunshine. They're everywhere, even in many of the supermarkets. **Bank of America** (call directory assistance for the bank nearest you) and **Wells Fargo** (1-800-242-4932) have the most locations sprinkled throughout the city, but **Glendale Federal, California Federal** and several others also figure prominently on the local scene. **Wells Fargo ATM's** have recently been installed in all of the Ralph's supermarkets and many Von's stores, which also appear every few miles no matter where you are in the city. And how much more convenient does it get—7-Eleven and many other convenience stores also have ATM machines that accept major bank cards.

INSIDER'S NOTE: *FIDELITY FEDERAL offers star-checking which gives you free ATM usage at your home bank and four wild cards—four freebies at other bank ATMs, that is. Also, there is no minimum balance. Call 1-800-434-3354.*

GAS

Call the **Southern California Gas Company** at 1-800-427-2200 ahead of time (about a week) to schedule a date for your gas to be turned on. Make sure to have your social security and driver's license numbers readily available. If you do not have any previous bills from California, you will be asked to put down a deposit, which varies depending on where it is that you are moving within L.A. To waive this deposit, have a letter of credit sent from your current utility company and include your new address. This letter can be sent to:

Southern California Gas Company
Attention: Collections
Box 61062
Anaheim, CA 92803

ELECTRICITY

Having electricity when you move in is essential. Sorting through boxes by candlelight is not as charming as it sounds. For most areas in L.A., **Edison** is the provider. Call 1-800-655-4555 and press 4 to start a new service (48-hour minimum). There is a $10 charge for startup, but again any deposit can be waived with a letter of credit from your current utility company. Send the letter to:

Southern California Edison
P.O. Box 410
Long Beach, CA 90801

WATER

Many places in L.A. include water and power in the rental fee. Make sure to ask about this when you sign your lease. If your rent does not cover these utilities, you'll need to call the **Department of Water and Power (DWP)** at 1-800-342-5397. To ensure weekend hookup, you must call the Thursday before. Otherwise, you only need a 24-hour notice. A deposit is not necessary if you have all your information ready on the phone and are credit-worthy.

INSIDER TIP: *If you want to install a new phone line in your place for a roommate, modem, or fax, ask the landlord about the jack situation so that when you call the phone company, you can help them determine if they need to physically send someone out.*

PHONE

When to install your phone is up to you. Sometimes the quiet is a welcome change, but having a phone, especially in such a spread-out city is a definite necessity. (Most people have more than one—this is a city of car-phone and bathroom-phone addicts). If you want your phone turned on the day you arrive at your new place, you must call well in advance—because if someone needs to actually come out, appointments are tough to get. You know the drill: they can come between 9 am and 12 pm or from 12 pm to 5 pm. The phone company does offer some night service, but those appointments are the first to go. The main telephone companies are **Pacific Bell** (1-800-559-2355) and **GTE** (1-800-223-6177). Both companies require a "turn on" fee, which can be deferred to monthly installment payments.

EARTHQUAKE!

There are always a few ants at any picnic, and paradise wouldn't seem so nice if there weren't some trouble.

We're talking about earthquakes. Take them as a lesson about our cosmic insignificance that puts things in perspective, or take them as a lesson about how some damn thing always goes wrong. Whatever you tell yourself now, however, you can't be psychologically prepared for surfing the earth's crust until that seismic wave hits. But you can be prepared to maximize your safety and make the best of it.

In the front of your telephone book is an earthquake survival guide that you should read carefully. For more information, contact the GOVERNOR'S OFFICE OF EMERGENCY SERVICES EARTHQUAKE PROGRAM at (818) 304-8383.

Here's the commonsense stuff.
Your earthquake preparedness kit for your home should include the following:
- *Fire extinguisher;*
- *Battery-operated radio with extra batteries;*
- *Flashlight with extra batteries;*
- *First aid kit;*
- *Three days' of drinking water (a gallon per person per day);*
- *A week's worth of canned food and a can opener;*
- *Extra eyeglasses and required medications;*
- *Wrenches to turn off gas and water supplies;*
- *Small bottle of bleach to disinfect drinking water;*
- *Blankets, warm clothes, and sturdy comfortable shoes.*

You should also have an earthquake kit in your car containing many of the same items.

BEFORE A QUAKE, YOU SHOULD KNOW:
- *The safest places in your home (away from windows and heavy items that could topple)*
- *Where your gas, electric, and water-main shutoffs are (and how to turn them off)*
- *Locations of nearest fire, police, and emergency medical facility.*

DURING A QUAKE:

- Indoors, duck and take cover under a sturdy desk, table, or other piece of furniture. Stay away from windows and mirrors. Don't rush outside. Don't use the elevator or the stairs while the building is shaking.

- Outdoors, move to open areas away from buildings and power lines.

- Driving, stop if it is safe, but not under (or on) a bridge, overpass, or tunnel. Don't park near trees and signs that may fall. In mountain areas, watch for falling rocks.

- Stay calm.

AFTER THE QUAKE:

- Put on your shoes to avoid cuts from broken glass and debris.

- Check household members (and neighbors) for injuries and supply first aid as necessary. If you smell gas, shut off the main valve; do not light matches or candles, or operate open-flame stoves.

- Stay away from downed power lines and damaged chimneys.

- Be careful when you open cupboards and closets—shifted contents can fall on you.

- Don't use phones unless it's a medical emergency; replace all phones that may have fallen off the hook lest they tie up the phone lines.

- Be prepared for aftershocks, which can do additional damage. And stay away from the beach, where quake-driven tidal waves can arise abruptly.

INSIDER TIP: *Renter's insurance has been very difficult to get since the Northridge quake because California Insurance companies took a huge loss but are still required by law to offer earthquake insurance when you sign up. Most companies have chosen not to offer renter's insurance at all so as to protect themselves in case there is another quake. This is a changing by the moment issue, especially in L.A. So call around when you get here to find out the latest.*

Questions to ask yourself before calling the phone company:

Do you want call-waiting?

Do you want to block 900 numbers?

Do you want to block caller ID?

CABLE

You must have cable TV in L.A.—how else will you keep up on the latest gossip and Hollywood news on the E! channel? This L.A. favorite is our MTV of the '90s. So popular are the E! channel personalities, they make Tabitha Soren look like a has-been. Even more than before, that is. And, well, you'll also get hooked up to CNN, ESPN, C-SPAN and some of those other trivial channels. Seriously, however, cable helps with bad reception and can cure the boredom blues. Movie channels cost more and are not all that necessary in a city where everyone catches the latest flick at a freebie screening.

Cable Companies

Century Cable—(310) 828-2111. There are no night hours
(8 am-12 pm and 12 pm-5 pm)

Continental Cable—(310) 649-5050. Call ahead for
Saturday appointments.

The monthly fee for basic cable usually runs around $25.

CELLULAR PHONE

It's certainly not a necessity, but you may feel left out without one. Everybody's talking to you cordless in L.A., and there's a good reason:

Prices are very competitive, so there are affordable deals. You can look like a wealthy businessman or woman without having to drain your bank account.

L.A. Cellular (the superstore: 12121 W. Pico Blvd., L.A., (310) 207-2213) and **Air Touch** (1-800-Airtouch or 247-8682) are the two services in the area. However, there are several other wholesalers who package deals using these carriers. Because it is so competitive, it is truly best to look in the Yellow Pages under "Cellular" and call around to find the best deal of the moment. The closer it is to a holiday, the better the deal. Here are a couple of leads to get your search started:
CelluLand, (310) 479-8700.
Active Cellular, 11801 W. Pico blvd., L.A., (310) 479-5922.

LOCAL TV STATIONS

Channel 2—CBS, *home of every show for those over 50.*

Channel 4—NBC, *home of "Must See TV."*

Channel 5—KTLA, *home of almost every syndicated sitcom—Saved by the Bell and the rest of them—and now the WB network, home of the saucy, spicy Spelling series, Savannah.*

Channel 7—ABC, *home of everything Disney—that's post merger.*

Channel 9—KCAL, *home of news at 8 in case you missed it at 4, 5, or 6 and don't want to wait until 10.*

Channel 11—Fox, *home of The Best Show You're Not Watching (according to TV Guide), Party of Five.*

Channel 13—KCOP, *home of the new Paramount network and Roseanne reruns.*

Channel 28—PBS. *Catch the nightly local public affairs news show, Life and Times (7:30 weeknights), to plunge you right into the issues of the day seen through L.A. eyes. A bit stodgy at times, but it stands in stark contrast to the local commercial stations' drooling coverage of stories about hero dogs, high-speed chases, heroic rescues, and grisly murders.*

THE INTERNET

So, now that you are connected to the outside world, it's time to get your computer hooked up. As with most things in the field of communications, this is a very competitive business. **America Online** (1-800-827-6364), **Prodigy** (1-800-776-3449), and **Compuserve** (1-800-848-8990) are the bigger names in the biz and are the easiest to use. In addition to connecting you to the Internet, each of these companies offers their own special services. Prices are constantly changing but are usually in the area of $19.95 for 20 hours a month. If you just want to use the Internet, it probably makes more sense to go with an independent supplier that has a much lower monthly fee and gives you unlimited access. However, these companies don't offer anything but Internet access. To set this up on your computer, you need a browser such as Mosaic or Netscape.

DAY CARE

If you're lucky, your place of employment offers day care. If you're not so lucky, at least your child's school provides extra long hour care. If you have neither of the above, you're luck hasn't completely run out, but it will take much more research and time to find the right place for your children. Ask around—other mothers are the best source for a first-hand account of day care centers. You might also want to call the local elementary school in your neighborhood and see if they have any suggestions. It is most important that the day care center you choose is licensed. For more information and referrals, contact the CHILD CARE RESOURCE CENTER in North Hollywood, (818) 762-0905.

Here's a few independent companies to check out:

The Loop—(213) 465-1311.

Caprica—(213) 266-0822.

L.A. Free Net—(213) 223-6511.

PARKING

Unfortunately, parking varies from city to city and neighborhood to neighborhood, and so do the permit departments. The best thing to do is ask your landlord about street parking and then plan accordingly. Parking permits can be ordered by contacting your **local city hall.** Parking restrictions are most significant in Beverly Hills, Santa Monica, and West Hollywood. Make sure you read the signs before you leave your car.

INSIDER TIP: *If you just want Internet access, get hold of an AMERICA ONLINE disc which offers a free month. Then download NETSCAPE and use it as your browser with an independent service. That way you'll avoid the cost of having to buy a browser.*

VOTER REGISTRATION

In liberal L.A., everyone has a vote . . . well, most of the time. **Register to vote** by calling (310) 462-2749. For absentee ballots: (310) 462-2748. For more information on upcoming national elections, check out **Project VoteSmart,** a national nonprofit organization that provides nonpartisan voting information services at no charge. Call the hotline, 1-800-622-SMART, or log on to the net (http://www.vote-smart.org) for up-to-date information on candidates running for president, congress, governor, or state legislature, in addition to finding out how a particular politician voted or where legislature is in the long process of "how a bill becomes a law."

GARBAGE AND RECYCLING

Garbage pickup varies, depending on where you live, so ask your landlord. If you live in an apartment, you probably don't have to worry about dragging your cans out to the curb. But you will have to worry about recycling—because that's what you do here in environmentally correct Los Angeles. L.A. County issues one yellow recycling bin to every home for curbside pickup of cans, bottles, and newspapers. If you live in an apartment, you will most likely have to devise your own plan. In L.A. county, call **1-800-552-5218** and press 5 for information on **recycling centers** near you. If you have **toxic items** to toss, call **1-800-98-TOXIC** for assistance.

NEWSPAPERS AND MAGAZINES

In addition to the publications we list here, keep your eyes peeled for the countless local neighborhood papers and newsletters (not to mention entertaining fanzines of every orientation), which can usually be found stacked at bookstores, cafes, and bars.

Los Angeles Times—L.A.'s primary daily paper covers the basics—and has a great Sunday Calendar section. Sports section gets the job done well, but the main news section is second-rate. The paper built its reputation on feature news and international coverage, but in recent years questionable editorial judgement and corporate downsizing have taken a toll. For home delivery, call (213) 626-2323.

Daily News—Well, it is daily, but it's better for human interest stories than hard news. For home delivery, call (818) 713-3000.

L.A. Weekly—The free citypaper for those who like to deviate from the mainstream. Averaging a hefty 150 pages, the well-written *Weekly* tends toward the kneejerk in its political and arts coverage, but is always worth picking up for its comprehensive entertainment listings and generally comprehensible reviews.

Los Angeles Reader—A free weekly with half the quality of the *Weekly*—and far less quantity.

Los Angeles—This glossy monthly covers a broad range of political and cultural issues, with a recent added emphasis on the Biz. Although demographically slightly skewed toward an older, upscale market, the magazine is great for entertainment listings, the annual **Dining Out Guide,** the **"Best of L.A.** issue, and special travel sections.

Buzz—A fun, squib-heavy Hollywood mag that dishes the dirt, gives up-to-the-minute Hollywood reports, and profiles everybody who's anybody on the local who's who list (and some others who populate the "who's that?" list).

INSIDER TIP: *If you're looking for a job, an apartment, or both, and you're not in town yet, check your library for the L.A. newspapers to get a head start.*

Venice Magazine—Beach community glossy monthly that's full of softball celebrity interviews and other diverting fluff.

BAM—Stellar music monthly with excellent reviews, gossip, interviews, and feature stories about the local and national music scene. *BAM*'s biz coverage and Local Music Focus page will update you in a double-quick hurry. Free at bars, cafes, and record stores.

Frontiers—Serious biweekly gay news and entertainment magazine that's free at bookstores and clubs. Sharp, pragmatic political focus.

Spunk—Amusingly scabrous mostly gay Westside freebie (sold at newsstands elsewhere in town and back east) with scads of entertaining gossip and flamboyant attitude.

Girl Guide—Free lesbian monthly, available at bookstores and clubs, packed with helpful entertainment listings, diverting columns, and news of special interest to women who dig women.

4-Front—Gay guys put together a nice little free mag for the boys. Vital club and restaurant listings, news snippets, and entertainment reviews.

JOB HUNTING RESOURCES

Moving gets so overwhelming, you sometimes forget the little things—like the fact that you'll need a job once you get here. The unavoidable job search should begin with the *L.A. Times* classified ads. For the entertainment industry, pick up *Variety* and the *Hollywood Reporter* daily.

Temporary agencies are also great sources for eventual full-time employment and also provide for a quick taste-testing of what's out there. **Appleone** (1250 Westwood Blvd., Westwood, (310) 477-0021 and other locations) and **Remedy** (11263 National Blvd., L.A., (310) 478-6565 and other locations) are two of the most well-known and often used agencies in the city. For entertainment placement, **All Star Agency** (205 S. Beverly Dr., Suite 204, Beverly Hills, (310) 271-5217) is one of the best especially because you don't have to shell out any of your own money.

TV TAPINGS

Dream of spinning the wheel on "THE PRICE IS RIGHT?" Or maybe you'd love to be a heckler in the audience of "POLITICALLY INCORRECT." Well, dream no more: CBS TELEVISION CITY (7800 Beverly Blvd., L.A.) offers free tickets for television show tapings with seating usually on a first come, first serve basis. For information, call (213) 852-2345.

INSIDER TIP: *For those who are serious about making their day job count, catering is your best bet. It gives you the in before you're really in. AMBROSIA, (310) 453-7007, and ALONG COMES MARY (213) 931-9082, are two of the biggest caterers in town. And whatever crowd WOLFGANG doesn't feed is sure to be kept from starving by the folks at PATINA.*

SO YOU WANT TO SERVE THOSE IN PICTURES

Full of excitement, you've decided to follow your dream and head to Hollywood. You know you could be the next Meryl Streep, Brad Pitt, or Steven Spielberg if someone would just give you a break. You're ready. So what do you do? Well, most likely you'll need to get a job so that while you are following your dream, you're also paying the rent. In L.A. (as in New York), you'll join a group of talented young hopefuls paying their rent by waiting tables. Those with the real "weight" serve the celebs at the best restaurants in town. They even arrange for their hours to be during power breakfast or lunch time. But getting a job at some of these places is almost as difficult as getting into law school—you need the right resume, experience, and even the right look. Still, you want to be discovered so you'll want a restaurant that serves the industry's best explorers. Here are some hot territories:

THE GRILL—It's where power movie moguls lunch to discuss upcoming deals. The time is ripe if you can work it. 9560 Dayton Way, Beverly Hills, (310) 276-0615.

JONES HOLLYWOOD—Mingle amongst this young crowd overeager to discuss business. 7205 Santa Monica Blvd., Hollywood, (213) 850-1727.

PINOT HOLLYWOOD—So close to Paramount, hope for osmosis. 1448 N. Gower St., Hollywood, (213) 461-8800.

CAFFE LUNA—Aside from the occasional celeb guests, it's a great place to network with other wanna-bes. 7463 Melrose Ave., L.A., (213) 655-8647.

MORTON'S—Some big movie execs trust their Morton's waiter more than their colleagues. Not bad! 8800 Melrose Ave., West Hollywood, (310) 276-5205.

INSIDER TIP: Never hand your script or head-shot to someone you are serving unless asked for it. Besides being annoying, it is a sure way to get fired. Still, you are allowed to be exceptionally charming, chatty, and attentive.

Chapter Five
SETTING UP
HOUSE
(or, Finding the Martha Stewart Within)

MAKING A HOME look like a home isn't easy when you don't have the budget of Martha Stewart. Still, if you are creative and willing to accessorize slowly (it takes a while, be patient), there's no reason you can't make your pad look like it belongs on the cover of *Town and Country*—well maybe not the cover but at least an inside shot. Most important, you want your place to feel like "you," but even you need the essentials.

FURNITURE

For mass furniture in all different styles and colors, trek over to **IKEA** (600 N. San Fernando Blvd., Burbank, (818) 842-4532). This cavernous warehouse store is a bit overwhelming, but the standard items here are perfect (shouldn't everyone have a halogen lamp?) to begin the furnishing process and their prices are very reasonable.

Plummer's (8876 Venice Blvd., L.A., (310) 837-0138) is another mainstream furniture hub to pick up the basics.

Once you've got a mattress, table, and a chair or two, you're ready to add some style. Furniture can be expensive, but you don't have to buy everything at once. Although it is tempting, resist. You can browse as much as you want, but only buy when you are truly in love with a piece—you're seeking a comfortable long-term relationship, not a flashy, shortlived fling. Here's a few places to cruise for dream furniture dates.

Casa—19824 Ventura Blvd., Woodland Hills, (818) 883-4681. Not many people know about this treasure chest filled with handcrafted bed frames, dining room tables, and several other ideas for accessorizing your house to the max. It's also a great place to shop for house-warming gifts.

Cost Plus—10860 Westwood Blvd., L.A., (310) 441-5115. It's a warehouse full of knick-knacks where you can sift through for some real finds if you have a knack.

Iron Maiden—8403½ 3rd St., L.A., (213) 655-9711. Iron furnishings—thus the name. Another place where it takes a little extra time to find something great.

Not So Far East—160 S. La Brea Blvd., L.A., (213) 933-8900. Recycled teak wood from Indonesia is the big draw at this upscale-yet-earthy furniture hub.

Pier 1 Imports—10984 Santa Monica Blvd., Westwood, and several other locations, (310) 478-6884. Wooden chairs, colorful throw pillows, tons of tchotchkes. Be careful not to overdose on wicker.

Modernism—13641 Ventura Blvd., Sherman Oaks, (818) 981-3757. It is cluttered when you walk in but only because there are so many fabulous pieces to trip over. From armoires to over-sized couches, this place is a true find.

Sofa-U-Love—11948 San Vicente Blvd., Brentwood, and other locations, (310) 207-2540. With such a cheesy name, you're libel to dismiss it. Don't. The prices are unbeatable for sofas, love-seats, chairs, and ottomans.

Standard Furniture—14900 Oxnard (at Kester), Van Nuys, (818) 781-1800. Discontinued furniture, like-new repos (bounced checks), and slightly damaged merchandise at way below what you'd find in department stores for the same stuff.

Pampa—10931 W. Pico Blvd., L.A., (310) 470-9545. A bit on the pricey side but some beautiful wooden pieces. It's a great place to check in with every once in awhile.

Z Gallerie—1426 Third St. Promenade, Santa Monica, and other locations, (310) 394-4685. Choose from an assortment of framed prints and over-priced furniture—but sometimes you just can't resist.

When you've got money to blow, head over to Robertson Blvd. (roughly between Beverly and Doheny) and the surrounding area, which has become one of the hottest spots in town for upscale clothing and serious furniture shopping. It's sort of the high-end upholstery district. Check out **Expressions** (157 N. Robertson Blvd., L.A., (310) 278-1135), **Paradise Rattan Furniture** (151 N. Robertson

Blvd., (310) 276-3435), and **Eclectica** (8745 W. Third St., L.A., (310) 275-1004)—all great places for the expensive decorator in you.

THE KITCHEN

Here are a few of the best kitchen-oriented stores in the city:

Crate and Barrel—Century City Mall, 10250 Santa Monica Blvd., and other locations, L.A., (310) 551-1100. As you probably already know, they have a great selection of dishes and kitchen accessories.

Pottery Barn—Century City Mall, 10250 Santa Monica Blvd., and other locations, (310) 552-0170. Along with the kitchen stuff, you can find beautiful candlesticks, vases, and pillows.

William Sonoma—317 N. Beverly Dr., Beverly Hills, and other locations, (310) 274-9127. It's a bit more expensive, but the kitchenware here is long-lasting. Best if you strive to be a gourmet but still useful if macaroni and cheese is your dish of choice.

INSIDER TIP: *If you are a serious chef and love to work in the kitchen, UTENSILS (250 N. Larchmont Blvd., L.A., (213) 461-8101) will be your candy store. The place carries everything you could ever want to cook with so you can make anything you ever want.*

LINENS

For linens and more, head for **Bed, Bath and Beyond** (11801 W. Olympic Boulevard, L.A., (310) 478-5767)—although it is difficult to leave with only what you came for. From comforters to place mats, it is easy to go crazy and buy, buy, buy. Once again, you don't have to get it all at once. Wait for things to go on sale (because they do) and you'll feel a lot better having paid less.

Stroud's (100 N. La Cienega Blvd., West Hollywood, and other locations, (310) 657-2422) is also a great place for sheets, towels, and more, and they also have significant sales, so check in regularly.

If you are willing to go more expensive, **Room With A View** (1600 Montana Ave., Santa Monica, (310) 998-5858) carries beautiful silks, quilts and handmade pillows.

INSIDER TIP: *When you don't have a lot of time and you don't have a lot of money, you can always rent furniture. BROOKS (11843 Wilshire Blvd., Brentwood, (310) 479-4494) is great for basic taste while NICK METROPOLIS (100 S. La Brea, L.A., (213) 938-4343) appeals to a more funky bunch. For appliances, check out WERTZ BROTHERS (11879 Santa Monica Blvd., L.A., (310) 477-4251).*

APPLIANCES

Probably the most important thing to do is to get all your electronic devices hooked up and running. Also if you need to buy major appliances, you'll want to do that as soon as possible—even a bachelor needs a refrigerator (we hope).

The major discount competitors are:

Best Buy—11301 W. Pico Blvd., L.A., (310) 268-9190,
and other locations.

Circuit City—3115 S. Sepulveda Blvd., L.A., (310) 391-3144,
and other locations.

Fry's Electronics—6100 Canoga Ave., Woodland Hills,
(818) 227-1000.

Adray's—11201 W. Pico Blvd., L.A., (310) 479-0797, and
other locations.

THRIFT STORES

One piece of good news concerning the out-migration of disaster-weary Angelenos in recent years is the boom in thrift stores hawking fine merchandise. From upscale to down, the market for other people's stuff has never been more bullish. If you've discovered the vintage advantage, you'll definitely want to frequent the thrifts. Fads being what they are, of course, we can't guarantee that these stores won't be picked over (or just plain be over) by the time you arrive, but rest assured there are scores more out there to pick up the slack—you'll soon discover your favorites. For now, you can make do with ours.

Wasteland—The spot to find Cosmo Kramer sweaters, Marcia Brady blouses, and frocks perhaps formerly worn by formerly Prince. This jumpin' Melrose recycling center is a mecca for the fashionably dissolute in all their grungy Technicolor splendor. The high-quality slightly pricey stock turns over at an astounding clip (shirts and slacks run upward of $20 a pop; dresses and jackets can cost quite a bit more); if you don't see anything you like, come back tomorrow. They buy clothes, too, so bear in mind that some of the stuff in your closet may have become "vintage" while you weren't looking. 7428 Melrose Avenue, (213) 653-3028.

INSIDER TIP: *Some of the best garage sales in town are located in Santa Monica, and they're usually listed in* **THE OUTLOOK,** *Santa Monica's daily.*

Good Old Times—For a more low-key approach to high-quality vintage wear, visit this cavern of earthly delights. The transplanted Dutch owners, Lisa and Chaim, have an excellent selection, with more emphasis on classic looks than on trends du jour. Don't get the wrong idea—however, you can still find your ornately detailed laceup leather pants and your Frankenstein fetish footwear and your quaintly loud, poly-print blouses. But there's also the option of tailored styles from the '40s and '50s. Ask politely and they'll let you enter leather-coat Valhalla in the back room. 7739 Santa Monica Blvd. (near Fairfax), (213) 654-7103.

Out of the Closet—They've opened a string of shops citywide-which has somewhat diluted the stock of vintage dresses, designer men's wear, discount furniture, and housewares—but this location remains the best. They have great sales and closeout racks where you can get shirts and blouses for a couple bucks, jackets and dresses for a couple more. The staff is young and trendy, so the groovy bargains that used to be commonplace are getting rarer. Still, there are many good things on tap, and if you pay a wee bit too much once in a while remember that the proceeds go to AIDS charities. 3160 Glendale Blvd., Atwater (and several other locations), (213) 664-4394.

St. Vincent DePaul Thrift Store—Funky furniture for the frugal, acres of fabulous (or was that shabulous?) frocks, and even the occasional used car can be had here. But the unique draw for scavengers is the As Is Yard out back where you will find many mysterious must-haves for chump change. 210 N. Ave. 21, (213) 224-6280.

Salvation Army—You can acquire many happenin' threads at this "Hipster Sally" if you beat Santa Monica's Starbucks beatnicks out of the sack (not difficult if you wake up before noon). The friendly staff doesn't know (or care?) what's hip, which spells bargains aplenty for diligent diggers. Furniture and housewares are hit and miss, but reasonably priced. 1658 11th St., Santa Moncia, (310) 450-7235.

Boys and Girls Club of Venice—Once the best place for fantastic oddball furniture, ultra-cheap! Unfortunately they caught on, but it's still a moderately priced spot for quirky living room essentials and decent office furnishings. Remains good for clothes and housewares. 2304 Lincoln Blvd., Venice, (310) 391-6302; also 3516 Centinela Ave., Mar Vista, (310) 915-7458.

Beverly Hills Hadassah Thrift—It's not in Beverly Hills, and thankfully neither are the prices. Tons of decent clothes and kitchen items, with a few nice furnishings lurking amid the shoddy. 1452 Lincoln Blvd., Santa Monica, (310) 395-3824.

Glendale Adventist Hospital Thrift Shop—Stellar selection, helpful staff, new stock every day, low prices—what else do you want in a thrift store? You want it situated in an obscure spot like this so it doesn't get picked over. 311 Vallejo Dr., Glendale, (818) 409-8056.

Disabled American Veterans Thrift Store—This store was better (and a bit cheaper) when it was across the street in a dumpy old space, but it's still pretty good gussied up. Well organized stock of clothing, books, housewares, and furniture. 6343 San Fernando Rd. (at Sonora), Glendale, (818) 244-2221.

Goodwill—A large store with an excellent selection of women's clothing—some of it very reasonably priced. As often happens at

FLEA MARKETS

It seems whenever you compliment someone on their furniture these days, they let you in on their secret: They shop at the flea markets. Still a great place to shop, even if the secret is out. Now at the flea markets, if you get what you pay for you probably paid too much.

BURBANK MONTHLY ANTIQUE MARKET—Fourth Sunday of every month, 8-3. Admission, $3. 1001 Riverside Dr., Burbank, (310) 455-2886.

PHILLIP DANE'S MELROSE MARKET—Every Sunday, 9-5. Admission, $2. Fairfax High School, at the corner of Melrose and Fairfax Aves., (213) 465-7665.

IVY SUBSTATION ANTIQUE MARKET—Second Saturday of every month, 8-3. Admission, $3. 9070 Venice Blvd., Culver City, (310) 455-2886.

LONG BEACH OUTDOOR ANTIQUE AND COLLECTIBLE MARKET— Third Sunday of every month, 6:30-3. Admission, $3.50. Veterans Memorial Stadium, Lakewood and Clark Aves., Long Beach, (213) 655-5703.

PASADENA CITY COLLEGE FLEA MARKET—First Sunday of every month, 8-3. Admission, free. 1570 E. Colorado Ave., Pasadena, (818) 585-7906.

ROSE BOWL FLEA MARKET—Second Sunday of every month, 6-4:30. Admission, $5-$10. 1001 Rose Bowl Dr., Pasadena, (213) 560-7469. It can get downright ruthless fighting over furniture. You must be prepared so bring some post-its and write your name on them beforehand. Then, when you know what you want, stick it on the furniture to mark your territory.

VALLEY INDOOR SWAP MEET—6701 Variel Ave., Canoga Park, (818) 340-9120. Some of it is junk but much of it is not. You have to weed through and you'll find some excellent deals on accessories, electronics, and clothes.

SANTA MONICA OUTDOOR ANTIQUE AND COLLECTIBLE MARKET— Fourth Sunday of every month, 8-3. Admission, $2.50-$4. Santa Monica Airport, Airport Ave. and Bundy Dr., Santa Monica, (213) 933-2511.

thrift stores, the stuff they think is nice isn't and the good stuff is hiding in the cheap crap. Happy hunting. 1535 S. Western Ave., (213) 732-1416.

INSIDER TIP: *HOLD EVERYTHING (Century City Shopping Mall, The Beverly Center, and other locations, (310) 652-5979). Organization is key to keeping your place neat and tidy. Welcome to creative storage wonderland. With all kinds of containers, boxes, and shelving, everything will find its place in your home.*

PLANTS

After you have a place to sit, a place to sleep, a place to eat, and a few things to beautify your place, it's probably time to think about a live-in roommate to improve the atmosphere—a plant that is. There are plenty of nurseries to choose from throughout L.A. Here are a few local bests:

Armstrong's—3226 Wilshire Blvd., Santa Monica, (310) 829-6766.

Lucky Plant—3113 Lincoln Blvd., Santa Monica, (310) 399-1145. Terrific deals on all kinds of plants and best of all—they deliver.

Mordigan Nurseries—6285 W. 3rd St., (213) 655-6027.

ART

Now that you've got the place furnished, the walls might seem a little bare. Buying art can be difficult and very expensive.

<u>Inexpensive:</u>

The **Third Street Promenade** in Santa Monica is a good place to start your search. With so many artsy boutiques, there are posters and prints all throughout the promenade in different little nooks and crannies.

Venice Beach is another strip to peruse looking for prints. While the tourists purchase "muscle beach" T-shirts and fluorescent-colored fanny packs, you too can join in the buying frenzy. There are several vendors who carry great old movie posters and classic photos. But please, limit your buying to art and maybe sunglasses—you are no longer a tourist.

Postermasters (2034 Cotner Ave., 1st floor, L.A., (310) 473-4911) is also a cheap way to put a little color on the walls.

L.A.'s Finest:

A step up the financial ladder may take you to various galleries. Here's a sampling of some of L.A.'s finest—within reason:

Bergamont Station—2525 Michigan Ave. Gallery A7, Santa Monica, (310) 453-6463

Dassin Gallery—Pacific Design Center, B-131-8687 Melrose Ave., West Hollywood, (310) 652-0203

Jason Vass Gallery—Okay, it's pricey but there are fabulous French movie posters in this chic Santa Monica sidewalk store. 1210 Montana Ave., Santa Monica, (310) 395-2048.

L.A. Louver—45 N. Venice Blvd., Venice, (310) 822-4955.

PaceWildenstein—9540 Wilshire Blvd., Beverly Hills, (310) 205-5522.

INSIDER TIP: *When you're ready to venture into the art world, it's a good idea to contact GENART, a relatively new organization that promotes the work of young artists. For more information, call (818) 786-9409.*

Framing

And when you're ready, take your works of art to one of these framing stores:

Fast Frame—2180 Westwood Blvd., L.A., (310) 470-0302, and several other locations.

FrameStore—11301 W. Olympic Blvd., L.A., (310) 477-8118, and several other locations. There are almost always discount coupons around so make sure and ask.

CLEANING SERVICES

Finally, when it's all put together and feels like a home, there's one more thing you might need: a cleaning service to put it all back together. Word of mouth is always a good way to find someone reliable. So ask your landlord or your colleagues. But if you're too shy, try these suggestions—just clean your sty.

Custom Maid—1-800-564-6484.

Maid With Joy—(310) 452-8621.

HomePerfect—(310) 788-0660.

PLACES OF WORSHIP

Freedom of religion is one of the most enthusiastically exercised freedoms Angelenos have. A random sample of some local approaches to the divine.

First African Methodist Episcopal L.A.: (213) 735-1251.

Baha'i, Beverly Hills: (310) 276-8186.

First Baptist, L.A.: (213) 384-2151.

Mount Baldy Zen Center: 909-985-6410.

L.A. Darma Zen Center: (213) 934-0330.

Hollywood Beverly Christian Church: (213) 469-5107.

Scientology Celebrity Center, Hollywood: (213) 960-3100.

St. Sophia Cathedral (Greek Orthodox), L.A.: (213) 737-2424.

St. Marks Glendale Episcopal: (818) 240-3860.

Islamic Center of Southern California: (213) 384-5783.

Santa Monica Evangelical Lutheran: (310) 451-1346.

L.A. Science of Mind, Beverly Hills: (213) 852-9055.

Sikh Dharma, Guru Ram Das Sharam: (213) 552-3416.

Theosophy: (213) 749-7244.

L.A. First Unitarian: (213) 389-1356.

United Church of Christ, Westwood Hills: (213) 474-7327.

L.A. United Pentecostal: (213) 257-0064.

Vedanta Society, Hollywood: (213) 465-7114.

Dial-a-Prayer: (213) 381-1191

Chapter Six
GOING OUT

LOS ANGELES IS AN INDUSTRY TOWN, no doubt about it. And, of course, you've got options. You can work on the supply side, helping create big-time Tinseltown product. Or you can play on the demand side. In other words, you go out and enjoy the fruits of all that high-priced Hollywood labor, whether directly, in the movie theater, or indirectly, elsewhere throughout the vast entertainment sprawl that is Los Angeles.

The palpable presence of the industry serves to raise the stakes across the board, adding a surging energy of sympathetic vibrations to the myriad facets of L.A.'s polymorphous entertainment scene until the whole town becomes a roiling vortex of jacked-up, hyper-driven, skull-freaking imagination.

In other words, there's lots to do.

ANNUAL EVENTS

As the song says, California loves to party. Here are a few of the many annual festivals and events around town. In addition to these, almost every community and neighborhood has its own block party or street fair, so check 'em out.

For more complete listings of goings-on, consult the front section of your telephone book, pick up one of the free weekly papers, or get your hands on a copy of Robert Badal's excellent book, *Romancing the Southland* (now out of print, but the library carries it).

January

Tournament of Roses Parade—As seen on TV. Pasadena, (818) 795-4147.

Los Angeles Auto Show—Cars R us. Downtown Convention Center, (213) 741-1151.

Kingdom Day Parade—Honoring Martin Luther King Jr. with a parade from Baldwin Hills Crenshaw Plaza to the Natural History Museum in Exposition Park, (213) 298-8777.

February

Black History Month Celebrations—10 of the city's 22 founding fathers were escaped slaves with Spanish surnames—an often overlooked historical fact. (213) 734-1164.

Kennel Club of Beverly Hills Dog Show—Fido or Fidon't? Canine competitors on display at the Sports Arena, (310) 748-6131.

Chinese New Year Celebration—Parade, street fair, music, and food, (213) 617-0396.

March

American Indian Festival and Market—Food, crafts, and native cultural traditions on display at the Natural History Museum, (213) 744-3488.

The Swallows return to Mission San Juan Capistrano—You've seen it on TV all these years, now you can be there in person. (714) 493-1111.

Los Angeles Marathon—Course runs through Hollywood, Silver Lake, Echo Park, and downtown. (310) 444-5544.

April

Fiesta Broadway—Downtown Latin block party celebrating being Latin. Music, food, and entertainment. A warm-up for Cinco de Mayo. (818) 793-9335.

Renaissance Pleasure Faire—Elaborate medieval fun featuring mock battles, cooking contests, jugglers, and fools as well as that ever popular event: wench lifting. 1-800-52-FAIRE.

ENTERTAINMENT FROM A TO Z

May

Cinco de Mayo—A great party, with lots of ethnic food, dancing, and music.

Ethnic Festival—The nation's largest multi-ethnic bash features music, food, and replicas of villages from around the world. (818) 712-0016.

Very Special Arts Festival—Disabled children from across the country sing, dance, and display their art. (213) 972-7389.

June

Christopher Street West Gay and Lesbian Pride Celebration—Parade, food, music, and more. (213) 656-6553.

Playboy Jazz Festival—The big names in mainstream jazz all turn up for this one. (310) 449-4070.

Summer Nights at the Ford—Nightly dance, theater, and music every night 'till September. John Anson Ford Theater, (213) 974-1343.

Summer Solstice Folk Music, Dance, and Storytelling Festival—The country's biggest participatory folk fest. (818) 342-7664.

Summerfest—Burbank does its darnedest to prove it can be fun. (818) 953-8763.

July

July Fourth Celebrations, citywide—(213) 881-2411.

Hollywood Bowl Summer Festival—A popular fave featuring jazz, classical, and pop performers who give it their all under the stars.

Lotus Festival—Asian-Pacific cultures are the focus in this festival at Echo Park. Food, music, and dragon-boat races in the lake. (213) 485-8744.

August

African Marketplace and Cultural Fair—This fest in the Crenshaw district takes us back to the motherland with music, storytelling, crafts, and food. (213) 734-1164.

Children's Festival of Art—Free performances and art activities are on tap at Barnsdall Art Park in Los Feliz. (213) 485-4474.

L.A. a la Carte—High-end street fete in Westwood Village features eats from some of the greater L.A. area's best restaurants. (714)-753-1860.

Nisei Week—Little Tokyo's big festival with dancing, drumming, martial arts—and maybe a little sushi. (213) 687-7193.

Watts Summer Festival—Get down to see the weird and wonderful Watts towers and see the neighborhood at its best. (213) 789-7304.

September

Fringe Festival—Interesting art and performance events are everywhere as this arty party sprawls citywide. (909) 397-9716.

Korean Festival—A Koreatown parade, some food, and a little tae kwon do. (213) 730-1495.

L.A. Classic Jazz Fest—America's classical music makes itself heard at various hot spots. (310) 521-6893.

"California is like breakfast cereal—what's not flakes is fruits and nuts."

GALLAGHER, COMEDIAN

October

Fall Festival—The Farmer's Market and Park La Brea go a little bit country with music and eats in a quasi-rustic mode. (213) 933-9211.

Halloween Street Fest and Parade—Come as you are (or wear a different costume) to gay L.A.'s big night out on the town. (213) 848-6308.

November

Doo Dah Parade—Mock the overblown Rose Parade with the rest of the smart alecks in Pasadena. (818) 796-2591.

Hollywood Christmas Parade—We don't have snow, so we find other ways to overdo it. (213) 469-8311.

Whole Life Expo—Spirituality, health and green issues go to market in this wild and wacky trade show. (310) 399-2992.

December

Beverly Hills Lighting Ceremony—Celebs and choral groups do their thing as Bev turns on the holiday decorations.

Los Posados—A candlelight procession depicting Mary and Joseph's journey to Bethlehem at the El Pueblo de Los Angeles Historic Monument Downtown. (213) 687-4344.

ART GALLERIES

There are more art galleries than gas stations in L.A., so it's easy to get your fill. For complete listings of specific shows, opening receptions, and gallery hours, consult the *L.A. Reader*, *Los Angeles* magazine, or the *L.A. Times*. You'll soon locate your favorites, but in the meantime it might be helpful to know that some galleries are conveniently clustered together and openings often fall on the same nights, thereby maximizing free wine-and-cheese opportunities.

Santa Monica

The side streets in this overgrown seaside town are thick with art galleries. Three good spots among many are gathered at Broadway near 20th. **Ruth Bachofner Gallery**, (310) 829-3300; **First Independent Gallery**, (310) 829-0345; and **Tatischeff/Rogers**, (310) 449-1240.

Bergamot Station

The best clump of galleries to be found on the Westside is at Bergamot Station (2525 Michigan Ave., Santa Monica). More than a dozen galleries, shops, and restaurants are huddled in a no-frills atmosphere. **The Gallery of Functional Art,** (310) 829-6990; **Track 16 Gallery,** (310) 264-4678; and **Patricia Faure Gallery,** (310) 449-1479 are three solid faves to check out, but the best strategy is just to get there and wander.

INSIDER TIP: *When you make a day doing the art thing at BERGAMOT, be sure to stop in at GALLERY CAFE. It's a popular lunch spot in the area great for healthy and some not-so-healthy California cooking. One of the hottest items on the menu: The Turkey Caesar burger.*

West Hollywood

Another brace of galleries can be found in West Hollywood near the confluence of Melrose and Santa Monica. Park and walk around—this is one of the best pedestrian areas in town. The neighborhood is tres gay and jumping. The galleries show a wide variety of stuff. **Gallery 825,** 825 La. Cienega Blvd., (310) 652-8272; **Koplin Gallery,** 464 N. Robertson Blvd., (310) 657-9843; **Margo Leavin Gallery;** 812 N. Robertson Blvd., (310) 273-0603; **George Stern Fine Arts,** 8920 Melrose Ave., (310) 276-2600; **Louis Stern Fine Arts,** 9002 Melrose Ave., (310) 276-0147.

La Brea

La Brea Avenue near 3rd Street is another prime spot to scope the art, grab a scone at a nearby cafe and scrutinize the passersby. A few to consider: **Jan Baum Gallery,** 170 S. La Brea Ave., (213) 932-0170; **Jan Kesner Gallery,** 164 N. La Brea Ave., (213) 938-6834; **Paul Kopeikin Gallery,** 170 S. La Brea Ave., (213) 937-0765; **Frank Lloyd Gallery,** 170 S. La Brea Ave., (213) 939-2189.

Other, or none of the above

PaceWildenstein—Many of the biggest and best modern shows go up at Pace. 9540 Wilshire Blvd., Beverly Hills, (310) 205-5522.

L.A. Louvre—They pronounce it loo-ver, which is a bit goofy, but they hang good stuff so we'll let it slide. 45 Venice Blvd., Venice, (310) 822-4955.

Los Angeles Central Library—The downtown library is an architectural wonder and an excellent gallery in its own right. 630 W. 5th St., (213) 228-7225.

BARS, BARS, BARS

L.A., as you've probably gathered by now, is both amorphous and polymorphous. And the city's bars and nightclubs echo this condition. Nightspots are spread willy-nilly and exist in every style and almost any imaginable hybrid of dance club, tavern, restaurant, live music venue, cafe, vaudeville hall, performance space-and kitchen sink. A spot that's a neighborly hangout at happy hour might become a drag club or a punk music bar or a throbbing techno-groove locus later in the evening. Many popular places try to be all things to all people with multiple-room entertainment complexes, and some actually suc-ceed at this precarious balancing act.

On the other hand, schizophrenia is an understandable response to the unremitting variety of experience in L.A. and nightclubs are no more immune than human beings. Recognizing these difficulties, the categories used here to describe nightspots are rather loose with a lot of overlap. Moreover, at many establishments the term "club" is used loosely, and refers to nightly moveable feasts that are deejay-driven and audience-validated. Be forewarned that dance clubs and their patrons are fickle and faddish, so the hot spot du jour could well be stone cold by the time you read this. For up-to-the-minute information, consult the comprehensive listings in the *L.A. Weekly*—or you could just ask around.

Bars, Acoustic/Folk

Canter's Kibbitz Room—Exploring the crazy premise that music sounds better when you can hear it. Who knows, maybe it'll catch on. 419 N. Fairfax Ave., (213) 651-2030.

Ghengis Cohen Cantina—Singer-songwriters galore for all the folk folk. 740 N. Fairfax Ave., (213) 653-0640.

McCabe's Guitar Shop—Not really a bar in the alcoholic sense of the word, but a great spot to sip coffee and soak up the best in unplugged country and rock—not to mention stuff that was never plugged in in the first place. 3101 Pico Blvd., Santa Monica, (310) 828-4403.

Bars, Blues

The delta of the Los Angeles river is not that large, but it has spawned our own desert style of low-humidity blues appreciation.

Babe and Ricky's Inn—A venerable joint that's been through a ton of changes over the years, still rockin' steady and true blue. 5259 Central Ave., (213) 235-4866.

B.B. King's Blues Club—Two stages of real blues and lots of authentic southern chow are the perfect antidote to the totally ersatz City Walk vibe. 100 Universal Center Dr., Universal City, (818) 6BBKING.

The Bailey—Mellow neighborhood ambiance and solid blues. 8771 W. Pico Blvd., (310) 275-2619.

Harvelle's—The oldest blues club on the Westside is a down-home mainstay. 1432 4th St., Santa Monica, (310) 395-1676.

Bars, Country

Culver Saloon—The yee-haw crowd stomps to live local country music. 11513 Washington Blvd., (310) 391-1519.

Jack's Cinnamon Cinder—Free dance lessons Tuesday and Thursday through Saturday. 4311 W. Magnolia Blvd., Burbank, (818) 845-1121.

Bars, Gay

L.A. gay bars run the gamut, run the gauntlet, and occasionally just plain run amok. Whatever you prefer. Here are a few faves, but for a more complete information consult the *Gay and Lesbian Community Yellow Pages*, or such publications as *Gay and Lesbian Times*, *Frontiers*, *4-Front*, and *Los Angeles Girl Guide*.

Apache—The natives are restless, and boys will be boys—most of the time. 11608 Ventura Blvd., Studio City, (818) 506-0404.

Axis—WeHo's biggest gay disco plays house, old-school, Latin, and sundry high-energy jams. Girl Bar rages on Fridays in this space with several bars, pool tables, and, of course, dancing. 652 N. Lapeer, West Hollywood, (310) 659-0471.

Checca—Gregarious and mostly gay. Kind of a drag—but only when it wants to be. 7231 Santa Monica, West Hollywood, (213) 850-7471.

Cobalt Cantina—This sweet little restaurant has a jumpin' bar. 4326 Sunset Blvd., Silver Lake, (213) 664-1189.

Connection—Friendly Westside neighborhood lesbian club with entertainment and dancing. 4363 Sepulveda Blvd., (310) 391-6817.

The Palms—West Hollywood's long-running lesbian fave. 8572 Santa Monica, West Hollywood, (310) 652-6188.

Probe—Dance all night to hot DJs from around the country. Saturday, especially, is gay men's night (but aren't they all when you are). 836 N. Highland, Hollywood, (213) 461-8301.

Rage—Everything a throbbing gay disco should be. 8911 Santa Monica Blvd., West Hollywood, (310) 652-7055.

7969—A bawdy place with a good bit of fun to be had—even for breeders. 7969 Santa Monica Blvd. West Hollywood, (213) 654-0280.

Bars, Jazz

There's much more to L.A.'s jazz scene than just the legacy of West Coast cool. We can heat it up and get experimental with the best of them, or just chill when that's what's called for. Consider these establishments when you want to sample the special Angeleno flavors of America's classical music:

Atlas Bar and Grill—A jumping social scene with bar in the back, dining, and music from trad to (occasionally) rad. 3670 Wilshire Blvd., (213) 380-8400.

The Baked Potato—A small spot where you can find some big talents. And the music isn't all that's hot—true to their name, they serve scads o' spuds put through countless culinary improvisational changes. 3787 Cahuenga Blvd. N., Hollywood., (818) 980-1615. Or, visit their other location at 26 E. Colorado Blvd., Pasadena, (818) 564-1122.

The Bel Age Hotel—The hotel's Club Brasserie restaurant offers excellent food, a fabulous view, jumping bar action, and, oh yeah, nice jazz. 1020 N. San Vicente Blvd. (310) 854-1111.

Catalina Bar and Grill—Big names who can really blow are always on hand in this small hall that's one of the town's best. 1640 Cahuenga Blvd. N., Hollywood, (213) 466-2210.

The Derby—Big and tall bands (and sumptuous cuisine). 4500 Los Feliz Blvd., Hollywood, (213) 663-8979.

5th Street Dick's Coffee Company—You won't really need the coffee—the music should keep you up at this swingin' place to catch late-night jams. 3347½ W. 43rd Place, (213) 296-3970.

Jax Bar and Grill—A mainstream mainstay. 339 N. Brand Blvd., Glendale, (818) 500-1604.

Jazz Bakery—A nice big space with sweets and sweet music— plus beer, wine, coffee, and sandwiches. 3233 Helms Ave. Culver City, (310) 271-9039.

St. Marks—A statue of Duke Ellington stands guard near the bandstand of this cool listening and libation station. 23 Windward Ave., Venice, (310) 452-2222.

Bars, Neighborhood

There are more neighborhood bars in L.A. than you can shake a swizzle stick at—here's a sample.

Circle Bar—A charmingly dank oval bar with jukebox spinning fab tunes while patrons spin fab yarns. Recently overrun by an infestation of young, beautiful people (doncha hate that?) after a rave-up in *Spin* magazine. 2926 Main St., Santa Monica, (310) 392-4898.

Good Luck Bar—Tinseltown flotsam and jetsam wash up at this cozy spot for your amusement. 1514 Hillhurst, (213) 666-3524.

Lava Lounge—Weird neighborhood bar for a weird neighborhood. Overpriced umbrella drinks and oddball clientele sometimes make you feel slightly screwed—but not in a bad way. 1533 N. La Brea Ave., Hollywood., (213) 876-6612.

Mark V Lounge—Westside neighborhood bar with Hollywood crowd intermingling as unobtrusively as they can. 5571 Sepulveda Blvd., Culver City, (310) 397-1291.

Sarna's Lounge—Serious darts, cheap drinks, and friendly pool in an unpretentious working-class corner bar. 10899 Venice Blvd., Culver City, (310) 839-6197.

Smog Cutter—A hard-drinkin', karaoke-singin', pool shootin' dive full of crusty regulars and charming bartendresses. If Bukowski were still alive, he might be drinking here. 864 N. Virgil Ave., Hollywood, (213) 660-4626.

Ye Olde Rustic Inn—Cozy and amusing Los Feliz spot for bargain drinks amidst a crowd that's a mix of goatee'd guys working hard to be cool and barstool lifers working hard on their cold drinks.

Bars, Rock and Alternative

Almost all of the next-big-things of the music world are rockin' the stages out here in L.A.—cuz this is where the biz is. Does that encourage people to get a little too slick? Yeah, sometimes, but it also ensures that we have a constant stream of wonderful sounds in our dozens of nightspots.

Alligator Lounge—A Westside mainstay, this is a key spot to loiter and listen. 3321 Pico Blvd. Santa Monica, (310) 449-1844.

Al's Bar—Hard-bitten hipster herd congregates here to suck down beer and wine while absorbing quaintly shabby atmosphere and thud-like tunes. 305 S. Hewitt St., Downtown, (213) 625-9703.

Bar Deluxe—Feel free to ignore the excellent menu and hang out near the big-ass fishtank while enjoying soothing libations and the fine, rootsy musical taste of the house DJs or live rock and alternative sounds. 1710 Las Palmas Ave., Hollywood, (213) 469-1991.

Century Club—The cover charge can be substantial at this celeb fave spot with four bars and top-notch live music, so call first. 10131 Constellation Blvd., Century City, (310) 553-600.

Coconut Teaser—It's a purple shack on Sunset that party-goers flock to after hours for a nightcap and some hard rock. 8117 Sunset Blvd., West Hollywood, (213) 654-4773.

Dragonfly—Pogo 'till it's a no-go at the club that proves punk isn't dead, it just smells funny. Recently, funk has made a welcome intrusion, if you'll pardon the oxymoron. 6510 Santa Monica Blvd., Hollywood, (213) 466-6111.

14 Below—Friendly folks, pool, darts, two full bars, and live music. 1348 14th St., Santa Monica, (310) 451-5040.

Hell's Gate—The place has really gone to hell—but we mean that in a good way. From agro-speed-metal to basic-Gothic deathrock, they run the musical gamut from A to B at this Hollyweird rock hovel. 6423 Yucca St., Hollywood, (213) 463-9661.

House of Blues—The food is South-by-Southwest paired with tasty blues-roots music and international sounds—from big names who often deserve to be much bigger. This is the nightspot you'll probably hear about more than any other; a tad bit of excess glitz, but everything else is Jake—as in Jake and Elwood Blues. 8430 Sunset Blvd., West Hollywood, (213) 650-0247.

Jack's Sugar Shack—More than a dozen brews on tap and count-less cocktails served up along with crowd-pleasing rockabilly, alt-rock, country, and blues. A Hollywood club without surplus attitude. 1707 Vine St., Hollywood, (213) 466-7005.

Largo—A more rockin' alternative to the folk that rules this stretch of the Bagel Belt (it's right across from Canter's). Largo is a cozy music spot with decent acoustics, but stay away from the straw-berry daiquiris. 432 N. Fairfax Ave., (213) 852-1073.

LunaPark—Three bars, two stages, a patio, and no Partridge Family in the pear tree—just the best in music and performance from slightly off-center. 665 N. Robertson Blvd. West Hollywood., (310) 652-0611.

Troubadour—A local music-scene landmark that's still alive and kicking it out with pop, country, folk, and alternative bands. 9081 Santa Monica Blvd., West Hollywood, (310) 276-1158.

Whiskey a Go Go—Bands have been playing the Whiskey since forever—and it's still not played out. 8901 Sunset Blvd. (310) 535-0579.

Bars, Upscale

"Money doesn't talk, it swears," to quote Bob Dylan. So you might as well just shut up and spend it if you've got it at some of these tony drinkeries.

Bar Marmont—8171 Sunset Blvd., Hollywood, (213) 650-0575. The trendy hot spot of the moment for the industry crowd.

The Bel-Air Hotel Bar—A prime location for celebrity spotting on Oscar day. They're all in town at once and they have to go some-where—and this is it for many of them. Don't make a nuisance of yourself. 701 Stone Canyon Rd., Bel Air, (310) 472-1211.

The Beverly Club—If Beverly Hills is making a come back, this may be one of the reasons why. Located in the heart of this ritzy city is a new Gen X club co-owned by Michael Sutton (formerly Stone of *General Hospital*). As you might imagine, he has a few friends who frequent the place giving the club a guaranteed good-looking crowd at all times. It's hip, it's new, and well, only time will tell how long the party continues. 424 N. Beverly Dr., Beverly Hills, (310) 275-8511.

The Four Seasons Hotel—The bar is always a hot spot for celebs, business tycoons and all others out for a good time. Whenever there is a movie junket (weekend for promoting an upcoming film), this is the venue of choice, which means Hollywood's most wanted are often running around the lobby. 300 S. Doheny Dr., (310) 273-2222.

The Gate—Hoppin' dance floor, murmur-prone conversation parlors, and hummin' outdoor patios. 643 N. La Cienega Blvd., (310) 289-8808.

Jones—Celebrities used to come here to drink, but now it's only people looking for celebrities—but they're fun to watch, too. Even those dining on thin-crust pizzas at the tables ringing the bar area know the score: Young Hollywood schmoozing and cruising is the free entertainment. 7205 Santa Monica, (213) 850-1727.

Monkey Bar—Before Hollywood Madam Heidi Fleiss was busted, it was the place for her and her clientele. Since then, things have calmed down at this restaurant/bar, but there's still action and familiar faces popping up on the scene. 8225 Beverly Blvd., (213) 658-6005.

red—Slightly smug wine bar with just a hint of fruitiness in the bouquet of the earnest top note offset by an audacious yet curiously down-to-earth verve in the finish, i.e., don't ask for the Riunite on ice, it wouldn't be nice. 7450 Beverly Blvd., (213) 937-0331.

Roxbury Live—Five bars and an upscale clientele ensure excellent people-watching if your plastic can handle the heat. There's music everywhere in this tri-level place, but check out the rock dungeon for the grooviest sounds. 8225 Sunset Blvd., West Hollywood, (213) 656-1750.

The Sunset Room—The hefty cover charge keeps gawking to a minimum (or at least limits it to those willing to spend the maximum). Consequently, the famous (and those who think they are) frequent this dressy dance club/bar/restaurant. 9229 Sunset Blvd., West Hollywood, (310) 271-8355.

Bars, Various and Sundry

Cat and Fiddle Pub—This popular English-style pub is sensational in the summer with a lively patio buzz. In the winter, play darts inside while sipping on some strong cider. Don't miss the live jazz jams on Sunday. 6530 Sunset Blvd., Hollywood, (213) 468-3800.

Cava—Young multi-ethnic crowd gathers for music events, with heavy action for the higher-mileage crowd at the bar waiting for dinner reservations. 8384 W. 3rd Street, (213) 467-4068.

Crooked Bar—Nestled 'neath the Coconut Teaser, the Crooked Bar provides a low-key escape (relatively speaking, of course) from the clubland craziness out on the strip. 8121 Sunset Blvd., West Hollywood, (213) 654-4773.

D.B. Cooper's Restaurant and Saloon—Throngs slosh and nosh in a kinda yuppie kinda sports bar kinda place. 3387 Motor Ave., Culver City, (310) 839-2500.

Dresden Room—A throng is always camped out to absorb martinis and capable piano-lounge music. Be a lizard—or just dress like one. 1760 N. Vermont Ave., (213) 665-4294.

Formosa Cafe—People who were famous decades ago used to hang out here, but they're all dead—in contrast to the lively crowd today. Umbrella drinks rule, and the patrons occasionally drool, but what do you want? 7156 Santa Monica Blvd., West Hollywood, (213) 850-9050.

George's—One of the best spots to find Lakers outside the forum, and a friendly hangout for folks without racial hang-ups. 7250 Melrose Ave., (213) 933-8420.

Mr. T's Bowl—Citing its mix of flush-faced weekday regulars and weekend rockin' ruffians cranking loud music from the stage, *L.A. Weekly* calls Mr. T's a "hangout for alcoholics of all ages." It's a multi-generational love fest! You gonna finish those beer nuts, or what? 5621½ N. Figueroa St., Highland Park, (213) 256-7561.

Bars, Microbreweries

No longer is man satisfied with simply a Miller or Bud. In the city that loves options and imports, microbreweries are all the rage.

Barney's Beanery—It's a legendary hangout in L.A. with a long list of beers that make for a long night. 8447 Santa Monica Blvd., (213) 654-2287.

Brewski's Brewing Co.—The young flock to this Friday night pick-up spot and the beer, well, it changes with the seasons. 73 Pier Ave., Hermosa Beach, (310) 318-2666.

Father's Office—It feels like a small town pub-intimate and cozy where everyone does know your name (after a visit or two.) 1018 Montana Ave., Santa Monica, (310) 451-9330.

Gordon Biersch Brewery—Chug a beer while sitting in a courtyard-a festive atmosphere always. 41 Hugus Alley, Pasadena, (818) 449-0052.

The Hamilton Gregg Brewworks—It's a do-it-yourself brewery where you can create everything including your very own custom label. Just don't expect instant results. It takes at least two weeks for the beer to ferment. 58 11th St., Hermosa Beach, (310) 376-0406.

Main Line Brewing Co.—1056 Westwood Blvd., Westwood, (310) 443-5401. It's a sports bar with tons of beers to choose from as well as attractive UCLA coeds. Know any guys who might like it here?

Westwood Brewing Company—1097 Glendon Ave., Westwood, (310) 209-2739. Recent competition for "the other" brewery in Westwood. This is a bit of an older crowd—a more mellow environment.

BEACHES

In Los Angeles there's a stretch of sand to suit any personality—you'll soon find your favorites. In the meantime, here's some raw data to get you oriented.

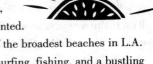

Manhattan State Beach—One of the broadest beaches in L.A. features 100 volleyball courts, surfing, fishing, and a bustling promenade. Manhattan Beach Blvd. and N. Ocean Dr.

Point Dune State Beach—Scenic cliffs, coves, and tidepools. Fine surfing and excellent snorkeling. Westward Beach Rd., Malibu.

Santa Monica State Beach—Thousands of strolling peds, bikers, and rollerbladers can't wreck this spot—especially if the wonders of nature you're most interested in are half-undressed homo sapiens. Palisades Beach Rd., (310) 394-3264.

Topanga State Beach—Surfing and swimming are favorite activities, especially near the spot where Topanga Creek hits the beach. Pacific Coast Highway and Topanga Canyon.

Venice City Beach—Dante's inferno with sunblock. A couple of good surf spots. Ocean Front Walk, Venice.

Will Rogers State Beach—Surfing, swimming, and volleyball plus a well-equipped workout area. PCH, Pacific Palisades.

Zuma Beach, Malibu—Heavy surf, beautifully curving coastline, and—you need a slurpee?—concessions. 30000 Pacific Coast Highway.

BOOKSTORES

Bookstores in L.A. have become increasingly social in recent years (and some have even managed to remain socially conscious). Well-attended reading series and poetry slams are on the rise. And many bookstores are copping a cappuccino-bar attitude (some have gone so far as installing espresso machines), which makes lingering and browsing a welcome option. Books may never be the next big thing, but you never know. (Movies, after all, are rumored to come from them.)

One thing that already has caught on, however, is books on tape. If you find yourself saddled with a long commute, this is a popular L.A. way to reclaim some of that wasted drive time.

What follows is a selection of some of the many specialty (and just plain special) bookstores, and a list of many other excellent bookshops.

A Different Light Lesbian and Gay Bookstore—Books, cards, periodicals, and videos that run the gamut from Gay to Z. 8853 Santa Monica Blvd., West Hollywood, (310) 854-6601.

Amok Books—"If it's out there it's in here," might be the slogan at Amok—that is, if they went in for mainstream pap like slogans. Dude, check yer head. Books and periodicals that feature cutting edge body-scarring artists, emerging neo-primitive folk-art styles, and sundry forms of multifarious youth-cult weirdness are on hand. One-stop shopping for all your arcane alternative-culture needs. 1764 N. Vermont Ave., (213) 665-0956.

Barnes & Noble—A delightful atmosphere—you'll feel like you are in your professor's very expensive and very extensive private library. Check out the adjoining store for videos and computer games. 8853 Santa Monica Blvd., West Hollywood, (310) 854-6601.

B. Dalton Bookseller—A mainstream bookstore that covers all subjects. 904 Westwood Blvd., (310) 208-7395, and several other locations.

Bodhi Tree Bookstore—Browse new and used spirituality from all points east and west at this friendly New Age mecca. The spot to get your aura detailed. An L.A. favorite with a complete selection of astrology, psychology, religion, self-healing, etc. Adjacent used book store is stocked with herbs and teas. 8585 Melrose Ave., West Hollywood, (310) 659-1733.

Book Soup—It usually looks more like a giant party than a bookstore. Open daily until midnight, Book Soup (no relation) specializes in film, art and literature, and foreign and domestic magazines. Be sure to stop by the Bistro, too. Make a night of it. 8818 W. Sunset Blvd., West Hollywood, (310) 659-3110.

Bookstar—Large selection in all areas—especially children's books. 100 N. La Cienega Blvd., L.A., (310) 289-1734 and several other locations.

Borders Books and Music—Once a local bookstore in the college town of Ann Arbor, Michigan, this place has definitely not lost its collegiate feel. There's a cafe, music, a study area and one of the largest selections of books in the city. 1360 Westwood Blvd., (310) 475-3444, and other locations.

Brentano's Book Store—With the classical music as background noise, there's a touch of class here that you won't find anywhere else. Because of its proximity to the movie theaters, Brentano's has become a favorite place to browse. They do such a great job with displays, it's hard to leave empty-handed. Century City Shopping Center, (310) 785-0204, and other locations.

Crown Books—An L.A. fixture—always dependable. Check phone book for the new and improved Super Crown featuring the same dependability with a much larger selection. 320 N. Canon Dr., Beverly Hills, (310) 278-1522, and several other locations.

Dutton's Brentwood Books—The best-sellers and wannabees both pass through here—as do thousands of customers. Helpful staff and an excellent selection of children's books. 11975 San Vicente Blvd., (310) 476-6263. Check out the other Dutton's, too. 5146 Laurel Canyon Blvd., North Hollywood, (213) 877-9222.

Hellhouse of Hollywood—They call themselves Satan's Supermarket of Horror, Occult and True Crime—hey, I thought that was Hollywood. Oh, it is. 6666 Hollywood Blvd., (213) 465-0550.

LA (The Bookstore)—Dedicated to the unruly subject of L.A., this bookstore is a mandatory stop for new arrivals. Whether it's wildlife or nightlife you're tracking, proprietor John Gabree has the essential info you're lacking. Free music and readings. 2433 Main St., Santa Monica, (310) 452-2665.

Larry Edmond's Bookshop—Everything to do with film and theater. 6644 Hollywood Blvd., (213) 463-3273.

Midnight Special—This great independent has a huge selection, fantastic atmosphere, and wonderful readings and events. And of course it's open late. Try this one before you hit the big chains. 1318 Third St. Promenade, Santa Monica, (310) 393-2923.

The Mysterious Bookshop—If mystery is your passion, indulge yourself here with fully stocked shelves of new, used, and hard-to-find stories. 8763 Beverly Blvd., L.A., (310) 659-2959.

Rizzoli Bookstore—Also a publisher, Rizzoli offers the best in books as gifts. Recently they published *A Thousand Days of Magic: Dressing Jacqueline Kennedy for the White House* and *Kate: The Kate Moss Book*. 9501 Wilshire Blvd., Santa Monica, (310) 278-2247.

Sam's Book City—5245 Lankershim Blvd., North Hollywood, (818) 985-6911.

Samuel French Theatre and Film Bookshop—Everything for the actor, filmmaker, and fan, from plays and screenplays to how-tos and biographies. Excellent browsing spot—and the books are interesting too! 11963 Ventura Blvd., Studio City, (818) 762-0535, or 7623 Sunset Blvd., (213) 876-0570.

Skylight Books—On the site of the old Chatterton's-an important literary and political bookstore in this part of town for more than

20 years—Skylight strives to fill the same quality niche. 1818 N. Vermont, Los Feliz, (213) 660-1175.

Waldenbooks—Another L.A. standby/1073 Broxton Ave., L.A., (310) 208-7295.

And all of the other bookstores in the known universe:

Coffeehouse Books—5437 W. 6th St., (213) 954-1780.

Cook's Library—8373 W. 3rd St., (213) 655-3141.

Federal Bookstore—Government Publications. Federal Building, Flower St., (213) 239-9844.

National Gay Archives—626 N. Robertson Blvd., West Hollywood, (310) 854-0271.

Sisterhood bookstore—1351 Westwood Blvd., West L.A., (310) 477-7300.

The Technical Book Company—Medical, legal, engineering, etc. 2056 Westwood Blvd., Westwood, (310) 475-5711.

Unicorn Bookstore—Gay. 8940 Santa Monica Blvd. West Hollywood, (310) 652-6253.

CIGARS

As that totally smokin' father of psychology, Sig Freud, pointed out, sometimes a cigar is just a cigar, and sometimes you just need a place to smoke one.

The Back Room at Gus's Smoke Shop—13420 Ventura Blvd., Sherman Oaks, (818) 789-1401. For $500 annually, it's a real treat to smoke out with Gus, an authentic cigar lover who knows his business and is a just great guy to know.

Brentwood Cigar Club—11606 Chayote St., Brentwood, (310) 440-3908. Relatively new on the stogie scene, this is a great place to pick up gifts for those obsessed with their habit— maybe even their own private locker.

Grand Havana Room—301 N. Canon Dr., Beverly Hills, (310) 274-8100. With a $2,000 initial fee and $150 monthly dues, it's not so surprising that this is the most exclusive of all the clubs. You must be a member or a guest of a member to ride up in the "secret" elevator that lifts off downstairs at the restaurant, On Canon. Those who have their own lockers: Jason Priestley, Tia Carrere, Arnold Schwarzenegger, Rick Dees, and Hulk Hogan to namedrop a few.

SMOOOOOKIN!

In this mostly no-smoking city, stogies somehow slip by. In fact, there are a few restaurants that actually promote cigars alongside their most famous entrees.

REMI (1451 3rd St. Promenade, Santa Monica, (310) 393-6545) offers up delicious Italian cuisine and welcomes cigar smokers with open arms. For the really serious, Jivan Tabibian, the cigar-loving manager, hosts a once-a-month evening of food, wine, and the best in cigars. Call ahead to make your reservation.

LOCANDA DEL LAGO (231 Arizona St., Santa Monica, (310) 451-3525) also allows cigar smoking alongside its Italian cooking.

And of course, Arnold Schwarzenegger's SCHATZI ON MAIN (3110 Main St., Santa Monica, (310) 399-4800) is pro-puffing. While dining on delicacies, choose from a variety of stogies. Also, call for information on the popular cigar nights held here.

And although the inside of CAFFE ROMA (350 N. Canon Dr., Beverly Hills, (310) 274-7834) is off limits to smokers, the patio is famous for cigar soirees. Every once in a while on a cool summer eve, you can catch Arnold and friends lighting up.

Hamilton's Wine Bar—9713 Santa Monica Blvd., Beverly Hills, (310) 278-0347. No membership fees, no cover charge—just a great place to smoke out. And you might even see owner George Hamilton puffing away next to you.

The Keep at Davidoff of Geneva—232 Rodeo Dr., Beverly Hills, (310) 278-8884. A private club for true cigar aficionados with a hefty price tag of $2,000 to join and $500 annual dues.

COFFEEHOUSES AND CAFES

Los Angeles is doing its part in the nationwide cafe boom, trying to meet our quota of one perky cappuccino parlor per city block. Some

SPACE-AGE,
RETRO-FUTURIST COFFEE SHOPS

L.A. being L.A.—the land of instant historical amnesia when it comes to anything but cars—many of the best examples of those spacious '50s coffee shops have been destroyed to make way for the new now. Car washes and bowling alleys around town sometimes are the best remaining examples of the style, but there are a few stellar survivors (and revivals) worthy of George Jetson.

ASTRO *is a bit more of a Greek diner on the inside, but the Space Age signage and the canted lines (as well as the vast windows on the patio) give it classic '50s Los Angeles feel. 2300 Fletcher Ave. (at Glendale), Silver Lake, (213) 663-9241.*

BEN FRANK'S COFFEE SHOP *has all the '50s touches in the Formica, light fixtures, and off-kilter angle of the bar. Rock around the clock at this 24-hour breakfast joint, which has become a favorite of the late-night Tinseltown rock 'n' roll crowd. 8585 Sunset Blvd., Hollywood, (310) 652-8808.*

DENNY'S—*We probably all know a little more about the Grand Slam breakfast than we'd care to admit, but Denny's distinctive sign, expansive windows, and sharply angled architecture make it a subdued example of the fine '50s style of California coffeeshop architecture that swept the nation. Stop in to reconsider the architecture—and you might as well have the Grand Slam while you're there. 5751 W. Sunset Blvd (213) 464-8435 (and many other locations).*

JOHNNY ROCKETS AND CAFE '50S *are two chains (in your yellow pages) that capture some of the gleaming optimistic spirit of the Jet Age—and their burgers are decent too.*

NORM'S, *a chain of excellent burger joints, is all bright lighting, gleaming Formica, and cushy booths that exemplify the '50s diner ideal of efficiency and low-rent glamour. The huge Norm's roadside sign, a jagged claw of triangles that looks like a plastic parody of flags flapping in a stiff breeze, is the strongest Space Age design aspect, which looks charmingly* corny with age. *1601 Lincoln Blvd., Santa Monica, (310) 450-0074 (and other locations).*

RAE'S—The jarringly bright orange booths and blue bar stools bordering an L-shaped counter take you right back to the '50s at this vintage coffeeshop. The worn futurism of the place makes it kind of homey, and the oblong sign out front simply screams 1958. *2901 Pico Blvd., Santa Monica (310) 828-7937.*

SHIPS, with its abstract rocketship logo on the sign outside, is a prime surviving Space Age futuristic diner. An angled formica service bar dominates the room in this 24-hour classic with toasters at every table. *10705 Washington Blvd., (310) 839-2347.*

SWINGERS—Embedded in the ground floor of the fabulous '50s-deco Beverly Laurel Motor Inn—used to be a more authentic shabby '50s diner that few ventured into. Remodeled into a groovy version of its former self, it's become home for a large herd of the grunge and the restless crowd of goatee people. But even if everything is now done here within the distancing quotation marks of irony, Swingers remains a nice stylish rehabilitation of a good old place. *8020 Beverly Blvd., (213) 633 5858.*

Sadly, the chains that best epitomize the bygone era of edgy optimism—such as COFFEE DAN's and GOOGIE—have dwindled or are now defunct, and their best examples have been remodeled into oblivion. But you can glimpse the faded glory of the coffee chop Modern style in Alan Hess's entertaining, sharply illustrated homage: Googie: Fifties Coffee Shop Architecture (Chronicle Books). And sometimes, after you become attuned to the look, you'll be able to catch glimpses of our Space Age future passed as you're driving around town.

old-school coffeehouses still exist, as well, sprinkled in below amid a few of our favorite cafes.

Anastasia's Asylum—Mostly mellow atmosphere and mostly veggie menu makes this a mostly good spot to veg out. Aspiring artists display their hang-ups on a rotating basis, and there's entertainment in the evenings. 1028 Wilshire Blvd., Santa Monica, (310) 394-7113.

Backdoor Bakery—Sidewalk scene-making and tasty pastries. 1710 Silver Lake Blvd., (213) 662-7927.

Bourgeois Pig—Work your vandyke (if you've got one) in this dark coffee bar with pool tables in the back. 5931 Franklin, Hollywood, (213) 962-6360.

Buzz—A fledgling mini-chain of Starbuck's wannabes (wanna-brews?) that gets the java done. 8000 Sunset Blvd., West Hollywood, (213) 656-7460; 8200 Santa Monica Blvd., West Hollywood, (213) 650-7742.

Cafe Tropical—Guava-cheese pie and high-octane Cuban coffee get the unpretentious locals piqued daily. Tattooed and talkative arty types predominate on weekend mornings. Excellent place to read the paper and get interrupted by pleasant convo. 2900 Sunset Blvd., Silver Lake (at Silver Lake Blvd.), (213) 661-8391.

Congo Square—Big beautiful tables and a young crowd to match. The action always percolates in the evenings thanks to throngs of peds on the Promenade. 1238 3rd St. Promenade, Santa Monica, (310) 395-5606.

Cyber Java—L.A.'s first online coffeehouse where you can sip cappuccino and cruise the web at the same time. What will they think of next? 1029 Abbot Kinney Blvd., Venice, (310) 581-1300.

Farmer's Market—Several java stations are scattered throughout this high-density hangout crammed with gawking tourists, shopping neighborhood walkovers, and fast-talking TV weasels from nearby CBS. And of course, you'll be there. 6333 W. 3rd St. (at Fairfax), (213) 933-9211.

Grounds Zero—Open-mic spoken word nights (call for schedule) are a highlight at these popular spots. 7554 Sunset Blvd., Hollywood, (213) 874-2261; 124 N. San Fernando Blvd., Burbank, (818) 567-4257.

Highland Grounds—Their patio is an excellent place for a morning cappuccino. Stop back later to sample the chow, or the fine acoustic music. 742 N. Highland Ave., Hollywood, (213) 466-1507.

Hollywood Moguls—Scene and herd. 1650 N. Schrader, Hollywood, (213) 465-7449.

Insomnia Cafe—Sleep is for wimps at this energetic java joint. The staff really can't be bothered to wait on you sometimes—and they charge for refills! Despite that, however, it's still a good people-watching perch. 7286 Beverly Blvd., (213) 931-4943.

Jabberjaw Coffeehouse/Art Gallery—Noisy bands and raucous youths gather to chug coffee and gaze in awe at the campy beauty of the paintings there. 3711 W. Pico Blvd., (213) 732-3463.

King's Road—A cafe where people go to be seen and overheard—with a great newsstand outside. Nice big scones and large vats of cafe au lait. Food, excellent; people watching, better. 8363 Beverly Blvd., (213) 655-9044.

Legal Grind—It's legal advice from the professionals for the cost of a cup of coffee, or maybe a double latte. You can't beat the prices at this coffeehouse gone *L.A. Law.* Started by Jeffrey Hughes, a young esquire, it's a place to seek legal counsel in a relaxed environment. Besides the many self-help law books, legal information, and lawyers sipping mochas beside you, Hughes has now announced his Attorney of the Day program, for which a local lawyer volunteers his/her time (can you believe it?) for two hours a day. 2640 Lincoln Blvd., Santa Monica, (310) 452-8160.

The Living Room—Fashionably funky types take their cappuccino breaks here when they tire of antique shopping along La Brea. 110 S. La Brea Ave., (213) 933-2933.

The News Room—Many of the industry types who hang here are already high on themselves, so why they need caffeine is something of a mystery. They hAve., however, scouted out a good location for the rest of us. 530 Wilshire Blvd., (310) 319-9100.

Novel Cafe—The aging "kids" behind the counter are occasionally overstocked on attitude, but that doesn't spoil this laptop-friendly, 24-hour used bookstore/coffeehouse with healthy soups, salads, and sandwiches. Always a scene, although time will tell how a recent ownership change with affect things. 212 Pier Ave., Santa Monica, (310) 396-8566.

Onyx Sequel—Loiter for hours over a coffee at this funky sidewalk cafe—you'll blend right in. 1804 Vermont, no phone.

Petterson's Frisch Rost—Comfy spot for jazz, folk, and word. 10019 Venice Blvd., Culver City, (310) 839-3359.

Stage Left Coffeehouse—Spacious coffee bar and restaurant with entertainment. Low-key fun with no cover. 208 N. Brand Blvd., Glendale, (818) 551-9791.

Starbucks—They're everywhere, they're in the phone book.

Van Go's Ear—24-hour hipsters hang for super breakfast, hyper java, and major whatever. 796 Main St., (310) 314-0022.

Wednesday's House—When the young and the restless need coffee, sweet snacks and bargain entertainment, they loiter here. 2409 Main St., (310) 452-4486.

COMEDY CLUBS

L.A. has so many comedy clubs it's not even funny. Or, wait, I mean it is . . . uh, anyway. Here are a few of the best (though not necessarily the brightest—comedy ain't no SAT test). Prices and showtimes vary and are subject to change, so do call first. (Note: many establishments have the built-in extra charge of a two-drink minimum, and cocktails at comedy spots are often pricey.)

Acme Comedy Theater—Sketch madness with names from TV comedy and other talented, if less-known, folk. 135 N. La Brea Ave., (213) 525-0202.

The Comedy Store—Multiple stages (shelf space?) ensure that the laughs are always well-stocked—with guaranteed low prices. 8433 Sunset Blvd., West Hollywood, (213) 656-6225.

Groundling Theater—TV-land's Phil Hartman, Pee Wee Herman, Jon Lovitz, and Elvira all got their start here at L.A.'s answer to Second City. You'll probably see the stars of tomorrow working their stuff in live sketches tonight. 7307 Melrose Ave., Hollywood, (213) 934-9700.

The Ice House—This granddaddy of comedy clubs hasn't gone geezerish, despite 35 years in show bidness. 24 N. Mentor Ave.,

Pasadena, (818) 577-1894.

The Improvisation—As seen on TV. All the biggest comedians have faced the firing squad in front of Bud Friedman's brick wall at one time or another. 8162 Melrose, (213) 651-2583

CONCERTS
Outdoor Concerts

Greek Theater—This venue in Griffith Park seats 6,200 and programs a wide variety of performances. 2700 Vermont Ave., Hollywood, (213) 665-1927.

Hollywood Bowl—Built into a canyon in the Hollywood Hills, this intimate little venue with perfect acoustics seats 18,000. Summer home of the L.A. Philharmonic. 2301 N. Highland Ave.

Irvine Meadows Amphitheater—Rock and pop concerts concerts an hour's drive south of L.A. 8800 Irvine Center Dr., Laguna Hills, (714) 855-4515.

Pacific Amphitheater—Forty miles south of town. 100 Sair Dr., Costa Mesa, (714) 979-5944.

Santa Monica Pier—Thursday night free summer concerts have become an institution. Call for schedule, (310) 458-8900.

Concerts and Events

For schedule and ticket information, call the numbers listed below, or consult *L.A. Weekly* or the *L.A. Times* for specific shows (as well as listings for many other concert venues).

Alex Theater—216 N. Brand Blvd., Glendale, (818) 243-2539

Dorothy Chandler Pavilion—The Music Center, 135 N. Grand Ave., (213) 972-7211.

Pantages Theater—6233 Hollywood Blvd. (at Vine), (213) 468-1770.

Pasadena Civic Auditorium—300 E. Green St., Pasadena, (818) 793-2122.

Shrine Auditorium—3228 Royal, (213) 749-5123.

Wilshire Ebell Theater—4401 W. 8th St., (213) 939-1128.

Wiltern Theater—3790 Wilshire Blvd., (310) 388-1400.

Universal Amphitheater—100 Universal City Plaza, Universal City, (818) 622-4440.

Buying Tickets

Ticketmaster, (213) 480-3232, is the most convenient way to get seats for just about anything, but you can often avoid their tacked-on service charges by calling venues directly. Other ticket-buying services include **Telecharge,** 1-800-762-7666; **Tickets LA,** (213) 660-8587; and **Good Time Tickets,** (213) 464-7383.

Discount Tickets

LA Theater Arts Hotline, (213) 688-2787, has a line on cheap seats, and many venues offer last-minute "rush" discounts on unsold seats for those willing to gamble on availability.

DANCE CLUBS

L.A. is the place to dance the night away, drive home, and fall asleep in a lawn chair in the back yard at daybreak—don't forget to apply sunscreen before you pass out from exhaustion or whatever. Use these nightspots to help you heat it up so you can work on your tan:

Crush Bar—Whether you're looking for '60s soul, '70s disco, '80s house, or the occasional shot of '90s Ave., you'll find it at the Crush. 1743 N. Cahuenga Blvd., Hollywood, (213) 461-9017.

The Garage—Diverse crowd of ultra-hip groovemeisters convenes just to be cool, meanwhile accidentally attending a nifty nightly parade of well-executed concept clubs. How does this happen? 4519 Santa Monica Blvd., Hollywood, (213) 683-3447.

Jewel's Catch One—Current late-night fave for mixed bag of gays, lesbians, and straight scenesters, with requisite gender-bending entertainment and the ever-popular high-energy dance thang thumping. 4067 Pico Blvd., (213) 734-8949.

LunaPark—This popular restaurant/bar/club goes through more changes than the I Ching. Any given night can deliver an endless variety of food, music, events, and people. If you're with friends, you're sure to have fun. Just watch out, *Los Angeles* Magazine voted it "Best place to be treated like dirt by imperious French bouncers." Now we're talking fun. 665 N. Robertson Blvd., West Hollywood, (310) 652-0611.

Opium Den—Young L.A.'s famed clubland entrepreneur Brent Bolthouse's latest place rocks with great DJs and an always packed house. 1605 N. Cosmo St., Hollywood, (213) 466-7800.

The Palace—An L.A. landmark where all kinds of bands have played. It's currently a Top 40 dance spot with a very young crowd. 1735 N. Vine St., Hollywood, (213) 462-3000.

Sanctuary—Lots of women with lots of plastic cruise the balcony bar, eyed by lots of men with lots of money. Lotsa luck. 180 N. Robertson Blvd., (310) 358-0303.

Viper Room—Johnny Depp's hyped-up club is sadly most famous as the spot where River Phoenix fell. Still, the stars continue to hang out here but mostly on weekdays (even then, however, they're often squirreled away in special VIP holding areas out of public view). Weekends bring the tourists as well as the high school kids eager to use their fake IDs. 8852 Sunset Blvd., West Hollywood, (310) 358-1880.

DANCE COMPANIES

Dance in L.A. is pretty much of a drive-through affair, with famous ensembles pulling off the expressway to do their star turns here at various venues. (Parking is always a problem.) The **UCLA Center for the Performing Arts** puts on an excellent art of dance series, which begins each September—call for info, (310) 825-2101.

DATE ACTIVITIES, Cheap and Inventive

Paddleboat rentals at Echo Park Lake are $8 per half-hour. The ducks and geese are your only competition out here—they're cute, but you're cuter for thinking of this quaint diversion. (213) 250-3578.

Instead of giving that special someone the cliche single red rose or the costlier dozen of the same, why not present him/her with the **World's Largest Rose Garden.** It's directly in front of the Natural History Museum at 900 Exposition Blvd., L.A., (213) 748-4772 (they start blooming in April).

Miniature Golf at Castle Park is always fun for some frivolous competition, but please, no wagering. 4989 Sepulveda Blvd., Sherman Oaks, (818) 905-1321; and, 12400 Van Owen St. North Hollywood, (818) 765-4000.

DELIS

Hello delis, you're lookin' swell, delis, it's so nice to see you so far from New York . . .

Art's Deli—A staple of Studio City. The original was severely damaged in the earthquake but Art's is back and as popular as ever. 12224 Ventura Blvd., Studio City, (818) 762-1221.

Canter's—This all-night place plays host to eclectic crowds at all hours. The food is everything deli food should be, but sometimes the people-watching is more of a draw than anything on the menu. 419 N. Fairfax Ave., (213) 651-2030.

Jerry's Famous Deli—Only in L.A. can a deli with valet parking, pay phones at every table, and Chinese food on the menu be really popular and wildly successful. 8701 Beverly Blvd., (310) 289-1811 (and other locations).

Junior's—This top-rated place is a constant—always good, always filling, and always filling up with customers. 2379 Westwood Blvd., (310) 475-5771.

Langer's—It's worth the trek if only to taste the best pastrami in L.A. 704 S. Alvarado St., Downtown., (213) 483-8050.

Nate 'n' Al's—This show-biz deli's reputation depends more on the deals that have been done here than on how the pastrami is done. The waitresses have been around forever and won't let you forget it. If you go on Sunday morning, be prepared to wait . . . and wait. You might even have to put yourself in turnaround—and walk out. 14 N. Beverly Dr., Beverly Hills, (310) 274-0101.

Stage Deli—Hidden away in the Century City mall, this New York transplant is pretty terrific and not very crowded.

BEST PLACES FOR THE ULTIMATE VEGGIE BURGER

NEWSROOM CAFE—120 N. Robertson Blvd., (310) 652-4444.

RED—7450 Beverly Blvd., (213) 937-0331.

THE SOURCE—301 W. Sunset Blvd., (213) 656-6388.

SWINGERS—8720 Beverly Blvd., (310)-653-5858.

THE SPOT, 110 2nd St., Hermosa Beach, (310) 376-2355.

A great Sunday morning alternative with excellent lox and
whitefish.10250 Santa Monica Blvd., (213) 553-3354.

EDUCATION

Area universities and colleges offer every degree imaginable—plus
extension classes, adult education, and sundry seminars. Even if you
aren't going to attend classes, however, universities are a good
resource to keep in mind for their lecture series and other cultural
events. In addition, many Southland learning institutions let non-stu-
dents use their libraries, a level of institutional civility unheard of in
most towns. For information and class schedules, contact:

UCLA, 405 Hilgard Ave., Westwood, (310) 825-4321.

USC, Exposition Blvd. and S. Vermont Ave., (213) 740-2300.

California State University LA, 5151 State University Dr.,
(213) 343-3000.

California State University Long Beach, 1250 Bellflower Blvd.,
Long Beach, (310) 985-4111.

California State University Northridge, 18111 Nordhoff St.,
Northridge, (818) 885-1200.

Pepperdine University, 24255 W. Pacific Coast Highway,
(310) 456-4000.

Community Colleges

Los Angeles City College, 855 N. Vermont Ave., (213) 953-4000.

Occidental College, 1600 Campus Road, Eagle Rock,
(213) 259-2500.

Santa Monica City College, 1900 Pico Blvd., Santa Monica,
(310) 452-9214.

West Los Angeles College, 4800 Freshman Dr., Culver City,
(310) 287-4200.

FAMILY FUN

Pueblo de Los Angeles—For those who believe L.A. has no history, shame on you. This is the first settlement in the city of angels,
and it is still an interesting site. Make sure to stroll down Olvera
Street to be a part of the constant fiesta of street vendors, delicious
eats, and lively music. For the small fee of nothing, talk a walk

through the Avila House, the oldest standing house in the city (it has been reconstructed once due to earthquake) decorated with authentic furniture of the period. Also located across the town square is the old fire station which kids will love. And visit the Pio Pico (yes, he's the Pico in Pico Boulevard) house, which was the first hotel in L.A. For one of the best free shows in L.A., come on a Sunday when there is always some kind of celebration at Our Lady Queen of the Angels Catholic church—another historic landmark. Broadway and E. Cesar Chavez Ave.

Fishermen's Village—So it isn't exactly up to par with the wharf in San Francisco—on a sunny day it's a solid substitute. Fish 'n' Chips, candied apples, and the beautiful blue Pacific background. For those who crave the sea, you can rent a boat or catch a ride with the pros. This can also be a fun lunch stop for bike riders and roller bladers who are exercising their way up the coast. 13723 Fiji Way, Marina Del Rey, (213) 823-5411

Los Angeles Zoo—If it feels like deja vu, you're not crazy—you're just a couch potato who needs to get out more. Why? Because this is where they filmed the opening of the television series *Three's Company*. When they weren't walking on the Santa Monica Pier, that perky threesome spent their days here. While the San Diego Wild Animal Park is by far the best zoo in California, L.A.'s zoo is still a fine way to spend some family togetherness. 5333 Zoo Dr., Los Feliz, (213) 666-4090.

FISHING

The fishing's pretty darn good here for a desert, but you gotta pick your spots. It helps if the spot you pick is on the Pacific, because lake and stream fishing is limited. Surf casting, deep-sea barge fishing, and pier fishing are more the ticket. Contact the **California Department of Fish and Game,** (310) 590-5171, for a license—they also supply info on fishing clubs, hot spots, and conditions. A few locations where you can match wits with wily, scale-encrusted, cold-blooded adversaries:

Lake Isabella in the Sequoia National Forest north of the Mojave is the largest freshwater lake in the state, and it's well-stocked with trout, bass, sunnies, and crappies.

Santa Monica Pier is a great place to stand around and take it all in. As songwriter Tom Waits once noted, albeit in a bar-room context, "Fishin' for a good time starts with throwin' out your line." Often, throwing out your line is all there is—call it the Zen of angling. Excursion boat fishing is also available for those who tire of the sound of one hand casting from the pier. (310) 458-8694.

Troutdale out in Agoura stocks the pond, passes you the rod and reel, and lets the trout teach you a few things. (818) 889-9993.

Ventura Sport Fishing Landing offers daylong boat fishing around the channel islands. (805) 644-7363.

FITNESS CLUBS

With the outdoors always an exercise and fitness option, it's a wonder anyone ever goes to the gym—but they do, by the thousands. A handful of favorites:

A Body Prepared—One of the many new places popping up all over L.A. that boasts of teaching the Pilates method, a new craze in the fitness world. So which celebs are in on the trend? Elizabeth Berkely, Christian Applegate and Vanessa Williams. (213) 930-2733.

Bally's Holiday Spa Health Clubs—A little cheaper than some others, but the facilities are not as nice as newer L.A. gyms. Call to find out about the location nearest you and the introductory specials they invariably offer, 1-800-777-1117.

Better Bodies—The purple curtains and interesting art on the walls make this small club look more like a coffeehouse than a sweat factory. There's no place for classes, but they do have a deal with Voight, useful if you're a member who craves aerobics. 11400 W. Olympic Blvd., (310) 473-1470.

Bodies in Motion—Rated best gym by *Boulevard Magazine*, it's mainly a place for classes—kickboxing, yoga, and step-aerobics. 10542 W. Pico Blvd., (310) 836-8000.

Family Fitness—This is a popular spot with businessmen and women. It's near Century City and has it all—especially great classes. 9911 W. Pico Blvd., (and other locations), (310) 553-7600.

SPINNING

Started a few years ago by exercise guru JOHNNY G., spinning has Angelenos dizzy with excitement. While riding on a stationary bike, you follow your instructor as he/she takes you through a cross-country-style ride sure to make you sweat. In fact, Johnny G.'s brochure reads, "You get so drenched, you literally have to empty the water out of your shoes. In Egypt, they call it flood season. Here, they call it SPINNING."

But lest you think L.A. is obsessed with physical exercise, Johnny G. makes sure to exercise your mind all the while you are in ped-aling purgatory. He keeps you motivated with self-affirmations. In fact his brochure asks, "Is it great legs or an awesome butt? Maybe just a lean healthy body with a strong mind! Is it cardiovascular training? Endurance or Strength? Maybe it's just group therapy." Exercise and therapy—it's the City of Angels combo special. JOHNNY G'S, 8729 W. Washington Blvd., The Helms Bakery Building, Culver City, (310) 559-5454.

Other places around to spin:
TODD TRAMP—624 N. La Cienega Blvd., (310) 657-4140
MAIN STREET—2215 Main St., Santa Monica, (310) 396-4747
VOIGHT FITNESS—980 N. La Cienega Blvd.,(310) 854-0741

Gold's Gym—Serious muscle mania especially in the morning when people come to lift before work. It's not all nice and pretty, but it's got all the equipment needed to pump you up. 60 Hampton Dr., Venice, and other locations, (310) 392-6004.

Great Shape—At this for-women-only gym, the clientele tends to be a bit older and the atmosphere very relaxed. 11980 San Vicente Blvd., Brentwood, (310) 820-6602.

LA Woman—It's all women all the time. It may get boring but if you are a serious work-out woman and aren't interested in the social scene of a gym, this just may be for you. 11650 Santa Monica Blvd., (310) 207-2279.

Spectrum Club—For just a little more money, you get a lot more. Great facilities, diverse classes, and plenty of beautiful bods. 2425 Olympic Blvd., Suite 1000 West, Santa Monica, (and other locations), (310) 829-4995.

Sports Club/LA—The Beverly Hills of gyms—better for networking than working-out. 1835 Sepulveda Blvd., (310) 473-1447.

Sports Connection—It's a young crowd here, mainly because the price fits into your budget. Still, the facilities are okay and the location is accessible. 2929 31st St., Santa Monica, (310) 450-4464.

YMCA, Westside Branch—If you're not into aesthetics, this place will be fine for you. The price is right and they have all the equipment of more expensive gyms, plus classes. It's just not the most upbeat atmosphere and certainly not a scene. 11311 La Grange Ave., (310) 477-1511.

FREE (AND ALMOST FREE) STUFF TO DO

Pier Pleasure—Thursday night summer concerts have become an institution at the Santa Monica pier—with big names and big crowds. Big fun. Call for schedule. (310) 458-8900.

No Money Symphony—You can often eavesdrop on rehearsals of the L.A. Philharmonic at the Hollywood Bowl for free around midday. Pack a lunch. 2301 N. Highland Ave., (213) 850-2000.

Free jazz, but it's cool—LACMA hosts jazz performances Fridays on the museum plaza as well as big band and chamber music on Sundays. (213) 857-6010.

Kiss and Makeup—The Max Factor Museum of Beauty is worth the price of admission just to see all the autographed photos of the stars—not to mention the collection of celebrity hairpieces. 166-68 Highland Ave., Hollywood, (213) 463-6668.

Shut Up and drive—Mulholland Dr., that is. Slither along this serpentine roadway that follows the spine of the Santa Monica Mountains from Hollywood west to the Pacific Coast Highway. Another entertaining roller-coaster ride is Sunset Boulevard west from Hollywood all the way to the Pacific.

No Life Records—Virgin and Tower may be the megastores when it comes to moving mountains of major-label product, but No Life Records is becoming a Hollywood hot spot for in-store indie

L.A.'S WORK-OUT GURUS

CHRIS STEELE OF STEELEBOXER— 2907 Washington Blvd., Marina del Rey, (310) 827-BOXR. He was one of the first in L.A. to teach kickboxing and is considered the best. With his wife, Patricia, Chris runs a one-room studio in Marina del Rey where he can whip anyone into shape. Michelle Pfeiffer turned to Chris to prepare for her role as Catwoman, and Sharon Stone has recently enlisted his help to tone herself up. And how did Antonio Sabato Jr. get that body? Chris Steele and maybe a little help from genetics. For an hour session, it's $100, which explains why the rich and famous are among Chris' clients. Still, everyone is welcome and everyone who knows Mr. Franklin (as in Ben, on the C-note) gets the star treatment.

KAREN VOIGHT OF VOIGHT FITNESS AND VOIGHT BY THE SEA— 980 N. La Cienega Blvd., (310) 854-0741. She's a local celebrity with an inspiring bod. Her studios are packed daily with men and women all faithful to their beloved Karen who has an addictive energy and a great spirit. Her workout tapes and recent book are famous worldwide, which may account for the fact that her class schedule is printed in several different languages. With original moves and a fast-paced beat to follow, it is easy to forget you are exercising your body and not just your mind. Along with Mark Stevens, another L.A. fitness guru, Karen worked with Elle McPherson on her recent workout video and well, it was a toss up when it came to who had the best bod.

PETER STEINFELD AT BETTER SHAPE UP—Rated the best personal trainer by Variety in 1995, Steinfeld (whose brother is the Jake in "Body By Jake") will work you out for some of the most intensive 30 minutes of your life. In his 16-plus years, Steinfeld has trained some of the best bodies in Hollywood. He pumped up Party of Five's Scott Wolf for White Squall and Madonna for her "True Blue" tour. But remember, working out like the stars doesn't come cheap. Each session: $200.

showcases, thanks to excellent acoustics, an excellent selection of underground pop, and an excellent price for the shows: free. 7209 Santa Monica Blvd., Hollywood, (213) 845-1200.

Could You Be More Pacific?—The Pacific Design Center is a lock to have displays of intriguing fashions, interior designs, and accessories in their more than 200 showrooms. High-quality architecture and design shows are often up and running at the center or across the plaza at the gallery—with free guided tours available. 8667 Melrose Ave., West Hollywood, (310) 657-0800.

I See London . . . —The Lingerie Museum at Frederick's of Hollywood not only traces the storied history of foundation undergarments, it also gets up close and personal with celebrity panties. 6608 Hollywood Blvd., (213) 466-8506.

GREAT ESCAPES

We love L.A., don't get us wrong, but sometimes this place starts to seem like a boil on a road-kill coyote's ass—that's when you need a vacation. Here are a few quick getaways that can help clear your head when the town starts to seem like Hell-A.

Upscale

Hotel del Coronado—You'll recognize it the minute you arrive— Hollywood has overexposed this spot in countless films. And it's easy to understand why. The charming building and grounds and a little bit of California's golden sunshine could convince you you're in Hawaii. But don't worry about jet lag, this paradise of swimming, golf, and all-around relaxation is only two hours away. 1500 Orange Ave., Coronado, 1-800-HOTEL-DEL; $154-$299.

Montecito Inn Montecito—Once a favorite hangout of Charlie Chaplin—who was also an original investor—he's left a lasting impression on this inn. The place is adorned with Chaplin memorabilia. It is small, quaint, and romantic—like the town itself (and maybe a bit like Chaplin in those same regards). The beach is a pleasant two-minute walk, and Santa Barbara's enchanting restaurants are nearby. Go hiking and biking by day, enjoy a robust meal in the evening, and then sleep away the day's pleasant exertions in a blanket of cool sea breezes. 1295 Coast Village Rd., Montecito,

1-800-843-2017); $150-$185 for doubles. Drive time from L.A.:
90 minutes.

Ritz-Carlton Laguna Niguel—Luxury, Laguna style—Gorgeous,
bright rooms (many with ocean views) and all the amenities:
swimming pools, sauna, fitness center, tennis courts, and a won-
derfully attentive staff. The grounds are immense and awash in
flowers. Laguna is a picturesque California coastal town with a
plethora of beachy cafes and fine dining. It is pricey, but for
romance, you'd have to fly to Europe to beat this. 1 Ritz Carlton
Dr., Dana Point, 1-800-241-3333, $215 and upwards. Drive
time: 1 hour.

Spindrift Inn—The only hotel located in the midst of historic
Cannery Row in Monterey, this romantic waterfront inn puts you
in the middle of quaint restaurants, happening nightclubs, and
the famous Monterey Bay Aquarium. The rooms feature canopy
beds and real wood-burning fire places. 652 Cannery Row,
Monterey, (408) 646-8900 or 1-800-841-1879, $149-$389.
Drive time: 4½ hours if you don't take the incredibly scenic
Pacific Coast Highway.

Ventana Inn (Big Sur)—Best for a three-day weekend, as it's a
ways up the coast. Despite the expense, this 243-acre resort just
may be paradise, considering the exceptional ocean views, a 4-
star restaurant, stellar service, and Japanese hot baths. It's a
peaceful (shall we say pacific?) place to unwind—or spark some
romance. 1-800-628-6500, $175 all the way up to $890 (suites
with private saunas). Drive time from L.A.: 4 hours if you don't
take PCH.

Modest

Highway One—Don't even bother moving to Los Angeles if you're
not planning to drive up Highway One sometime—we don't want
your kind here. This slinky sliver of enchanted highway hugs the
California coast all the way, and the stretch from L.A. through
Big Sur up to Monterey is incredibly varied and aesthetically
astounding. If you don't have money to stay in some schmaltzy
spa or swank hotel, don't sweat it. The options: cheap motel,
your car's back seat, the beach at Big Sur (but beware the tide;

also, the cops occasionally roust illegal beach campers, but just move on to a different spot and the odds are great they'll never see you again in this lightly patrolled area). Cut corners on cuisine by packing a cooler or stopping at any roadhouse that looks enticing. Stop rolling northward whenever you feel like it, and head home. The good news? Even going back the way you just came, everything looks completely different. It's called a new perspective—keep it in mind when you get back to town.

Joshua Tree National Monument—If you start to think L.A. is a little strange, Joshua Tree will show you how bizarre the desert can be if left to its own twisted devices. This National Monument in the Mojave (about 150 miles from town) is like a trip back in time—some kind of trip anyway. If you stay at a cheap motel in a nearby nowhere town like Paradise Valley or Twenty-nine Palms and dine at crusty roadside diners, you'll be going the whole nine yards of desolate desert escape (as seen in countless films—think *Baghdad Cafe*, but less amiable). Take plenty of water for you and don't overheat your auto. Joshua Tree visitors info, (619) 367-7511.

Catalina Island—The place is cute as a button and swimming in Mediterranean charm (this is the Pacific, right?). The hotels on the island are pricey, so it's really only a low-budget escape if you make it a daytrip. (Roundtrip fare is $23 from Catalina Cruises, (310) 253-9800; about an hour each way.) But there's more than enough doing in Catalina to overstuff a day. Or you can just dawdle like a lazy tourist in a seaside town, which you are. Walk and gawk at the beautiful circular Casino, or stop and have a sandwich at the Channel House terrace overlooking Avalon Bay while you decide what, if anything, to do next. You got your glass-bottom boat trips, you got your fly fishing, you got your restaurants to sample, you got your hiking and camping. You got yourself a change of pace. Visitor info, (310) 510-1520; California Discovery Tours, 1-800-322-3434.

Sprawl Hop—Take advantage of L.A.'s biggest disadvantage—the sprawl—by visiting one of the nearby communities that we haven't had the space to detail in this slender yet indispensable volume. Check in to a budget motel and see the sights of

Pasadena, or Laguna Beach, or . . . Hey, come to think of it, just vegging out in Encino can be relaxing if you've never been there.

MISCELLANEOUS FUN

The Rose Bowl Parade—This parade on New Year's Day in Pasadena is a world-famous spectator event, but if you want to participate, volunteers are always needed to help build the floats. A couple of the big floatmakers are Festival Artists, (818) 334-9388, and C.E. Bent and Sons, (818) 793-3174. Also, after the parade, you can view the floats up close without all those annoying marching bands and washed up celebrities. January 2nd and 3rd the floats are on display from 9 a.m. to 4 p.m. at the intersection of Sierra Madre and Washington Blvd.

Whale Watching Cruises—The majesty of these migrating aquatic giants is awe inspiring, and there are a number of different day cruises from late December to March. Try: Catalina Cruises, (213) 253-9800; Los Angeles Harbor Cruises, Ports O' Call Village, San Pedro, (310) 831-0996; Spirit Cruises, Ports O' Call Village, San Pedro, (310) 831-1073; Fisherman's Wharf Boat Dock, Marina del Rey, (310) 822-3625; Sea Landing Aquatic Center, Santa Barbara, (805) 963-3564.

For land lubbers, the prime spot for whale watching is the Point Vicente Interpretive Center. There's a nifty picnic area nearby, so bring the binocs, pack a lunch, and make a day of it. 31501 Palos Verdes Dr., W. Rancho Palos Verdes, (310) 377-5370.

MOVIES

Of the dozens upon dozens of movie houses listed in the *Los Angeles Times* or *L.A. Weekly*, most will be showing big-budget behemoths destined to evaporate from memory the minute you're done watching them. There are many theaters that show more challenging, offbeat, or overlooked films. And second-run theaters and revival houses help you save money and promote cultural diversity by preserving alternative venues.

Movie Theaters with the Best Art Films

Nuart, 11272 Santa Monica Blvd., (310) .478-6379.

Aero, 1328 Montana Ave., Santa Monica, (310) 395-4990.

Wilshire, 8440 Wilshire Blvd., L.A., (213) 468-1716.

New Beverly Cinema, 7165 Beverly Blvd., (213) 938-4038.

Bing Theater, 5905 Wilshire Blvd., (213) 857-6010.

UCLA Film and Television Archive, Melnitz Theater,
   (310) 206-FILM.

INSIDER TIP: *If you think a movie is going to sell out, call 777-FILM (or, from the Valley, 444-FILM) and order tickets by phone on your credit card. They charge a dollar for the service, but it sure beats driving across town to find a sold-out show.*

Imax Theater

The five-story-high, 70-foot-wide screen puts you inside the experience for state-of-the-art intensity. **Museum of Science and Industry,** 700 State Dr., Exposition Park, (213) 744-2014.

Action-Flick Pick

Vista Theater is a classic big, big screen made better by management's smart move of removing every other row of seats. Even if Vlade Divac sits in front of you, you'll still be able to see. 4473 Sunset Dr., Hollywood, (213) 660-6639.

INSIDER TIP: *It's a quiet riot when SILENT MOVIE puts on an old favorite. Movie buffs have made this a popular hangout for those who are truly cool. 611 Fairfax Ave., (213) 653-2389.*

MUSEUMS
Art

The Craft and Folk Art Museum—With more than 3,000 objects
   from all over the world, this museum makes for an interesting day,

especially for the family. 5800 Wilshire Blvd., (213) 937-5544.

Getty Museum—17985 Pacific Coast Highway, Malibu. (310) 458-2003. Call ahead for a reservation.

Huntington Library, Art Collections and Botanical Gardens—So beautiful are the grounds, you feel like you're on vacation. After a stroll through the rose or cactus gardens, view the renowned art collection that includes Blue Boy and Pinkie, or stop in the library to see their Gutenberg Bible or a first printing of Shakespeare's plays. 1151 Oxford St., San Marino, (818) 405-2141.

Los Angeles County Museum of Art (LACMA)—L.A.'s largest art museum boasts two outdoor sculpture gardens and a wealth of 19th- and 20th-century European paintings. Also note the children's art classes offered on weekends. 5905 Wilshire Blvd., (213) 857-6000.

Museum of Neon Art—501 W. Olympic Blvd., (213) 489-9918. No, it's not an ode to nightlife in Vegas, it is an actual museum dedicated to expression through light and motion. You can even take an introductory class in neon design and technique or go touring with the museum to see the famous neon signs of L.A.

Norton Simon Museum—Picasso graphics, Monet paintings, and more. 411 W. Colorado Blvd., Pasadena, (818) 449-6840.

UCLA's Armand Hammer Museum of Art and Cultural Center—There's always an interesting exhibit on hand at this multicultural haven. 10899 Wilshire Blvd., Westwood, (310) 443-7000.

Miscellaneous Museums

California Museum of Science and Industry—A wonderful day for the family or those just plain curious about our history of technical advances in science, medicine, and engineering—with plenty of hands-on exhibits. 700 State Dr., Exposition Park, (213) 744-7400.

Carole and Barry Kaye Museum of Miniatures—Small is beautiful indeed. Big little worlds that fill 14,000 square feet with costumes, homes, dolls, furniture. A quirky favorite with a great gift shop. 5900 Wilshire Blvd., (213) 937-6464.

Children's Museum—Leave it to the children of this city to make diversity work. This fabulous hands-on museum is filled with kids from all walks of life and together they seem to have a great time playing. It's a perfect adventure to take the kids on for some quality time. 310 N. Main St., (213) 687-8800.

Gene Autry Western Heritage Museum—This museum focuses on the American West and is a great family outing. Educational, interesting, and lots of fun. 4700 Western Heritage Way, Griffith Park, (213) 667-2000.

George C. Page Museum of La Brea Discoveries—Actually part of the Natural History Museum, the La Brea tar-pits outside the museum are an L.A. landmark. Inside, check out fossils and bones and learn all about L.A. in the dinosaur age. Bring along the kids for a dino-mite time. 5801 Wilshire Blvd., (213) 857-6306.

Museum of Afro-American History and Culture—Rotating exhibits and interesting lectures explore the contributions of Black Americans. 600 State Dr., Exposition Park, (213) 744-7432.

Museum of Flying—Call ahead, because there are always different exhibits and the occasional air show. The kids will love it. 2772 Donald Douglas Loop., Santa Monica, (310) 392-3882.

Museum of Jurassic Technology—Noted for being L.A.'s kookiest museum, this dynamite learning center is a must, if only for a souvenir from the off-beat gift shop. 9341 Venice Blvd., Culver City, (310) 836-6131.

Museum of Television and Radio—This brand-new museum is a font of information. In addition to fun exhibits, this is a resource center where you can let your fingers do the walking. 465 N. Beverly Dr., Beverly Hills, (310) 786-1000.

Petersen Automotive Museum—In a city that worships cars, this museum is a must-see. With an extensive collection of turn of the century automobiles and Harley-Davidsons, it's the car lover's dream. Call ahead to find out about specific vehicle shows. 6060 Wilshire Blvd., (213) 930-CARS.

Simon Wiesenthal Center's Museum of Tolerance—Focusing on the horror of the Holocaust, the museum examines the larger scope of racism and prejudice with a 2½ hour tour. Call for schedule. 9786 W. Pico Blvd., (310) 553-8403.

Hollywood Wax Museum—As if there weren't enough celebs in town. Still, it's wacky and fun to go with a rowdy crowd. Open Sun.-Thurs. 10 am-midnight and Fri. and Sat. 10 am-2 am. 6767 Hollywood Blvd., Hollywood, (213) 462-8860.

Natural History Museum of Los Angeles County—A fantastic collection filled with dinosaur fossils and more. A fun and educational day for mom, dad, and the kids. 900 Exposition Blvd., (213) 744-3466.

Skirball Museum—This brand new location recently opened to high praise and fanfare. Tracing Jewish life from antiquity to America, the museum does an excellent job of bringing the American immigration experience to life. So patriotic in fact, you come out humming Neil Diamond's "They're Coming to America." 2701 N. Sepulveda Blvd., (213) 471-6732.

Watts Towers—Sam Rodia's towers, assembled from salvaged pipes, concrete, ceramic tiles, and glass bottles into nearly hundred-foot spires, are worth a trip into a sometimes-dicey neighborhood. Rodia, a plasterer by trade, always remained mum about his motivation for building these gargantuan curiosities. View the ultimate folk-art icon, L.A.'s own little Stonehenge, and make your own best guess. Watts Towers Art Center, 1727 E. 107th St., (213) 847-4646.

MUSIC
Rock, Pop and Alternative Bands

Los Angeles is always threatening to shatter into its constituent parts (just before it fuses into a previously unimaginable new amalgam), and the music scene is like that. Rock in L.A.—from hardcore to metal to speed-gore to pop to R&B to rap to folk-rock to surfabilly to whatever's next—is like a candy store for fans. And, more odiously, for the record company weasels always sniffing out the next big stink. Music lovers sometimes barely get a chance to enjoy a group before they become so famous we can't get in to see them anymore. Another caveat: By the time you read this, or by tomorrow, any of the groups mentioned here may have broken up or have had breakthrough chart success. C'est L.A. vie.

ON LOCATION WITH 90210 AND MELROSE PLACE

Being based in L.A. both on and off screen makes it easier for these shows to shoot all over L.A. Here's a look at some of the more memorable spots:

WEST BEVERLY HIGH SCHOOL—Would you believe there is no W. Beverly High? It's true—the cast and crew transformed Torrance High School from a local industrial town school into the elite institution attended by the gang. 2200 Carson St., Torrance.

THE PEACH PIT—No, it's not a real place—although L.A. does have it's own Apple Pan (rumored to be the source of this fictitious hang-out). While the interiors are shot on a sound-stage, the exterior shots are of a neighborhood diner in Old Town Pasadena, miles away from Beverly Hills. Rose City Diner has since been bull-dozed and turned into a Ruby's diner which has a completely new exterior. Wherever is the famous click going to meet for their mega-burgers?

CALIFORNIA UNIVERSITY—Sorry this doesn't exist either. In fact, Occidental College has never looked as good as it does each week for various scenes of the Beverly Hills brats hard at work at their prestigious University, .1600 Campus Rd., Eagle Rock.

KELLY AND STEVE'S MANSIONS—Most disappointing of all, those beautiful mansions that Kelly and Steve grew up in—well they are actually over the hill in (818) land. The Valley, that is— Sherman Oaks and Encino respectively.

SHOOTERS—Hard to believe that something on Melrose Place is based in reality, but Shooters is— well almost. While it is not called Shooters, there is a bar on Melrose Avenue that fronts for Jake's ultra-cool hang-out, FELLINI'S ON MELROSE, 6810 Melrose Ave., L.A.

D AND D ADVERTISING—Never doubt Aaron Spelling's brilliance— He has saved himself some cash by using his own Spelling Enter-tainment Building as the outside of Amanda's unconventional, to say the least, advertising agency, 5700 Wilshire Blvd., L.A.

THE APARTMENT COMPLEX—While the outside does exist (but not in L.A. county), the inside is located far from the glamour of Hollywood on a soundstage in Valencia. Don't despair—they're really is a working pool!

To keep up to date with what's happening in the local music scene, consult the free local music magazine *BAM,* or the omnipresent *L.A. Weekly*.

One of the prime scenes du jour is something called **poptopia,** which may be a fruity beverage of some sort, or might just be a convenient handle for a herd of nerdy melody-crazed rockers ever in search of the hummable. Among the groups often mentioned (and heard) in this loosely linked movement are **The Shakes, Pink Fuzz, PG 13, The Negro Problem, Velouria, Wondermints,** and **Baby Lemonade** (there are literally 100 more).

A Few Other Current Notables

Arty pop band **That Dog** has a nice following, and their folk-rap, pop-star pal Beck occasionally turns up at their shows.

Many folks enjoy the hillbilly-punk of **Hellhound.**

You can explore the sounds of **generation-XTC** (the band, not the drug) with **The Sugarplastic**—being derivative has never been so sweet.

Another smart pop band to watch is **Mrs. God,** and it's fun just to read their band name in the paper.

Vida—often the life of the party—is a veteran outfit that includes ex-members of **Minutemen** and **Black Flag.** They tend to establish a complex groove and solo like maniacs. Nice original tunes and a couple of swell Zappa covers.

Descendants—Led by actor Tate Donovan, their sound is traditional Irish—fiddle and all. Catch them Thursday nights at Molly Malone's on Fairfax.

Zelda's R-and-B-based originals and rockin' live show is strongly recommended by the *L.A. Weekly*. Check 'em out.

Young Dubliners—It's an Irish folk-rock group with a likable persona and those adorable smiles. Catch them regularly at the House of Blues.

Frosted—Fronted by ex-Go Go Jane Weidlin (the smart one, or was that Kate Jackson?), currently causing a stir.

Ex-X man **John Doe** always has something cooking (currently a local-music TV show) as does his ex-, **Exene Cervenka,** the other key ex-X member (who often does poetry readings and opened a hillbilly hipster retail shop in Silver Lake called You've Got Bad Taste).

The Plimsouls—the greatest L.A. band that got big but never huge—occasionally regroup, so watch for that.

There's also at least one other movement to keep an eye on. **Rock en Espanol**—a gaggle of groups with a Latin touch and rock 'n' roll roots-is mixing pop, rock, R & B, soca, salsa, and whatever else is handy for enthusiastic crowds at various venues. Sixty percent of L.A.'s young people are Latino, so you might want to stop in and peep the wave of the future.

Funk

James Brown, Sly Stone, and George Clinton got the ball rolling—and samples lifted from those three have been fueling rap hits for the past 15 years.

Consequently, most funk these days is a DJ deal, but there are still some out there doin' it all the way live.

The Viper Room house-band **Bootie Quake** is a slammin' cover combo that has that funky '70s groove tattooed into their brains.

Afreaka Nature does that P-funk update deal for those that gots to get funked up (better late than whatever).

There's more funky stuff out there, too, for those of us who need it; sometimes it's in the Afro-Brazilian clubs or the reggae joints.

Jazz

The big names always do concerts and shows in Los Angeles. But the local jazz scene is also packed with studio session players dropping in on sets by friends, or putting together their own small groups to explore sonic regions they don't get to visit as hired guns for dog-food commercials and whatnot. Their angst is our joy—always the bittersweet irony of any blues-derived music.

Ex-Crusader **Joe Sample** can be found R & B-ing his adventurous jazzy self in sundry hot spots (well, they're hot when he's there).

Guitar slinger **Kevin Eubanks** gigs regularly around town after his day job on *The Tonight Show* as Chin-Boy's sidekick.

The **Cecilia Coleman Quartet,** raves the weekly *L.A. View,* is led by one of Los Angeles's most impressive young jazz pianists, which is why you should check out CC's stuff as soon as you get to town.

Opera

Recently marking its 10th anniversary, the **Los Angeles Opera's** season runs from September to June at the Dorothy Chandler Pavilion. 135 N. Grand Ave., (213) 972-7211. Tickets are also sold through Ticketmaster, (213) 480-3232.

PARKS

Armand Hammer Golf Course and Park—Seniors enjoy the golf course, where they set up camp almost every weekend with picnic tables and umbrellas. Meanwhile, it looks like a mommy-and-me class at the other end of the park, with a swing-set and more just for tots. 601 Club View Dr., Beverly Hills.

Descanso Gardens—A placid lake, a soothing waterfall, a Japanese tea house, and 165 astonishing acres of flowers—azaleas, roses, and especially camellias. Thirty acres of California oaks and a five acre rose garden ensure that the birds and the bees love it. You too. 1418 Descanso Dr., (at Verdugo Blvd.), Glendale, (818) 952-4400.

Griffith Park—In the city's largest and most famous park, there is no excuse for being bored. You can ride on a pony (or a full-size horse), hop on the Travel Town train, picnic with family and friends, go in circles on the merry-go-round, or start your game of anything. 4730 Crystal Springs Dr. (near Los Feliz Blvd. and Riverside Dr.), (213) 665-5188.

Los Angeles Arboretum—From the concrete jungle to the literal kind is just a short drive. The arboretum offers 127 lush acres that display all of our luxuriant foliage (native and imported) to best advantage. Plus, we've got the Hollywood angle. Not only is the house from *Fantasy Island* here, but so is the lake from *The African Queen* where Bogie got the willies from those creepy leeches. 301 N. Baldwin Ave., Arcadia, (818) 821-3222.

Pan Pacific Park—This huge park sits next to the La Brea tar pits and attracts families, couples, and individuals—especially on Sunday, when the park turns into an entertainment center. Hard bodies rollerblade by while young children practice their baseball swings and others opt for a game of soccer.

Roxbury Park—It may be a Beverly Hills park, but everybody is welcome and plenty of people take advantage of these beautiful grounds where children run freely and it isn't uncommon for a pick-up game of any sort to be going on. 471 S. Roxbury Dr., Beverly Hills.

Parks for Bike Riding

The Beach—Whether you bring your own or rent from the dozens of places that line the bike path, you're in for a day of sun and fun. Just remember that in order to keep the fun in sun, you must wear sun block. The main bike path extends all the way from Redondo Beach down south to Malibu up north, but you can catch it just about everywhere in between. If you tend to get bored staring end-lessly at the water, you'll want to start your ride around Washington Blvd. and head north so you pass through the hoopla of Venice Beach. The only downside to this ride is that you'll have to tolerate clueless pedestrians. Ride all the way to the Santa Monica pier, where you can have some lunch and take a ride on a Ferris wheel—maybe not in that order, however. If you want to avoid the crowds, start your ride around the pier and head north up to Malibu, where it is a bit quieter. Note: Unlike Venice, there are not many places to rent bikes right off the path in Malibu.

Burbank Trail—Begin right where Alameda meets Mariposa. Then you're off cycling on a path that takes you through parks, down suburban side streets and right past the movie studios.

Griffith Park—Okay, so this park has it all, but the bike trail along Griffith Park Dr., also deserves mention. While passing through Travel Town, the L.A. Zoo and the golf course, you may want to stop for a picnic lunch. A great ride for kids, too. See page 178.

Kenneth Newell Bikeway—If you've always wanted to see the Rose Bowl, this is a unique way to catch a glimpse. Follow this trail through the Arroyo Seco Canyon for a challenging cardiovascular workout. When you finish, head into Old Town Pasadena for some breakfast or lunch at the many outdoor cafes and juice bars.

San Vicente—Don't let the runners have all the fun. Join the hundreds who come out to play on weekends along this long and winding road leading down to the beach. It's probably best to start at Bundy and San Vicente to avoid busy intersections and then roll west. For those who want a little longer ride, Wilshire and San Vicente is also a good place to get set and go.

PLANETARIUMS

Griffith Park Observatory—Besides being famous as the spot where James Dean saved Sal Mineo in *Rebel Without a Cause*, there are actual astronomy exhibits, a huge Foucault's pendulum, and various shows in the planetarium including a late night laser show. But if you really want to rock the house, ask 'em to demonstrate the Tesla coil. It's cool. 2800 E. Observatory Road, Griffith Park, (213) 664-1191.

POOL HALLS

Hollywood Athletic Club—Fun, young, with a mostly industry-obsessed crowd—as well as seriously obsessed pool shooters (celebrities and regular folk) who know how to pick up their cues. 6525 Sunset Blvd., Hollywood, (213) 962-6600.

Hollywood Billiards—In a previous life, Hollywood Billiards was a serious pool shark-infested dive at Hollywood and Western, but the brand-new place a little further down the road is a slightly-yuppified, squeaky-clean 24-hour hall with 42 tables, courtyard dining, live music, and 80 brews on tap. Hollywood Blvd. at the 101 Freeway, (213) 465-0115.

Q's—Collegiate and friendly haunt where youths can rack up a few drinks while they work on their game. 11835 Wilshire Blvd., West L.A., (310) 477-7550.

Yankee Doodles—Young and fun sports bar provides a great place to pick up the stick—and maybe something else. 1410 3rd St. Promenade, Santa Monica, (310) 394-4632.

Also, see BARS, with pool tables.

RADIO STATIONS

For those who are tuned into it, Los Angeles has the best variety of fine radio stations in the country. A few totally excellent radio waves to surf:

KBIG: 104.3—Adult contemporary.

KCRW: 89.9—Enjoy block programming in various genres: jazz, pop, reggae, and classical. Or, get it all at once with the Morning Becomes Eclectic show—weekdays 9 to noon—a local institution for adventurous music lovers. The city's most popular public radio station.

KEZY: 95.9.

KFPK—Pacifica Network station broadcasts progressive talk

shows, alternative and ethnic music programs, and
sundry curiosities.

KLOS: 95.5—The infamous station that gave Kato his own talk-
show is also the home of Howard Stern in the morning and
Susan Olsen (Cindy Brady) in the afternoon. As you might
imagine, the ratings drop a bit when Howard goes off the air.

KLON: 88.1—Excellent jazz and blues station that supports the
local scene.

KPCC: 89.3—Noncommercial, listener-supported jazz, blues, and
international sounds.

KROQ: 106.7—The biggie of alternative rock—a great station for
decades, currently in a slight down period.

Star 98.7—A new yuppie station with top 40, classic hits, and some
retro tunes. A little too much Hootie and the Blowfish, though.

KUSC: 91.5—Fine college station plays amazing mix of music.

KIIS: 102.7—Top 40 pop all the time with popular DJs and a
young audience that blast this station from the high-school
parking lots.

KOST: 103.5—They're big on telling you to relax and enjoy your
music (easy listening) along "the coast." At night, their love
songs and dedications are so sugary, your teeth will hurt.

KSCA: 101.9—A great mix of alternative and classic music that's
gaining in popularity.

INSIDER TIP: *KLON radio, 88.1 FM, sponsors fantastic
jazz caravans (and blues treks as well) that bus you
around to 20-odd clubs in a single night for a paltry $12.
This is a fantastic musical appetizer platter for newcomers to the city (or for locals fresh on the scene) that
lets you scope out places you'll want to return to later.
Of course you're welcome to step off the caravan at any
point. (310) 985-1686.*

RECORD AND MUSIC STORES

Aron's—Immense turnover in used CDs and an enormous

FASHIONABLE FOUR EYES

Sunglasses are a fashion statement in L.A. An outfit is simply not complete without the perfect shades. Many people even insist on wearing their sunglasses indoors. While the sun is strong here, you won't need your eyewear while you're inside (unless your say, Sharon Stone). But you do need sunglasses year round. If you're not into fancy shmancy, check out the sidewalk shops lining Venice Beach. They have great styles for knock-off prices. Also try sporting goods stores, department stores, and even The Gap for cheaper versions of the latest styles.

If you've got money to spend, L.A. is full of high-class, high-priced eyeglass shops. OPTICAL DESIGNS (1235 Montana Ave., Santa Monica, (310) 393-4322) has great styles for you and your kids—there's an adjoining store full of glasses for the little tykes.

OPTICAL OUTLOOK (8555 W. Sunset Blvd., West Hollywood, (310) 652-9144 and several other locations) is a popular chain where you are sure to "see" something you like. Where do the stars go to get their sun spectacles? OLIVER PEOPLES (8642 W. Sunset Blvd., West Hollywood, (310) 657-2553) and LA Eyeworks (7470 Melrose Ave., (213) 653-8255). In addition to sunglasses, you should always wear sun block when you know you are going to be outside. Don't avoid it because you are dying for a tan. Even if you wear a high number, you'll still get color, just maybe not skin cancer.

selection. Great cheap vinyl in the back. 1150 N. Highland Ave., Hollywood, (213) 469-4700.

Borders Books & Music Cafe—Stoke on latte and nab some tunes or tomes. 330 S. La Cienega Blvd. (also in Westwood), (310) 659-4046.

Counterpoint—New and used records, CDs, and books. Fun browsing and the Bourgeois Pig Cafe is a couple of doors down. 5911 Franklin Ave., (213) 957-7965.

Eastside Records—Friendly little place full of funky hipsters. 1813 Hillhurst Ave., Los Feliz, (213) 913-7461.

No Life Records—Fab in-stores and alternative everything. 7209 Santa Monica Blvd., West Hollywood, (213) 845-1200.

Platterpuss Records—They've been here for decades, so stop in this little shop and enjoy the good vibe, the great selection and the competitive prices. 2204 Lincoln, Santa Monica, (310) 396-2528.

Record Collector—Specializing in classical and jazz. 1158 N. Highland Ave., (213) 467-2875.

Record Store—New and used, good selection. 1511 S. La Cienega Blvd., (310) 652-6198.

Rhino Records—Good prices paid for your used stuff and tons of other people's stuff passing through so you can take your pick. 1720 Westwood Blvd., (310) 474-8685.

Rockaway Records—New and used CDs with listening station. Gets the job done, snotty clerks and all. 2395 Glendale Blvd., Silver Lake, (213) 664-3232.

Tempo—Well-stocked and convenient. 7064 Sunset Blvd. (and other locations), (213) 467-9742.

Tower Records—Reliable chain of megastores with its own quirky attitude and merchandise. 8801 W. Sunset Blvd. (and other locations), (310) 657-7300.

Virgin Megastore—Mega is the operative prefix. 8000 W. Sunset Blvd., Hollywood, (213) 650-8666.

RESTAURANTS

In addition to driving around endlessly, Angelenos love restaurants. And remember, we're only scratching the surface.

Food key: $=pennies plus (under $10), $$=reasonable, $$$=ouch!, $$$$=major damage.

American

Patrick's Roadhouse—Often referred to as a power breakfast spot, the power actually refers first to the breakfast and then to the people eating it. Huge portions of eggs, pancakes, and other brunch favorites are served up with colorful owner Bill Fischler always good for a notable quotable. And well, the diners are pretty powerful too—Katzenberg and Clinton, just to name two. 106 Entrada Dr., Santa Monica, (310) 459-4544. $

CALIFORNIA CUISINE

Everyone serves it up so you better get hip to the idea of Asian-style spring rolls filled with seasonal Southern Cal vegetables in a French sauce or thin-crust pizza with goat cheese and smoked salmon. Here in L.A., this type of culturally diverse cooking that attempts to be light and healthy is called California Cuisine. Usually credited with this innovation in food is Wolfgang Puck, who has gone from Spago and Chinois to the freezer section. Yes, you can now buy prepackaged versions of his creations, which were supposedly based on the idea of using seasonal, fresh ingredients, at your local supermarket. But for the full effect of this cuisine, it's best to actually go into the restaurants, as the decor has its own flavor—although whether the decor is tasteful or tasteless is an ongoing debate.

Chinese

If you don't find a Chinese place you like here, don't worry, a half an hour later another one will open up.

Bamboo—The Valley's answer to fantastic Chinese cooking—the moo shu will melt in your mouth and the sweet and sour shrimp is to die. 14010 Ventura Blvd., Sherman Oaks, (818) 788-0202. $$

Joss—Typical Chinese cuisine with delicious dim sum. 9255 Sunset Blvd., (310) 276-1886. $$

J.R. Seafood—Much more than just excellent seafood, and the prices are very right. 11001 Santa Monica Blvd., West L.A., (310) 268-2463. $

The Mandarin—This bustling L.A. favorite is a great choice when you have friends in town—or when you just crave good Chinese. 430 N. Camden Dr., Beverly Hills, (213) 272-0267. $$$

Mon Kee—Where better to get real Cantonese cooking than in Chinatown? Mon Kee is one of the first places to settle here since Chinatown migrated to this side of town, and you'll be glad it's still standing after you taste the seafood. 679 Spring St., Chinatown, (213) 628-6717. $$$

Mr. Chow LA—Better known for its place on the social circuit than for its high rating on the food chain. 344 N. Camden Dr., Beverly Hills, (310) 278-9911. $$$

The Panda Inn—Once one of the most popular spots in town, the Panda lost that original momentum, but the food remains good. Their Panda Express takeout cafes, however, have picked up the slack, offering the same taste for less cash. Westside Pavillion, 10800 W. Pico Blvd. and other locations, (310) 470-7790. $$

French

Pinot Bistro—A popular spot in the Valley, this French bistro's most treasured dish is Pappa al Pomodoro, an old Tuscan soup. 12969 Ventura Blvd., Studio City, (818) 990-0500. $$

BAKERIES

BEVERLYWOOD BAKERY—9128 W. Pico Blvd., (310) 550-9842. The absolute best for egg bread and corn rye.

MANI'S—8801 Santa Monica Blvd., West Hollywood, (310) 659-5955. A charming place with a variety of coffees and baked goods. For those who like it low-fat, there is plenty to choose from.

BREADWORKS-1601 Montana Ave., Santa Monica, 260-1931. A variety of breads from olive to sun-dried tomato to raisin-nut—and they're all delicious.

DIAMOND BAKERY—335 N. Fairfax Ave.,(310) 655-0534.

LA BREA BAKERY—624 S. La Brea Ave., (310) 939-6813. Consistently cited as the best bakery in Los Angeles—the breads are heavenly.

SWEET LADY JANE BAKERY—8360 Melrose Ave., (310) 653-7145

Greek

Cafe Athens—Break a plate and join in the fun at this Greek festival-like dining spot. 1000 Wilshire Blvd., Santa Monica, (310) 395-1000. $$

The Great Greek—When you are not dancing and singing with the waiters, you'll enjoy traditional Greek cuisine. Such a lively place, it is perfect for a birthday or any other celebration. 13362 Ventura Blvd., Sherman Oaks, (818) 905-5250. $$

Le Petit Greek—Specialty salads to rival all others. If you like feta, this place is for you. 127 N. Larchmont Blvd., Hancock Park, (213) 464-5160. $$

Indian

Anarbagh—Relatively new on the Indian scene, it's not as good as some of the others, but then again, it probably still has some improving to do. 22721 Ventura Blvd., Woodland Hills, (818) 224-3929. $$

Bombay Cafe—Always top-rated, this spicy cuisine is about as authentic as you can get while dining on Indian in Santa Monica. 12113 Santa Monica Blvd., Santa Monica, (310) 820-2070. $

India's Oven—Excellent, economical fare with polite yet painfully relentless service. Tandoori chicken is a crowd pleaser and their buriyanis are outstanding. 7231 Beverly Blvd., (213) 936-1000. $$

Shalimar—Basic Mughlai style dishes including lamb tikka and Karahi beef. For those who don't eat meat, the vegetable and bean dishes are sharply seasoned and flavorful. 23011 Ventura Blvd., Woodland Hills, (818) 225-7794. $$

Italian

Caffe Luna—The service is so-so but the back patio is delightful on a warm evening. Most important, the focaccia bread they serve up is better than most desserts. 7463 Melrose Ave., (213) 655-8647. $$

Chianti—It has appeared on *Melrose Place* so often, you'd think Aaron Spelling owned the place. Well, he doesn't and the crowd here is anything but *90210* or *Melrose* groupies. It's a great place for romance and fine dining. Also try Cucina next door for a more casual option-they share the same kitchen. 7383 Melrose Ave., (213) 653-8333. $$

Dan Tana's—An old Hollywood favorite probably because it feels like you're on the set of *The Godfather* with its dark lighting and enticing Italian aromas. Noted for having the best steak in town, they're only open for dinner. 9071 Santa Monica Blvd., West Hollywood, (310) 275-9444. $$$

I Cugini—Enjoying fine Italian dining while gazing upon the blue Pacific is a perfect way to spend an evening. 1501 Ocean Ave., Santa Monica, (310) 451-4595. $$

Il Moro—Northern Italian cuisine tucked into West L.A.—perfect for business lunches. 11400 W. Olympic Blvd., West L.A., (310) 575-3530. $$

Locanda Veneta—While you might be sitting on top of the person next to you, nothing can beat the Venetian cuisine served up here. Try the linguini with rock shrimp, asparagus and tomatoes or the crab ravioli. It's a town favorite and so is the chef. 8638 W. 3rd St., (310) 274-1893. $$

Orso—Tops in high-end pizza and pasta. Its great in warm weather when the patio dominates although it does get pretty crowded. 8706 W. 3rd St., (310) 274-7144. $$$

Pane e Vino—An electric crowd is always on hand, full of baby moguls and other execs halfway up the ladder. The patio is full of energy, the food isn't. 8265 Beverly Blvd., (213) 651-4600. $$$

Peppone—One of the original power restaurants, which is now draining its battery. Still, the food is delicious and the wine list quite complete. 11628 Barrington Ct., Brentwood, (310) 476-7379. $$

Posto—It's a casual place for traditional Italian cuisine—and excellent soups. 14928 Ventura Blvd., Sherman Oaks, (818) 784-4400. $$

Trattoria Amici—One of the places Hugh Grant heads when he is in town . . . with Elizabeth Hurley. 469 N. Doheny Dr., Beverly Hills, (310) 858-0271. $$$

Japanese

America's sushi craze began out here, so it's hardly surprising that we do Japanese better than anyone this side of the Pacific.

Asahi Ramen—A favorite ramen dive—huge portions of Japanese noodles for nothing prices. One of many popular Asian places on the bustling Sawtelle strip. 2027 Sawtelle Blvd., (310) 479-2231. $

Asakuma—Located in the Westside's own "Little Tokyo," this is a favorite with locals who boast of the comprehensive sushi bar. 11701 Wilshire Blvd., (310) 826-0013. $$

Asanebo—It's not sushi, it's sashimi, and it is a delicious alternative to a typical Japanese meal. 11941 Ventura Blvd., Studio City, (818) 760-3348. $$$

Crazy Fish—Not enough tables, not enough people working, and still young Westsiders flock for their weekly fix of sushi. Best bet: Order to go. 9105 W. Olympic Blvd., Beverly Hills, (310) 550-8547. $$

Ginza Sushiko—It's by appointment only, which should be your first clue that prices make this place exclusive. Patrons claim it's the best sushi in town, but so few can actually afford to eat here that it is best known for the price, not the sushi. 218 N. Rodeo Dr., Beverly Hills, (310) 247-8939. $$$$

Katsu—Consistently rated the best sushi in L.A.—it's often crowded with a Hollywood crowd. 1972 N. Hillhurst Ave., (213) 665-1891. $$

Ramenya—The absolute best bowl of Japanese noodles in the city—it's no wonder there is always a line. 11555 W. Olympic Blvd., (310) 575-9337. $

Sushi House—You'll probably have to wait . . . but it is well worth it. The sushi is fresh and light-feeling. 12013 W. Pico Blvd., (310) 479-1507. $$

Sushi Nozawa—Don't be fooled by the strip-mall exterior, the sushi is for real. Try one of the specials, guaranteed to be out of this world. 11288 Ventura Blvd., Ste. C, Studio City, (818) 508-7017. $$

Teru-Sushi—One of the first sushi bars that made it chic to eat raw fish still packs 'em in. Wonderful specials but they're gonna cost you. 11940 Ventura Blvd., Studio City, (818) 763-6201. $$$

Yabu—According to *The Hollywood Reporter AFM Weekend Guide*, this is the best and most authentic Japanese noodle house on the

Westside. The paper reports that Sheryl Crow and Tea Leoni prefer these noodles to all others. 11820 W. Pico Blvd., L.A., (310) 473-9757. $$

Yuu—A nothing on the outside, this sushi/saki bar is noted for being authentic and delicious at the same time.

Kosher

The Milky Way—This kosher dairy restaurant garners quite a bit of attention in town. Its owner is a nice woman named Leah Adler who happens to be Steven Spielberg's mom. Does that make her E.T.'s grandma? Happy to answer all your questions, she's almost always working the room. 9108 W. Pico Blvd., (310) 859-0004. $

Mosaique—An elegant restaurant with what some call the best kosher kitchen in town. 8164 W. 3rd St., (213) 951-1133. $$

Pat's—At this Italian eatery, you'll find it hard to believe the meals are kosher. The food is tasty, well-seasoned and the atmosphere is quite conducive for a first date. 9233 W. Pico Blvd., L.A., (310) 205-8705. $$

Pico Kosher Deli—While others claim to be the real thing, this place truly is. 8826 W. Pico Blvd., (310) 273-9381. $

Mexican

Authentic Cafe—California-style Mexican food—that means Mexican food made with the utmost in culinary creative latitude. You must try their authentic, well, original tamales. 7605 Beverly Blvd., (213) 939-4626. $

El Coyote—Huge portions, a full bar, and a young, energetic crowd. 7312 Beverly Blvd., (213) 939-2255. $

Lucy's Drive-In—Tasty 24-hour drive-thru Mexican place, without the grease. 1373 S. La Brea (at Pico), (310) 938-4337. $

Mexica—While it's not the best Mex in the city, it is a fun place to start off the night with appetizers and drinks. 7313 Beverly Blvd., L.A., (213) 933-7385. $$

Poquito Mas—So close to Universal, it becomes the place of choice for movie execs at the lunch hour. 10651 Magnolia Blvd., North Hollywood, (818) 994-8226. $

TOTALLY MEXCELLENT

So close to the border, it was bound to happen. Angelenos have gone loco for Mexican food. Incorporated into almost every menu in the city, south-of-the-border cuisine abounds in L.A. Whether it's served off a roadside truck, in a small neighborhood dive, or in a trendy Beverly Hills bistro, here's a list of some of the best Mexican delights in town:

BAJA FRESH—For take-out or a quick bite, undeniably the best in L.A. 475 N. Beverly Dr., Beverly Hills, (310) 858-6690 (and other locations).$

EL CHOLO—Voted the best margaritas in Los Angeles Magazine's, "Best of L.A.," El Cholo is just as famous locally for its no holds barred authentic Mexican cooking. 1121 S. Western Ave., (213) 734-2773. $

EL TORITO GRILL—Delicious dishes with homemade guacamole made at your table to your liking. And instead of chips beforehand, they offer warmed tortillas, not to mention their speciality: lobster fajitas. It is L.A., after all. Check out the bar on Friday nights—it's hopping. 9595 Wilshire Blvd., Beverly Hills, (310) 550-1599. $$

KAY N' DAVE'S—In keeping with perfect Santa Monica etiquette, this small eatery is laid-back and politically correct. They don't use lard or animal shortening in any of their food and they're happy to make your meal to order. The portions are large and everything tastes just right. 262 26th St., Santa Monica, (310) 260-1355. $

LA SERENATA DI GARIBALDI—In the heart of East L.A., this is Mexican cooking with an emphasis on seafood. Judging by the Mexican clientele, the food is for real. 1842 E. 1st St., (213) 265-2887. $

OLVERA—Fiesta! This place is always moving and shaking. The bar is packed and the crowd eating here is energized. Located behind the House of Blues, there is constant activity and overflow. The food is Mexican served up with L.A. style. 8426 Sunset Blvd., West Hollywood, (213) 656-3055. $$

Pizza Places

What you might call "California" pizza is lighter of crust than what's preferred in some other regions, and, yes, many of our establishments do go over the top with trendy froufrou toppings like caviar, sun-dried tomatoes, pineapple-rumaki, moo shu chicken etc., etc., etc. But when it comes to pizza we must once again echo that rap music snooper star, Mr. Doggy Dogg, that it's All Good. Any kind of pizza—East Coast, West Coast, old school, new school, by the slice, by the pound. Buy the pizza; it's A.G.

Antonio's—Just like Mama used to make. Not that many people know about this, so don't tell anybody. 13619 Ventura Blvd., (818) 788-1103. $

Hard Times Pizza—Great slices on site, though, mysteriously, delivered pizzas don't have the same flavor at all. This is New York-style pizza (both flat and Sicilian) without the excess grease you get in the Apple at places like Ray's. 2664 Griffith Park Blvd., Silver Lake, (213) 661-5656.

Jacopo's—Pizza, pasta, and salads—perfect when you don't want to cook but feel like a hot meal. They deliver. 11676 Olympic Blvd., L.A., (310) 477-2111.

Johnnie's New York Cafe Pizzeria—So close to Century City that it is perfect for informal business lunches. If you like it simple, try "Johnnie's Favorite." For those who crave gourmet pizza, try the "Roasted Veggie" which includes Japanese eggplant, zucchini, and red and yellow bell peppers. 10251 Santa Monica Blvd., and other locations, (310) 553-1188. $

Mama's Original Pizza and Pasta—Not really that original, but

darn good anyway. 7212 Melrose, Hollywood, (213) 937-MAMA; 3311 Motor Ave., West L.A., (310) 204-MAMA.

Maria's Italian Kitchen—Named best pizza on KIIS-FM radio, this chain of restaurants is actually best when you are in a jam, because they deliver and they offer a lot more than just pizza. 10761 Pico Blvd., Westwood, (310) 441-3663. $

New York Pizza and Pasta—Tucked away in a nothing strip mall, the food is fantastic, the people who work there are more than friendly, and they deliver. Try the meatball sub— only if you are really really hungry. 11078 Santa Monica Blvd., (310) 444-0050. $

Pizza Buona—Family place cranks out good 'za with tangy sauce and nicely substantial crust that is occasionally marred by slow delivery. 2200 W. Sunset (at Alvarado), Echo Park, (213) 413-0800.

Pizza Go—Dependable takeout in mid-Wilshire. (213) 381-5131.

Pizza Man—Will deliver anywhere or suggest an alternative. (213) 380-5723 or (213) 388-1414.

Santo Pietro's Pizza—Perfectly casual pizza in a pleasant side-walk cafe situation up in the hills. 2954 Beverly Glen Circle (south of Mulholland), (310) 474-4349.

Shakey's Pizza—Venerable chain offering serviceable slabs of hot starch and molten cheese. 7001 Santa Monica Blvd., Hollywood, (213) 463-1104; 5170 W. Sunset Blvd., Hollywood, (213) 663-2145; 6052 W. Olympic Blvd., (213) 937-4234.

And of course, L.A. is awash in well-known national chain delivery places that 1) are makin' it great; 2) nobody knows like; 3) are staunch advocates of pizza-pizza. They're all in the book—just not this one.

Thai

Chan Dara—It's a bit on the spicy side, but the food here is some of the best Thai in the city. Satay is the appetizer of choice, and the crispy noodles, the curry dishes and the pad Thai are all very popular. 1511 N. Cahuenga Blvd., Hollywood and other locations, (213) 464-8585. $

Jitlada—It's one of the first Thai restaurants to gain attention and still worthy. 5233 Sunset Blvd., (213) 667-9809. $$

Sompun—It's a mother-daughter-run business that depends on generations of fantastic recipes. You must try the fish cakes. 4156 Santa Monica Blvd., L.A., and other locations, (213) 669-9906.

Tommy Tang's—A fun place with great dishes, especially the pad Thai. On the weekends, there is usually a large gay crowd at the bar. 7473 Melrose Ave., and other locations, (213) 651-1810. $$

Vim—It's not exactly the place to go for a night out on the town. Ambiance is meager but the food is fantastic. 831 S. Vermont Ave., (213) 386-2338. $

Various

Aunt Kizzy's Back Porch—Located in a mall, this is "real" Southern home cooking—so good and so fattening. But once in a while, it is a treat. Now, get back to the gym to work off that chicken fat. 4325 Glencoe Ave., Marina del Rey, (310) 578-1005. $

Babalu—It's a different kind of eating at this Caribbean spot—spicy and seasoned. You'd have to be a jerk not to like the ch_cken. 1002 Montana Ave., Santa Monica, (310) 395-2500. $

Cava Restaurant and Tapas Bar—Paella, tortillas, sangria—Viva Espana! 8384 W. 3rd St., (213) 658-8898. $$

Dar Maghreb—It's a Moroccan experience with belly dancers and minimal silverware. Oh, and the food is pretty tasty too. 7651 Sunset Blvd., (213) 876-7651. $$

Indo Cafe—Spicy Indonesian cuisine at very reasonable prices. Extraordinary variety of Pacific Rim hybrid dishes and interesting specials. 10428½ National Blvd., (310) 815-1290. $

Rincon Criollo—Named as the "Cuban Food to Make you Forget That Other Place" by *L.A. Weekly*. It's their oblique way of calling it the best in the city. 4361 Sepulveda Blvd., Culver City, (310) 391-4478. $$

Vegetarian

A Votre Sant—They do serve chicken, but the menu caters to veg-heads. Quite popular for breakfast. 345 N. La Brea Ave., L.A. and other locations, (213) 857-0412. $$

Bodhi Gardens—Outstanding vegetarian Asian food in an Eagle Rock mini-mall. 1498 W. Sunset Blvd., (213) 250-9023.$

Planet Organica—It's veggie takeout: meatless sausages and meatballs, eggplant Parmesan. 1437 3rd Street Promenade, Santa Monica, (310) 576-0059. $

Real Food Daily—Started by former actress Ann Gentry, this isn't a place for the low-maintenance. Actually, Woody Harrelson, and Al Pacino have been spotted feasting on Gentry's tasty vegan creations. A menu must: Fishless sushi—because everyone in this town has to have his/her fix. 514 Santa Monica Blvd., Santa Monica, (310) 451-7544. $$

Date Restaurants

Abiquiu—Once the L.A. trendy spot Bikini, it has been re-opened post quake as the same sassy Southwestern eatery. But there is something very new on the menu: the "Get Shorty" tamale named for the film, which shot the memorable scene wherein Chili Palmer successfully pushed a stunt man down the long staircase. Everybody wants to be in pictures. 1413 5th St., Santa Monica, (310) 395-8611. $$

Barefoot Bar and Grill—Oh so California with two patios, Cal-cuisine, and a prime location for people watching. 8722 W. Third St., (310) 276-6223. $$

Bistro Bar at Citrus—Michel Richard's less casual Citrus with the same Franco-California bistro style cooking that made him famous. In fact, the only difference is that you sit in the bar area of Citrus with a semi-different menu and end up paying less. 6703 Melrose Ave., (213) 857-0034. $$

Ca'Brea—Opened by the same people who brought L.A. Locanda Veneta, this northern Italian cafe-style eatery is simply divine, although like its predecessor it has a tendency to get crowded and noisy. 346 S. La Brea Ave., (213) 938-2863. $$

Ca'Del Sole—Excellent Italian cuisine with a cozy atmosphere (fireplace and all) and heavenly tiramisu. 4100 Cahuenga Blvd., North Hollywood, (818) 985-4669. $$

Coogie's—It's where the Malibu crowd goes for a casual dinner or a power breakfast. The service is excellent and the

Cal culinary creations are tasty and filling. 23755 W. Malibu Rd., Malibu, (310) 317-1444. $$

Eclipse—Another Aaron Spelling favorite, judging from the number of times it's been used in all of his series. Perhaps he just likes the look of this mostly Mediterranean celebrity favorite. They call the food "cuisine of the sun," which is simply another take on California cuisine. 8800 Melrose Ave., (310) 724-5959. $$$

Jackson's Farm—It's a less casual version of Jackson's with the greatest corn chowder in town and decadent desserts. 439 N. Beverly Dr., Beverly Hills, (310) 273-5578. $$

La Cachette—This French favorite is relatively new on the scene. Judging from the rave reviews, it's likely here to stay. 10506 S. Santa Monica Blvd., (310) 470-4992. $$

LA Farm—You'll start off with warm bread and pate at this Franco-California dining spot located next door to Caravan Pictures, which brings an industry crowd overflow at lunch. For dinner, it remains busy but it's low-hum and laid-back. 3000 Olympic Blvd., Santa Monica, (310) 449-4000. $$

Marmalade Cafe—A typical California cafe: salads, pastas, and popular brunch foods. 710 Montana Ave., Santa Monica (and other locations), (310) 395-9196. $

Modada—It's over-done and some would say over-rated. Still it's a trendy grazing spot for the Hollywood herd with Sam Marvin, whom *Buzz* magazine named the "Unheralded Chef of the Year.". 8115 Melrose Ave., West Hollywood, (213) 653-4612. $$$

Pastina—A small Italian cafe with delicious pastas, a delightful atmos-phere, and a staff that makes you feel like you're dining at your aunt and uncle's. 2260 Westwood Blvd., (310) 441-4655. $

Twin Palms—How did Cindy Costner make out in her divorce from Kevin? Well, she couldn't have done badly, since she got their share in this popular, Cal-French restaurant. The patio is a delight and the bar is quite the pickup scene. 101 W. Green St., Pasadena, (818) 577-2567. $$

Vida—The menu is eccentric, the food quite tasty, and the atmosphere relaxed. This is where Hollywood's young would-be moguls plan world conquest over high-end eats. 1930 Hillhurst Ave., Los Feliz, (213) 660-4446. $$$

Typhoon—Best to order family style at this lively Cal-Asian spot settled within view of the runways at Santa Monica Airport. The service is fantastic and the blackened catfish divine. Order the famed mashed potatoes with whatever you end up getting. 3221 Donald Douglas Loop S., Santa Monica, (310) 390-6565. $$

L.A. LANDMARKS IN FOOD

APPLE PAN—They come in droves for a burger at this shack of a restaurant where many believe the burger was born. 90210's Peach Pit doesn't seem that original an idea after a visit to this L.A. staple. 10801 W. Pico Blvd., (310) 475-3585. $

MUSSO AND FRANK GRILL—It's been a Hollywood hangout since 1919. It's one of those places where you wish the walls could talk . . . about the famous who've sipped the famed martinis at the bar. 6667 Hollywood Blvd., (213) 467-7788. $$

ORIGINAL PANTRY CAFE—The best hint that this joint is part of ancient L.A. history probably is that they serve diner-style cuisine with all the fat and cholesterol retained—talk about a blast from the past. Still, adipose-fretting Angelenos line up for their fatty fare share. As for the waitresses. "We've been here since the beginning, honey." 877 S. Figueroa St., (213) 972-9279. $

PHILIPPE THE ORIGINAL—They say they invented the French-dip sandwich at this L.A dive, and with one bite, you'll understand that "Original" in the name. It's delicious! You can't say you've lived in L.A. until you've been to Philippe's. 1001 N. Alameda St., (213) 628-3781.$

PINK'S FAMOUS CHILI DOGS—In a city known for being health conscious, you'll have to throw all your eating habits out the window to fully enjoy this popular hot dog standout that serves up meaty dogs and thick chili. 709 N. La Brea Ave., (213) 931-4223. $

TAIL O' THE PUP—More famous for the architecture than the food. (The stand is shaped like a giant hot dog). 329 N. San Vicente, West Hollywood, (213) 652-4517. $

INSIDER TIP: *For the perfect date you don't have to fly to Venice to enjoy a romantic gondola ride. Not many people know this but Long Beach has its own flow of canals. GONDOLA GETAWAY offers an hour-long ride with the all the amenities, making for a great Italian imitation. For $55 for the first couple and $10 for additional couples up to six, the price is certainly less than a round trip ticket on ALITALIA. For more information or reservations, call (310) 433-9595. If you don't want your night to end here, head over to San Pedro for dinner at PAPADAKIS. It's a couple's place for traditional Greek cuisine, maybe even the best this side of the Mediterranean. 301 W. 6th St., San Pedro.*

Chain Restaurants to Try

Restaurateurs know a good thing when we see it, so they tend to open versions of their successful joints all across town. For the eating public, that's a good thing.

Baja Fresh—Healthy-ish Mexican dishes with tasty guacamole and sensational salsas. 475 N. Beverly Dr., Beverly Hills, (310) 858-6690, and other locations. $

California Pizza Kitchen—The now-national chain mixes California cooking with Italian favorites. Top picks: Moo shu Chicken Calzone or Barbecue Chicken Pizza. 121 N. La Cienega Blvd., (310) 854-6555, and other locations. $

Cheesecake Factory—Huge portions of everything—the menu is the size of a book. Filling and flavorful salads (the Chinese chicken salad is the flavor of choice) and decadent cheesecakes with scads of different flavors. 364 N. Beverly Dr., Beverly Hills, (310) 278-7270, and other locations. $

Chin-Chin—Healthy Chinese food. They'll make it how you want it. But be forewarned: it can be bland when cooked without oil or sauce. 8618 Sunset Blvd., West Hollywood, (310) 652-1818 and other locations. $

Crocodile Cafe—Another California cuisine joint with all the trendy dishes: Pizzas, dumplings, and Chinese chicken salad. 201 N. San Fernando Blvd., Burbank, (818) 843-7999, and other locations. $

Houston's—A basic California eatery with everything from ribs to their own version of the Oriental chicken salad. There is really only one "must" on the menu—you must indulge and order the spinach dip as an appetizer for the table. Century City Mall, 10250 Santa Monica Blvd., (310) 557-1285. $

Islands—Great burgers, salads, and soft tacos if you can bear eating under posters of perfect bikini-clad women. The most popular item on the menu is probably the Pelican chicken sandwich, but you must order their legendary fries, seasoned to perfection. 10948 W. Pico Blvd., and other locations, (310) 474-1144. $

Johnny Rockets—Burgers, chili, and fries, not to mention a delicious (and very fattening) tuna sandwich. 7507 Melrose Ave., West Hollywood, and other locations, (213) 651-3361. $

Louise's Trattoria—Cafe-style Italian cooking with pastas, salads, and focaccia sandwiches. The challenge: try not to load up on their incredibly fattening and incredibly delicious bread. 11645 San Vicente Blvd., 826-2000, and other locations.$

INSIDER TIP: *On Sunday nights, the popular chain restaurants such as CALIFORNIA PIZZA KITCHEN, CHEESE-CAKE FACTORY, and LOUISE'S are packed. To avoid the mob scene, order your food to go. It is quick, easy, fast-and you eat when you want.*

Koo Koo Roo—Healthy and succulent rotisserie chicken that's become something of a fad. While it's a bit on the overpriced side, you'll hardly feel like you are eating fast food—despite the fact that you are. It's great when you need to eat fast or don't feel like cooking after work. Try the new turkey burrito or the less-talked-about but delicious vegetable soup. 2002 Wilshire Blvd., Santa Monica, (310) 453-8767, and several other locations. $

Rosti—They are popping up everywhere these days, and that's good news, because you can order to go and pick it up on the way home. Good Italian meals, especially the pastas and risotto. 7475 Beverly Blvd, (213) 938-8335, and other locations. $

THE QUEST FOR THE PERFECT CHINESE CHICKEN SALAD

There's hardly a restaurant in town that doesn't serve its own style Chinese chicken salad. If at first you can't find it on the menu, be sure to check for pseudonyms such as "Oriental chicken salad," "Asian mixed greens" or "Thai style chicken salad." Whatever they call it, Angelenos devour it. So get with the program and try a few of the best of the bunch.

CHEESECAKE FACTORY—364 N. Beverly Dr., Beverly Hills, (310) 278-7270. It's a little on the heavy side, but when you are hungry, it is not only filling, but absolutely delicious. Filled with won-ton and rice noodles, the dressing is a thick, tasty sauce more akin to a plum sauce than anything else. Insider Tip: Ask for the dressing on the side so you can dip your warm bread in it. Few things in life are better!

GEORGE E. WONG—11929 Santa Monica Blvd., Santa Monica, (310) 477-4434. Rated the best Chinese chicken salad by Los Angeles Magazine, you can't beat the tangy ginger dressing. And for vegetarians, they're happy to 86 the chicken.

FEAST FROM THE EAST—1949 Westwood Blvd., Westwood, (310) 475-0400. Don't judge a book by it's cover and don't judge the food by the restaurant's atmosphere. There's not much going on here except for excellent food. At lunch, people flock all in search of the famous Chinese chicken salad with what is rumored to be the best sesame dressing in the city.

STANLEY'S—13817 Ventura Blvd., Sherman Oaks, (818) 986-4623. This salad has been famous in the valley for years and it still holds. The dressing (light, yet sweet) is tossed into a bowl of lettuce, mandarin oranges, rice noodles and chicken. And it tastes even better, along with the hot, fresh bread that is served up first

Nicest Restaurants in Town

As in any big city, there's never a shortage of upscale patrons eager to drop top dollar for prestige dining. When you'd like to join them for a special occasion, here's your crib sheet.

Arnie Morton's of Chicago—A steakhouse with the largest portions of any restaurant in town and side dishes of the same proportions. 435 S. La Cienega Blvd., (310) 246-1501. $$$$

Buffalo Club—The first clue is the unlisted phone number-they'll let you know if they'll allow you to dine here. If you can surmount that barrier, you'll nosh expensively amidst L.A.'s rich and famous. 1520 Olympic Blvd., Santa Monica, (310) 450-8600. $$$

Cafe Bizou—Generally considered one of the city's best new restaurant, this Valley hideaway has become a popular dining spot. New French cuisine with "new" French customer service. 14016 Ventura Blvd., Sherman Oaks, (818) 788-3536. $$$

Cafe Pinot—Downtown's answer to trendy California Cuisine with a French twist. The food feels light yet filling. Be sure to try the Kumamoto oysters. 700 W. 5th St.,(213) 239-6500. $$$

Camelions—Enjoy Cal-French delights in this enchanted cottage perfect for romance. A special place for bridal showers or private parties. 246 26th St., Santa Monica, (310) 3950746. $$$

Campanile—Connected to the La Brea Bakery, the breads alone make for a delicious meal. But there's a lot more. 624 S. La Brea Ave., (213) 938-1447. $$$

Chaya Brasserie—Located next to Cedars-Sinai Hospital, the crowd is a blend of L.A. docs and their famous patients. Cal-French cooking with specialities. 8741 Alden Dr., (310) 859-8833. Also try Chaya Venice, at 110 Navy St., (310) 396-1179. $$$

Chinois On Main—A Wolfgang Puck creation with unique dishes and over-decorated plates. But be prepared: It is very small and very crowded all the time. 2709 Main St., (310) 392-9025. $$$

Citrus—Michel Richard's Franco-California cuisine creation has remained popular and good, transcending all trends. 6703 Melrose Ave., (213) 857-0034. $$$

Drai's—This Franco-California spot is a favorite of the moment-meaning the industry crowd calls it home. Still, owner Victor Drai, who knows how to work the room, keeps all of his customers happy—he won't bump you at last minute just to get a star in. 730 N. La Cienega Blvd., (310) 358-8585. $$$

Engine Co. No. 28—Businessmen and women wheel and deal at this downtown firehouse turned restaurant. True American classics: meatloaf, potatoes, and lots of beef. 644 S. Figueroa St., (213) 624-6996. $$

Georgia—It's expensive Southern cooking that has become one of the hottest spots in town—Johnnie Cochran hosted his victory party here after the verdict. Collard greens have never looked so good and cost so much. 7250 Melrose Ave., (213) 933-8420. $$$

The Grill on the Alley—If you need an agent, you're likely to find one here on any given day at the lunch hour. In close proximity to the agencies, this is "the" power lunch spot for traditional American dishes. 9560 Dayton Way, Beverly Hills, (310) 276-0615. $$$

The Ivy—Danny Devito had them whip up a special omelet in *Get Shorty*, but ordering from the menu is probably your best bet with delicious dishes such as the lime chicken and grilled vegetable salad. Also try Ivy at the Shore. It's a bit more relaxed and less snotty. 113 N. Robertson Blvd., (310) 274-8303. $$$

Jackson's—Opened by Alan Jackson, son of L.A. talk-show host Michael Jackson, the cuisine is quite good—try the crab ravioli. 8908 Beverly Blvd., (310) 550-8142.$$

L'Orangerie—It's tres French and tres fancy . . . and tres cher. 903 N. La Cienega Blvd., (310) 652-9770. $$$$

Morton's—It's not the basic menu that drives the show biz crowd here—it's the fact that this is power dining institution in a milieu that is overwhelmingly trendy. You come here to deal, to be seen, or to pretend you don't want to be seen. 8764 Melrose Ave., (310) 276-5205. $$$$

The Palm—An old favorite of L.A.'s rich and famous, which still serves up what some say is the best steak and lobster in town. 9001 Santa Monica Blvd., (310) 550-8811. $$$

Patina—Ask anyone for the best restaurant in town and you'll almost always be directed here. Franco-California cuisine with real substance and taste. For special occasions, they'll even cater. 5955 Melrose Ave., (213) 467-1108. $$$

WHEN YOU'RE NOT CHECKING IN, CHECK THESE OUT

Hotels in L.A. are meeting places, whether it's to do business or catch up with old friends. The following restaurants are rated among the top in L.A. and if you're having too good of a time, you can always stay the night.

BEL-AIR HOTEL—Secluded in the hills of Bel Air, you're in for quite a romantic evening at this Cal-French, top-rated restaurant set in one of the most beautiful hotels around. 710 Stone Canyon Rd., Bel Air, (310) 472-1211. $$$$

THE BELVEDERE AT THE PENINSULA—When you don't opt for a seat at the bar, which is almost impossible to get anyway, The Belvedere is the place to be. The pricey menu is first-rate French-Cal bistro. 9882 Little Santa Monica Blvd., Beverly Hills, (310) 273-4888. $$$

CHECKERS AT WYNDHAM—One of the reasons to go downtown for a night. With such reasonable prices (call ahead for deals), the Franco-American cooking tastes even better, although it is pretty good to start. 535 S. Grand Ave., (213) 624-0000. $$$

ONE PICO AT SHUTTERS ON THE BEACH—Relaxed is the feeling at this delightful beachfront restaurant that is perfect for brunch and elegant for dinner. One Pico Blvd., Santa Monica, (310) 587-1717. $$

POLO LOUNGE AT THE BEVERLY HILLS HOTEL—Along with the less formal Polo Grill, this is probably one of the most famous places to eat in L.A. Whether it's for a power breakfast or a dinner date, the food is always superb and the waiters simply, a delight. 9641 Sunset Blvd., Beverly Hills, (310) 276-2251. $$$

REGENT DINING ROOM AT THE REGENT BEVERLY WILSHIRE— Fancy continental cuisine and prime people watching with a terrific afternoon tea. A delightful spot for bridal showers or other special occasions. 9500 Wilshire Blvd., Beverly Hills, (310) 274-8179. $$$

Matsuhisa—The perfect place to go when your friend visits and it's on the expense account. Excellent Japanese food at expensive L.A.—actually New York prices. Ouch!/Yum! 129 N. La Cienega Blvd., 659-9639. $$$

McCormick and Schmick's—In a city that lacks popular seafood dining spots, this is as close as it gets. A nice place to wine and dine business associates. Two Rodeo Collection, 206 N. Rodeo Dr., Beverly Hills, (310) 859-0434, and a location downtown. $$$

Rex II Ristorante—In *Pretty Woman*, this is where Julia Roberts sent her escargot gliding across the room. A beautiful looking restaurant, it used to be the scene for L.A.'s elite. While it's less trendy these days, the Italian cuisine is delicious—and better be at their never-changing astronomical prices. 617 S. Olive St., (213) 627-2300. $$$$

Spago—It's the place where Wolfgang Puck created California cuisine, and people, especially tourists, still flock here to taste the original. 8795 Sunset Blvd., West Hollywood, (310) 652-4025. $$$

Valentino—An exceptional fine-dining experience with superb multicourse meals and a world-class wine list. 3115 Pico Blvd., Santa Monica, (310) 829-4313. $$$

Xiomara—With a different menu every night, you're never sure what to expect at this French bistro—except quality and creativity. 69 N. Raymond Ave., Pasadena, (818) 796-2520. $$$

Sandwich Places

Sandbags—11640 San Vicente Blvd., Brentwood, (310) 207-4888. Gidget gone crazy with sandwiches made out of everything but the kitchen sink. Try the Albuquerque Turkey and the Navajo Chicken. For those less daring, the basics are great too. Other locations. $

California Sunburger—1001 Gayley Ave., Westwood, (310) 208-1020. You don't have a lot of time, you don't have a lot of money and you don't do the golden arches thing. This is the perfect stop for a quick lunch that won't interfere with your waistline. It's not a veggie burger—it's a sunburger (made from sunflower seeds) and it's great. Also on the menu, made-to-order smoothies and middle-eastern delights. $

SKATING, ICE RINKS

Just because you move to the desert doesn't mean you've got to give up winter sports. Lace 'em up.

Culver Ice Rink—4545 Sepulveda Blvd., Culver City, (310) 398-5718.

Ice Capades Chalets—6100 Laurel Canyon Blvd., North Hollywood, (818) 985-5555.

Pickwick Ice Arena—1001 Riverside Dr., Burbank, (818) 846-0032.

Roller Rinks

Wheeling and dealing of a different sort.

Moonlight Rollerway—5110 San Fernando Rd., Glendale, (818) 241-3630.

World on Wheels—4645½ Venice Blvd., (213) 933-3333.

SKIING

Even our little local peaks make the mountains back East look like speed bumps. A few of our most convenient options:

Big Bear Lake—The resorts in the Big Bear Lake area are only two hours from downtown Los Angeles. Make the smooth transition from show biz to snow biz at one of these: **Bear Mountain** (909) 585-2519, lodgings (909) 866-5877; **Snow Valley** (909) 867-2751, lodgings (909) 878-3000; **Snow Forest** (909) 866-8891, lodgings (909) 878-3000; or **Snow Summit** (909) 866-5766, lodgings, (909) 878-3000.

Mammoth Mountain—Five-hour drive for excellent skiing, the best in the area by most accounts. More than 3,000-foot vertical drop and some good long runs. (619) 934-2571.

Wrightwood—Like Big Bear, this area is also a mere two hours from the 'hood. Check out **Mountain High** (714) 972-9242, lodgings (619) 249-547, and **Ski Sunrise** (619) 249-6150. Both offer decent commuter shussing.

SPORTS, PARTICIPATION

Amateur Athletic Foundation—If you're trying to raise a team or raise money for one, these folks can help. 2141 W. Adams Blvd., (213) 730-9600.

You can find an organized game by calling local park and rec departments. **L.A. County:** (213) 738-2961. **Los Angeles Municipal Sports:** (213) 485-4871 or (213) 485-5515. For other areas, consult the chapter on Essential Numbers.

Horseback Riding

KC Malibu Stables—400 N. Kanan Rd, Malibu. A guided trail ride in Malibu Creek State Park with a gorgeous view of the Channel Islands.

Sunset Ranch—3400 N. Beachwood Dr., Hollywood, (213) 469-5450. Most famous for their Moonlight Dinner ride, which follows a trail through Griffith Park and lasts about five hours. Why so long? Well, you must stop for margaritas and Mexican cooking along the way.

SPORTS, SPECTATOR

As the recent defections of the NFL Raiders and Rams shows, the phrase "go team" has taken on sardonic overtones of late in professional sports. There's no telling who the home team will be next week and whether they'll remain in their stadiums or blackmail the taxpayers into buying them new arenas packed withprofit-margin-enhancing skyboxes. For now, these are our teams, their stadiums, and how to contact them. Go team, or not—it's your call.

Professional Teams

California Angels—Anaheim Stadium, 2000 Gene Autry Way (near Katella Ave.), Anaheim (714) 634-2000.

The Los Angeles Clippers—Los Angeles Sports Arena, 3939 S. Figueroa St. (at Martin Luther King Jr. Blvd.), (213) 748-0500.

Los Angeles Dodgers—Dodger Stadium, 1000 Elysian Park Blvd., (213) 224-1500; box office, (213) 224-1448.

Los Angeles Lakers—The Great Western Forum, 3900 W. Manchester Blvd. (at Prairie Ave.), Inglewood, (310) 419-3100;

box office, (310) 419-3100.

The Mighty Ducks—Arrowhead Pond, 2695 E. Katella Ave., Anaheim, (714) 740-2700.

College Teams

UCLA Bruins Basketball runs at Pauley Pavilion, 650 Westwood Plaza (at Strathmore Pl.), (310) 825-2101. Football Bruins play at the Rose Bowl in Pasadena, (818) 793-7193.

USC Trojans Hoopsters tip off at the Sports Arena, 3939 S. Figueroa St. (at Martin Luther King Jr. Blvd.), (213) 743-2620. Football Trojans play at the Coliseum, 3911 S. Figueroa St., (213) 747-7111.

INSIDER TIP: *The* SURFERS JOURNAL *offers up quarterly reports for all the different regions, with detailed information on the best surf spots, conditions, and helpful hints on the surrounding areas. The price is $6 and you can either pay in advance or by credit card. Call (714) 361-0331. Also, weekend surfers can wake up to "*SURF PATROL*" radio show (*KMAX 107.1 FM*, 5 to 7 a.m.), offering surf reports, surf news, and of course surf music.*

SURFING

The top surf spots (the locals tell us):

Malibu, The Point

Topanga (where Topanga Canyon meets Pacific Coast Hwy.)

Zuma State Beach (deep into Malibu past Kanan Rd.)

County Line (L.A./Ventura)

El Porto (aka, El Polluto)

2nd Jetty (Santa Monica)

Breakwater (Venice)

Leo Carrillo (35000 W. Pacific Coast Hwy.)

Zeros (below Leo Carrillo)

Sunset, at Gladstone's (17300 Pacific Coast Hwy., Pacific Palisades).

For more information on where to surf or for specific directions, call the **Department of Beaches and Harbors** at (310) 305-9503. For current updates on surfing conditions, call (310) 379-8471.

Surf Shops

Zuma Jays—For the experienced surfer, they've got everything you need. Ditto for the novice; they rent wet suits, boogie boards, or surf boards to outfit you like a pro. 22775 Pacific Coast Hwy., Malibu, (310) 456-8044.

Boarding House—Brand-name gear, rentals, and lessons. 2619 Main Street, Santa Monica (at Ocean Park), (310) 392-5646.

Val Surf and Sport—4810 Whitsett Ave., North Hollywood, (818) 769-6977.

Horizons West—2011 Main St., Santa Monica, (310) 392-1122.

Surfing Environmentalism

Contact the **Surfrider Foundation**—Malibu at 100 Wilshire Blvd., Santa Monica, (310) 451-1010.

INSIDER TIP: *Pollution is a huge problem in the Santa Monica Bay, especially after the rains, so surfers beware. Wave riders here are prone to ear and eye infections. For more information, contact HEAL THE BAY at (310) 581-4188.*

SYMPHONY

One of the nation's best symphonies, the **Los Angeles Philharmonic,** led by Esa-Pekka Salonen, performs all the major warhorses of the symphonic repertoire. Dorothy Chandler Pavillion, 135 N. Grand Ave., (213) 850-2000.

TENNIS

In other parts of the country, tennis has a very privileged and—OK, let's be blunt—a snotty reputation. But out here it's not such a big deal. Tthere are plenty of courts and plenty of other things for condescending rich jerks to be snotty about.

There are dozens of low-cost or no-cost municipal courts

sprinkled throughout the city. **Echo Park Lake Rec Center** has six courts, (213) 250-3578; **Central Hollywood's Poinsettia Rec Center** has eight courts, (213) 876-5014; **Queen Anne Rec Center** in **Mid-Wilshire** has four courts, (213) 934-0130; **Cheviot Hills Recreation Center,** with fourteen lighted courts is the biggest and busiest in the city, (310) 836-8879. For specific info about these and many other locations, contact the city parks and rec department at (213) 485-5515. (The tennis courts at **Santa Monica's Palisades Park,** (310) 458-8311, are such an extraordinarily relaxing place to hit a few that your stroke will probably feel better than it is.)

There are also many private clubs citywide that often provide better-maintained facilities and various amenities such as private lessons, consultation with a tennis pro, on-site snack shops, and loads of atmosphere. Three to consider:

Private Clubs

The Racquet Center—20 tennis courts as well as racquetball and handball courts. 10933 Ventura Blvd., Studio City, (818) 760-2303.

The Tennis Place—16 tennis courts, ball machines, private lessons, and leagues. 5880 W. 3rd St. L.A. (213) 931-1715.

Marina Tennis—11 courts, lessons, and ball machine rentals. 13199 Mindanao Way, Marina del Rey, (310) 822-2255.

And the Southern California Tennis Association at (310) 206-3838 has information about many other area clubs.

THEATER

Theater groups are about as rare as sunny days in L.A., so you'll always have options. Sure you can line up to see some lumbering Broadway retread by Android Load Whatever, but why not hold the hubris, take a risk, and stumble into a little theater in your neighborhood (wherever that turns out to be). We don't have the space to list them all here, and anyway little theater groups have the life expectancy of mayflies, but below are a few of our more established venues. For complete listings and reviews, consult the *L.A. Weekly* or *The Times,* or you can call the **LA Theater Arts Hotline,** at

TOURIST TRAFFIC JAMS

UNIVERSAL STUDIOS—If you've never been, it's a must-do attraction, and after you pay the sky-high admission fee of $34 at the front gate, you are truly in for a treat. Once a short tour of the studio movie sets, the tram ride now lasts a little over an hour and takes you by such famous spots as Beaver Cleaver's house and the Bates Motel from Psycho. Word to the wary, beware of flash floods and an extra hungry shark they call Jaws. Not to worry, however, it's all part of the magical world of movie-making. Highlights: Back to the Future—The Ride and the new Jurassic Park—The Ride, an incredible waterborne adventure which cost Universal over $100 million and boasts such spectacular effects as an Ultrasaurus who measures as tall as a five-story building from just neck to head and an 18-foot-tall Stegosaurus, 40 feet long from nose to tail. 100 Universal City Plaza, (818) 508-9600.

DISNEYLAND—You're so close, how can you not? Mickey Mouse, Space Mountain, fresh candy apples, It's a Small World—it's the real thing. But take heed, it is an expensive day out in Anaheim and prices in the park are just as high as the park's admission ($34 for adults). Check local papers for any discount promotions. (1313 S. Harbor Blvd., Anaheim, (714) 999-4565.

VENICE BEACH—Hopefully, the sun will be shining when you set foot on this Mardi Gras-esque boardwalk. Sun brings out the people and this is one of the greatest people-watching shows on earth. Stroll by muscle beach to see where Arnold Schwarzenegger once pumped up, and catch any of the side shows that range from rollerblading stunts to fire-eating comedians.

MELROSE AVENUE—It is still a site to see. Once the runway for punk rockers to strut their stuff, things have calmed down along this trendy street, so much so that most people look more like they're right off of Melrose Place than on this once-freakish Avenue. Still, you can catch a blast from the past on any given day. There's great thrift shops, crowded cafes, and expensive boutiques. A fun stop for lunch and a little shopping.

RODEO DR.—In Pretty Woman, Julia Roberts asks her happy

hooker roommate Kit where she should go shopping in Beverly Hills. Kit replies, "Rodeo Dr., baby." She's right. The only catch is: You'll need lots of money. So many tourists opt for window shopping instead, which is almost as fun. Lined with such names as Gucci, Tiffany's, Ralph Lauren, and Cartier you can't help but stare . . . and that's about it. For actual purchasing, head one block east to Beverly Dr., where the stores are less expensive and the cafes and restaurants are plentiful.

STAR-GAZING

You don't need a telescope to find the stars in L.A. They are everywhere; you just need to know where to look. Lucky for you, we'll give you a head start.

THE BIGG CHILL FROZEN YOGURT SHOP or THE COFFEE BEAN AND TEA LEAF NEXT DOOR. Judging by the number of celeb sightings, you might think this shopping center located at Ventura Blvd. and Laurel Canyon is the "studio" in Studio City. The place is crawling with soap opera hunks, famous teens and sitcom stars. 12050 Ventura Blvd., Studio City.

CENTURY CITY SHOPPING CENTER. It is almost a guarantee—the stars have to shop too, and many of them do it here. At night, the movie theaters are also a lucky people-watching zone. 10250 Santa Monica Blvd.

FRED SEGAL. The prices are high, the salespeople are snotty, and the place is dripping with attitude and products that are ecology-conscious. Put it all together and you've got a hot shopping spot for L.A.'s famous faces. The clothes look like something you might see on Friends and well, who knows? You very well could run into a friend. 8118 Melrose Ave., (213) 655-3734.

THE IVY. Looking around, you feel like you are at a photo shoot for People magazine. From TV stars to mega-celebs, gazing was never made so easy. For a less uptight crowd, try The Ivy at the Shore. Important to note, dining like the stars means paying like the stars—through the nose. And one word of caution, no cameras allowed. 113 N. Robertson Blvd., (310) 274-8303 or 1541 Ocean Ave., Santa Monica, (310) 393-3113.

(213) 688-2787, which gives you a touchtone phone run-through of what's playing all over our town.

Actors' Gang Workshop—6209 Santa Monica Blvd.,
(213) 466-1767

Ahmanson Theatre—135 N. Grand Ave., (213) 972-0700.

The Geffen Playhouse—10886 Le Conte Ave., Westwood,
(310) 208-5454.

Highways—1651 18th St. Santa Monica, (213) 660-8587.

Mark Taper Forum—135 N. Grand Ave., (213) 365-3500

A Noise Within—234 S. Brand Blvd., Glendale, (818) 546-1924

Odyssey Theater—2055 S. Sepulveda Blvd., (310) 477-2055

Pantages Theater—6233 Hollywood Blvd., Hollywood,
(213) 365-3500.

Pasadena Playhouse—39 S. El Molino Ave., Pasadena,
(818) 356-PLAY

Shubert Theater—2020 Ave. of the Stars, 1-800-762-7666 and
1-800-233-3123.

Theatre/Theater—1713 Cahuenga Blvd., (213) 466-1767.

THEME PARKS

Our movies have become non-stop thrill rides and our theme parks have become . . . movies. Psychologists call this condition roller-coaster reversal, an increasingly prevalent syndrome that hasn't quite become universal, or Disney.

Adventure City—It's a bit of a drive, but the little ones love the petting farm, the puppet shows, the rollercoaster, and the arts and crafts. And what is it about kids and train rides? 1238 S. Beach Blvd., Anaheim, (714) 236-9300.

Disneyland—Rodent-inspired theme park features attractions based on *Pocahontas*, *The Lion King*, *Toy Story*, et al., for the cross-marketed, synergistic kid in us all. Adults, $34; children 3 to 11, $26; So. Cal. residents, $24. Ball Rd. at Santa Ana Freeway, Anaheim, (213) 626-8605, ext. 4565, or (714) 781-4565.

Knott's Berry Farm—Dinosaurs, Camp Snoopy, and rides, rides, rides. Did we mention the rides? Adults, $29; children 3-11, $19; So. Cal. residents, $23 (kids $17). 8039 Beach Blvd.,

Buena Park, (714) 220-5200.

Queen Mary Seaport—Historic luxury liner turned hotel and shopping center. Adults, $10; kids 4 to 11, $6. 1126 Queens Highway, Long Beach, (310) 435-3511.

Raging Waters—Giant water slides and rides mean big damp fun in the desert. 111 Raging Water Dr., San Dimas, (714) 592-6453.

Sea World—Attractions aplenty and aqua shows featuring whales, dolphins, sea lions, otters, and walruses. Get up early, pack the kids in the car, and go. Adults, $30; kids, $22. Mission Bay, San Diego, (619) 226-3901, or (714) 939-6212.

Six Flags Magic Mountain—Dozens of scary rides, some of which are not even tied in to movies—probably just an oversight. Adults, $32, kids under 4 feet, $15. Magic Mountain Parkway, Interstate 5, Valencia, (818) 367-5965.

Universal Studios Hollywood—Backdraft to the Future doused by the Flintstones in Waterworld—or something like that. Citywalk actually seems relaxing after the orchestrated film-fun attractions. Adults, $33; kids 3-11, $25. Hollywood Freeway at Lankershim Blvd., Universal City, (818) 508-9600.

VOLUNTEERING

There are hundreds upon hundreds of places that could use your help. Ask around and you'll likely find something that perfectly suits your temperament, sympathies, and talents.

The Volunteer Center of Los Angeles—Find a nonprofit organization that needs you In Central L.A., call (213) 484-2849; Downtown, (213) 485-6984; East/Northeast L.A., (213) 484-2849; West L.A., (310) 398-4155.

AIDS Project Los Angeles (APLA)—(213) 993-1600. Responsible for such philanthropic successes as the annual Aids Walk and Dance-A-Thon, this is an organization that can never have enough people helping.

American Cancer Society—1-800-227-2345. There are so many different groups to help out under this organization. Call and ask how you can help out.

Big Brothers of Greater Los Angeles—(213) 258-3333, and Big Sisters of Los Angeles—(213) 933-5749. These are wonderful organizations but can require a lot of time, so be ready to commit yourself if you choose to take on the responsibility of a big brother or sister.

Heal the Bay—2701 Ocean Park Blvd., Santa Monica, (310) 581-4188. This environmental organization is very active in southern California—Ted Danson and Ed Begley Jr. are just a few of the celebrities who believe in healing our oceans.

Los Angeles Gay and Lesbian Community Services Center—7676 Hollywood Blvd., West Hollywood, (213) 255-7251.

The Rape Foundation—1223 Wilshire Blvd., Suite 410, Santa Monica, (310) 451-0042. This is an umbrella organization that includes The Stuart House, a model used around the country for dealing with sexually abused children. While the annual fundraisers look like a who's who in Hollywood, the volunteers are truly the heart of this successful organization.

WALKING TOURS OF L.A.

If you'd like to do something really revolutionary in L.A., try walking. And the best place to start a revolution is at the grassroots level—in your own neighborhood. Wherever you settle, you'll be confronted by our uniquely jumbled styles of architecture, the exotic cornucopia of native and imported plant life, and the beautifully preserved Cars That Time Forgot parked everywhere. Once you begin to weary of your own pleasant neighborhood, it's time to drive to someone else's neighborhood, park the car, and stroll about. Hollywood Hills, Downtown, Silver Lake, Hancock Park, Santa Monica, Beverly Hills—they all have their charms.

Once you've gotten past the aw-shucks/gee-whiz-L.A.-is-beautiful-and-pleasant phase, it's time to turn to architecture walks. You couldn't do any better than picking up David Gebhard and Robert Winter's Architecture in *L.A.*, *A Compleat Guide* (Gibbs Smith), which walks you through the historic buildings of every city neighborhood. In addition, the **Los Angeles Conservancy** (213) 623-2489) organizes architectural tours of downtown landmarks, 1920s-era movie theaters in the Historic Theater District, and various other often-menaced wonders of the city.

Speaking of which, there's also nature—in both domesticated and wild guises. **Griffith Park** (213) 665-5188), **Elysian Park** (213) 225-2044), and any beach you can reach all offer instant respites from the workaday tumult that is L.A. There are also several prime hiking areas that are more rugged, or at least more rustic:

Angeles National Forest—Up on the northern border of L.A. County, this 695,000-acre forest is packed with hiking and horseback riding trails, countless canyons, several lakes and streams—all manner of recreational opportunities. (818) 574-5200.

Malibu Creek State Park—Hiking trails and a nice little lake up in the chaparral. (818) 706-8809.

Santa Monica Mountains National Recreation Area— With 65,000 acres of public parkland, you should find some-place to walk. (818) 597-9192, ext. 201.

Topanga State Park—Explore the wilds right in town—but watch out for rattlesnakes, they're rumored to be more dangerous than film executives. One of the most popular hikes of the moment is Paseo Mirarmar. Going west on Sunset, this long and winding road is on your left just before you hit the Pacific. Drive to the top and park at the dead end. From here on in, you'll have to huff and puff your way to the top of this steep climb. It's like doing the treadmill on the highest incline at times, but the view is much better. (310) 455-2465.

Verdugo Mountains—Just north of Burbank and Glendale, these mountains are home to popular pedestrian destinations La Tuna Canyon and Wildwood Canyon Park, as well as several other park and rec areas. 1-800-533-7275.

Other paths among the many walks of life include:

Nursery Nature Walks—A great way to teach your children nature appreciation. Offering walks for families with newborns, young children, and physically and mentally challenged chil-dren, volunteers will lead you down the path of nature and wonder. (310) 998-1151.

The Wilderness Institute—Arranges wildflower gazing treks to various Southern California sites., (818) 991-7327. Wildflower lovers also have the benefit of an information hotline, (818) 768-3533, that tells what's blooming where and when, which is a service of the Theodore Payne Foundation for Wild Flowers, (818) 768-1802.

The Antelope Valley Poppy Reserve—is a sight to behold in early April. Call for info: 805-724-1180.

Will Rogers State Historic Park—(310) 454-8212 This place never met a hiker it didn't like.

Chapter Seven
ESSENTIAL NUMBERS

NOTHING EVER GOES EXACTLY AS PLANNED, and we all need a little help once in a while. When your number comes up, some of these numbers might come in handy. For general information and 24-hour referrals citywide: (213) 686-0950 or 1-800-339-6996. TDD for deaf callers 1-800-660-4026.

Police:

In a life-threatening emergency situation call 911 or 485-2121, but for other eventualities, try these numbers:

Los Angeles:

Metro Area: (213) 626-5273

Harbor Area: (310) 832-5273

San Fernando Valley: (818) 994-5273

E. Los Angeles: (213) 264-4145

W. Los Angeles: (310) 451-5273

Crime Reports and Info: (213) 485-7227

Burglary: (213) 485-2524

Auto Theft: (213) 485-2507

Other Communities:

Beverly Hills: (310) 550-4951

West Hollywood: (310) 855-8850; (213) 650-4142.

Culver City: (310) 837-1221.

Burbank: (818) 238-3333.

Glendale: (818) 548-4840.

Pasadena: (818) 405-4501

Santa Monica: (310) 395-9931.

Earthquake: **Preparedness Information:** (213) 773-7273

Fire: **To report a fire,** call 911, or (213) 483-6721.

Hospitals, Veterinary:

Cahuenga Pet Hospital, 825 Cahuenga Blvd., Hollywood, (213) 462-0660.

Center-Sinai Animal Hospital, 10737 Venice Blvd., (310) 559-3770

Culver City Animal Hospital, 5830 W. Washington Blvd., Culver City, (310) 836-4551.

Echo Park Pet Hospital, 1739 Glendale Blvd., (213) 663-1107.

Larchmont Animal Clinic, 316 N. Larchmont, (213) 463-4889.

Los Feliz Small Animal Hospital, 3166 Los Feliz Blvd., (213) 664-3309.

VCA Robertson Blvd. Animal Hospital, 656 N. Robertson, Blvd., L.A., (310) 659-2260.

Santa Monica Dog and Cat Hospital, 2010 Broadway, Santa Monica, (310) 453-5459.

Doctors:

First of all, ask your hometown doctor if he or she knows of, or would recommend any physicians in Los Angeles. Failing that, get a referral from a friend or co-worker.

A third options is the **Physicians Referral Service:** (310) 657-6464.

Complaints, **Medical Board of California:** 1-800-633-2322.

Dentists:

Again, the best option would be a referral from your hometown dentist or a friend or co-worker. But as a newcomer, you may well be short on personal contacts. If so, try, **1-800-DENTIST.** This referral service is paid for by participating dentists, so you're not going to get a totally objective view, but if you don't have anything else to go on, it's better than nothing.

Community Services:

AIDS Healthcare Foundation: (213) 462-2273, 1-800-243-2101.

AIDS Project Los Angeles: (213) 876-2437, or 1-800-922-2437 in English, or 1-800-400-7432 in Spanish.

Alcoholics Anonymous: (213) 936-4343.

American Civil Liberties Union: (213) 977-9500.

Chamber of Commerce: (213) 580-7500.
Child Care Information and Referral:
(213) 413-0777 or (213) 299-0199.

Consumer Information and Complaints:
Better Business Bureau, 714-527-0680;
Attorney General's Public Inquiry
Unit: 1-800-952-5225; California Dept.
of Consumer Affairs, 1-800-952-5210;
L.A. County Consumer Affairs, (213)
974-1452; U.S. Consumer Product
Safety Commission, 1-800-638-2772.

DMV: (213) 744-2000.

Earthquake and Disaster Preparedness:
Governor's Office of Emergency
Services Earthquake Program, (818)
304-8383; L.A. County, (213) 974-1120;
FEMA, 1-800-299-1160.

Federal Information Center: (213) 894-3800.

Free Clinic, Los Angeles: (213) 653-1990.

Gay Bashing Complaints: (213) 848-6470.

Health Service, L.A. County: (213) 250-
8055, or 1-800-564-6600.

Housing:
California Fair Employment and
Housing Department (discrimination
cases), 1-800-884-1684; Federal HUD
discrimination hotline, 1-800-669-9777;
Legal Aid Foundation, (213) 487-7609;
Eviction Defense Center, (213) 387-
9038; LA City Housing Department
(rent stabilization), (213) 847-7368.

Immigration and Naturalization Service:
1-800-755-0777.

Mental Health:
L.A. County 24-Hour Psychiatric
Emergency, 1-800-854-7771; informa-
tion and referral, (213) 738-4961;
Patients Rights Advocacy Program,
(213) 738-4888.

National Organization for Women (NOW):
(310) 657-3894.

Suicide Prevention, 24 hours: (213) 381-
5111.

Planned Parenthood: (213) 226-0800.

Poison Control Center, 24 hours:
(213) 222-3212, or 1-800-777-6476.

Rape and Battering Hotline, 24 hours:
(213) 626-3393 or (310) 392-8381. Rosa
Parks Sexual Assault Center, 24 hours:
(213) 295-4673.

Recycling Information, City of L.A.:
1-800-773-2489.

Recycling, Santa Monica: (310) 453-
9677.

Unemployment Claims and Job Service:
(213) 744-2600.

Volunteer Center of Los Angeles (places volunteers in nonprofit organizations):

Central L.A., (213) 484-2849;
Downtown, (213) 485-6984; East/North-
east L.A., (213) 484-2849; West L.A.,
(310) 398-4155.

Voter Registration Information:
1-800-345-8683.

Waste Alert Hotline (to report illegal dump-
ing of toxic substances): 1-800-698-6942,
or 1-800-303-0003.

Departments of Parks and Recreation L.A.
County: (213) 738-2961.
Los Angeles: General, (213) 485-5515;
Camp Info, (213) 485-4853; Municipal
Sports, (213) 485-4871; Griffith Park,
(213) 665-5188.
Beverly Hills: (310) 285-2537.
Burbank: (818) 238-5300.
Culver City: (310) 253-6650.
Santa Monica: (310) 458-8311.
West Hollywood: (310) 848-6471.
Glendale: (818) 548-5300.

Lawyers:
Lawyer Referral Service:
(213) 387-3325.
Legal Complaints, State Bar of
California:
1-800-843-9053.
Lesbian Law Project: (213) 993-7670

Mayor's Office: 200 N. Spring Street,
(213) 485-5175.

Miscellaneous:
Arts Hotline: (213) 688-2787.
Time of Day: (213) 853-1212.
Weather: (213) 554-1212.
L.A. County Parks Service:
(213) 744-4211.
State Parks Service: (213) 6293342.
Forest Service Info: (818) 790-1151 or
(818) 796-5541.
National Parks Service: (819) 888-
3770.
West Hollywood Information:
(213) 848-6496.

Visitors Info:
Los Angeles: (213) 689-8822.
Beverly Hills: (310) 271-8174.
Long Beach: (310) 436-3645.
Marina del Rey: (310) 305-9545.
Pasadena: (818) 795-9311.
Hollywood Chamber of Commerce:
(213) 469-8311.
L.A. County Information Center:
(213) 974-1311.

ACKNOWLEDGMENTS

Amanda's Acknowledgments: There are a lot of people who proved to be invaluable resources to me in putting together this book. I want to thank all of them—in particular my friends and family—for helping to fill this guide with an overflow of information and for putting up with my stressful side. Thanks to my co-writer for his wacky vocabulary and hours upon hours of work. Most of all, I dedicate this book to my favorite Michigan alums (and best friends) who have promised to make this a bestseller and to Jeremy, the love of my life, for his patience, support, and . . . computer.

Jeff's Thanks To: The Los Angeles Police and the Department of Motor Vehicles, both of whom could embroil us in costly and complicated red tape if we didn't thank them properly; the millions of people of the city(s) of Los Angeles, without whom none of this would have been necessary; my co-author Amanda Rudolph, whose energy, expertise, and enthusiasm were inspirational; and personal thanks to Norm and Liz Reid (as well as Nancy Reid Green and the rest of the Reid family), Frieda Landau, Jeremiah Creedon, Will Nixon, Emma Segal, David Dokken, and especially to Tina King.

BIBLIOGRAPHY

Acting is Everything, An Actor's Guidebook For a Successful Career in Los Angeles by Judy Kerr (September Publishing)

Architecture in L.A., A Compleat Guide by David Gebhard and Robert Winter (Peregrine Smith Books)

City of Quartz by Mike Davis (Vintage)

Googie: Fifties Coffee Shop Architecture by Alan Hess (Chronicle Books)

How to Meet and Hang Out with the Stars: A Totally Unauthorized Guide by Bret Saxon and Steve Stein (Citadel Press)

I Love Los Angeles Guide by Marilyn J. Appleberg (Collier)

L.A. Shortcuts: The Guidebook for Drivers Who Hate to Wait by Brian Roberts and Richard Schwadel (Red Car Press)

Los Angeles Access (HarperCollins)

Los Angeles: Biography of a City by John and LaRee Caughery (University of California Press)

Mysterious California: Strange Places and Eerie Phenomena in the Golden State by Mike Marinacci (Panpipes Press)

Romancing the Southland by Robert Badal (Douglas A. Campbell)

The Beach Towns: A Walker's Guide to LA's Beach Communities by Robert John Pierson

Wall Art: Mega Murals and Supergraphics by Betty and Stefan Merken (Running Press)

INDEX

Editor's Note: If you're looking for any of the following services—Schools, Police Stations, Post Offices, Hospitals, Libraries, Parking Information, Garages, Banks and ATMs, Cafes, Delis, Coffeeshops, and Diners, Community Resources, Convenience Stores, Synagogues, Churches, Pharmacies, Dry cleaners, Laundromats, Gas Stations, Grocery Stores, Hardware Stores, Video Stores, Beer and Liquor stores—go to the neighborhood in which you're looking, and turn to the *Essential Resources* Pages.